Advertising at War

THE HISTORY OF COMMUNICATION

Robert W. McChesney and
John C. Nerone, editors

*A list of books in the series appears
at the end of this book.*

Advertising at War

BUSINESS, CONSUMERS,
AND GOVERNMENT
IN THE 1940S

INGER L. STOLE

UNIVERSITY OF ILLINOIS PRESS
Urbana, Chicago, and Springfield

Library of Congress Cataloging-in-Publication Data
Stole, Inger L.
Advertising at war : business, consumers, and government
in the 1940s / Inger L. Stole.
p.   cm.—(The history of communication)
Includes bibliographical references and index.
ISBN 978-0-252-03712-2 (cloth)
ISBN 978-0-252-07865-1 (pbk.)
1. Advertising Council—History.
2. Advertising—United States—History—20th century.
3. World War, 1939–1945—United States—Propaganda.
4. Corporations—Public relations—United States—
History—20th century.
5. United States—History—1933–1945.
I. Title.
HF5813.U6S767   2012
940.54'88973—dc23   2012030961

Contents

Illustrations

Acknowledgments

The writing of acknowledgments is a reflective and humbling endeavor. I could never have written this book had it not been for the help and support from a long list of people. I thank James L. Baughman, Stephen Vaughn, and the late Ivan Preston for guidance during the very early stages of this project, and Mark H. Leff and the late Robert Griffith for their scholarly inspiration. I also thank Kendra Boileau for encouraging me to develop an initial monograph on WWII advertising into a full-length book.

Energized by a joint grant from the American Council on Consumer Interests and Consumers Union in the spring of 2009, I visited the latter's archival collection in Yonkers, New York. Roberta Piccoli and Robert Huerster made me feel extremely welcome and accommodated my research needs in ways that went far beyond expectations. I owe them and Rob Schneider a world of thanks. I am also beholden to Larry Kirsch for being an early and steadfast supporter and to the Media Education Foundation for its faith in the project.

Support from the Campus Research Board at the University of Illinois provided time off for writing and helped pay for the cost of book illustrations, and the University Archives at the University of Illinois provided valuable assistance in locating images and obtaining permission to reprint images from the Advertising Council collection, housed at its facilities. Thanks in particular to Nancy Adelman, Emma Brooks, and Rory Grennan. At the University of Illinois I am also indebted to my department chair, David Tewksbury, to Amy Holland for always being extremely helpful, and to John Nerone, Dan Schiller, and Pat Gill. Molly C. Niesen provided valuable assistance and feedback during various stages of the project, as did Brian Dolber. My colleague Susan G. Davis deserves special thanks. Her friendship and support have been unwavering, and her tireless work for social change continues to be an inspiration.

This book would not be what it is without Peggy Ann Brown's assistance in maneuvering the maze of archival collections in Washington, D.C., and I owe thanks to Sarah Rundell for help in copying material from the Thurman Arnold Papers at the American Heritage Center at the University of Wyoming and to Sandy Eklund for assistance with the Donald E. Montgomery Papers at the Walter P. Reuther Library at Wayne State University in Detroit. I am similarly indebted to Carrie Marsh at the Honnold/Mudd Library in Claremont, California, and to Peter Burton for helping with the tedious task of organizing an overwhelming amount of documents as I was preparing to write the first draft.

I am grateful for valuable feedback from two anonymous manuscript reviewers and to Marissa Lowe, Robert Gross, and Christine Lamberson for their help in carefully checking notes and citations for accuracy. Christine provided additional help in locating copies of the advertisements that are included in this book. A special thanks goes to Jane Lyle, who patiently copyedited the first drafts of every chapter and brought messy notes to my attention. Without her help, it would have would have taken twice as long to get this book to its present shape. At the University of Illinois Press, I am grateful to Willis G. Regier, who assumed editorial responsibility for my manuscript after Kendra Boileau accepted an out-of-town promotion, to production manager Jennifer L. Reichlin, and to Jane M. Curran for her invaluable help with the final copyediting.

I owe a world of gratitude to friends for reminding me that life is more than work. Particular thanks go to Pat DiBiase, Allen Ruff, John Nichols, Mary Bottari, Lisa Graves, Kelly Park Snyder, Janice Peck, Mari Jo Buhle, Paul Buhle, Anne Mork, Rick Baker, Jeff Liggon, Jean Rothschild, Matt Rothschild, Kim Curtis, Rene Sandler, and Amy Roges. Thanks also to Nancy Ranum, Kathy Riddiough, Cathy Sullivan, Hanna Diament-Talmadge, Sandra Austin-Phillips, and Eileen Kennedy.

Last, but not least, I want to thank my daughters, Amy and Lucy, and my husband, Bob McChesney, for their love and support.

Advertising at War

The past two decades have witnessed an increased interest in advertising and consumer issues across scholarly disciplines. Fields ranging from business and advertising to sociology, American studies, history, mass communication, art history, anthropology, and psychology are recognizing the centrality of consumption and consumer-related issues to their scholarly pursuits. Most scholars explore these issues from contemporary perspectives, although the recent appearance of historical accounts suggests the emergence of additional approaches.[1] To date, however, the historical approach has favored the decades flanking World War II, leaving advertising and consumer issues that emerged in connection with war conditions largely undocumented.[2]

Thus, scholars have yet to provide a comprehensive account of the advertising industry's behavior in the larger social, economic, and political context of the war or to explore the significance of these events for helping advertising to become an inviolable American institution in the postwar era. *Advertising at War: Business, Consumers, and Government in the 1940s* therefore casts a wider net, mapping the ongoing tensions between advertisers, regulators, and consumer activists during the war and chronicling how advertisers turned a situation that by all rational accounts should have worked to their disadvantage into a priceless opportunity to cement their place in a postwar society defined by advertising and the consumer products it promoted. Advertising achieved this status between 1942 and 1945, economically at first, and then politically and culturally. A successful campaign to achieve favorable laws and regulations eliminated any realistic threat to the institution's role in the economic system. This campaign included a significant public relations component, which was aimed at defining advertising as quintessentially *democratic* and *American*. The process had the crucial and enthusiastic support of the commercial media, especially the news media, and was complete by the middle of the twentieth century.

The focus of this book, then, is on the political maneuverings of the American advertising industry during World War II. While the specific images produced by the industry during this period played an important role, they are not my main focus. My goal is to uncover the significant political and economic forces that shaped the industry, or what Frank W. Fox has so aptly termed "the ad behind the ad," the use of advertising to bolster the corporate system behind the products.[3]

Sources and Terms

The scarcity of existing scholarship has forced me to rely rather heavily on archival sources, newspaper accounts, and trade publications. The latter have both advantages and limitations. Trade magazines tend to be extremely sensitive, even alarmist, at times; their editors are prone to overstatement and exaggeration. They do, however, provide us with an opportunity to learn what industry leaders and the publications themselves wanted their less influential colleagues to know and think. Because trade publications frequently quote influential industry leaders, giving us glimpses into their concerns and strategies, they are an invaluable source for reconstructing an industry's past.

Issues surrounding World War II advertising involved a range of groups and organizations, which often had conflicting agendas. Thus it has been necessary for me to use several different archival collections to reconstruct individual and collective narratives. The Ad Council Papers, housed at the University of Illinois, have yielded excellent material, as have the papers of Advertising Council member Thomas D'Arcy Brophy, located at the State Historical Society of Wisconsin in Madison. The Records of the Office of War Information at the National Archives II have been invaluable in the task of mapping government perspectives on wartime advertising, as have the records of several other government agencies, including the Federal Trade Commission and the Department of the Treasury. The Consumers Union Archives in Yonkers, New York, has offered great insights into the organized critique of wartime advertising, and several collections at the Harry S. Truman Library and Museum in Independence, Missouri, have aided my understanding of the relationship between advertisers and the government in the immediate postwar era.

Throughout the book, the terms *advertisers, advertising, manufacturers, business,* and *advertising industry* are frequently used. By *advertising* I mean the practice of promoting brand-name goods or services that are being offered for sale. Advertisements are typically prepared by creative talent at advertising agencies and placed in select mass media by strategic planners. *Advertisers* are the manufacturers that approve and pay for advertisements and advertising campaigns prepared by said advertising agencies. They also keep a close eye on political developments that might affect their business. I use *advertising industry, business,* and *business community* as general, and sometimes interchangeable, terms to describe the shared interests of advertisers and advertising agencies, generally organized by their trade associations. While I explore the overlapping interests between the advertising industry and the commercial mass media, my main focus is on the former.[4]

Advertising and the "Ambiguity of Competition"

In order to appreciate the controversies over advertising's economic role that emerged and continued into WWII, it is important to keep in mind that advertising as we know it barely existed before the final decades of the nineteenth century. There was no "Madison Avenue" with its panoply of advertising agencies, powerful trade associations, and broadcast media dependent upon national brand advertising. Commercial advertising was a relatively small enterprise with no federal regulation in 1906 when the Food and Drugs Act was passed. That measure did not address advertising, but only the labeling of products. Eight years later, the newly established Federal Trade Commission Act provided the Federal Trade Commission (FTC) with regulatory powers over advertising, but the agency was mandated to intervene only in cases where one business used advertising to gain unfair advantage over another. It thus lacked the jurisdiction to intervene on consumers' behalf when they were misled, wronged, or even harmed by false and misleading advertising. As consumer advertising became more common, rapidly developing into a multibillion-dollar industry, and people found themselves dependent upon manufacturers for information about many of their everyday purchases, the need for consumer protection became apparent.[5] Advertising was now a controversial industry, and more than a little unpopular.

To begin to understand the ensuing criticism of advertising, we must ask why it exists and what role it plays in the economy. While this may appear to be a simple question, such was not the case in the late 1930s, when advertising's economic role was the subject of considerable confusion. This uncertainty reflected what has come to be called the "ambiguity of competition": the opposite meanings ascribed to competition in economic theory, on the one hand, and in the popular vernacular of businesspeople and the general public, on the other.[6]

Advertising must be understood first and foremost as a business expense. But it is much more than that. The United States has had a private-enterprise economy throughout its history, but national advertising emerged as a dominant institution only in the twentieth century. Advertising was in use before then, of course, but there was much less of it, and a significant proportion of the ads were akin to what today is called classified advertising, that is, dry, factual reports informing costumers about products and their availability. A merchant might place a notice in the local paper informing customers about a new shipment of lace, tea, or spices, for example. Following the Civil War, modern advertising began its climb to prominence. By around 1890, the market situation had changed from one in which there were many local manufacturers producing a variety of consumer products for local consumption to one that was dominated by fewer and larger companies. It did not take long, however, before these large producers were faced with the problem of sustaining growth. Limited outlets hampered the distribution of their goods, and this, in turn, threatened capital investment in machinery, labor, and products. Manufacturers realized that they needed to seek national markets—in effect to cast a wider net. Thus they turned to national advertising.[7]

This explanation is good as far as it goes, but it fails to convey exactly why some industries featured a great deal of advertising and others showed less interest. It also fails to explain why advertising became a mandatory business expense for firms in so many industries. To get to the bottom of the issue, it is necessary to understand the transition from an economy dominated by relatively competitive markets to one dominated by what economists refer to as oligopolistic markets. Under oligopoly, a handful of firms dominate the industry, and their size and power allow them to prevent new businesses from entering the market and effectively challenging them. It is a multiheaded monopoly as much as it is a competitive market as understood in economic theory.

At the time of the American Revolution, 90 percent of American enterprise was agricultural, and most producers operated in what economists regarded as competitive markets. Producers in such markets were not engaged in a personal rivalry. None of them had any control over market prices, so each of them produced as much as possible and was forced to sell at the existing market price. The hallmark of competitive markets is that new players can enter them at any time. If an industry becomes especially profitable, new firms will enter the market. This, in turn, will increase the overall supply, lead to a lower market price, and cause a reduction in individual profits. The ongoing competition and lower prices may benefit consumers, but the businesses themselves are powerless before market forces. While a pure monopoly or something proximate is the dream of any capitalist, for both economic and political reasons—monopoly was deemed illegal with the passage of the 1890 Sherman Antitrust Act—oligopoly became the order of the day.

When the U.S. Constitution was written, only twenty-two American corporations existed; it was not until after the Civil War that they became more common.[8] Changes in technology, communications, and transportation facilitated the creation of giant corporations, which in turn agglomerated into bigger units, even monopolies, which collided sharply with traditional concepts of business competition: "the American Way."[9] Although less than 25 percent of all American manufacturing establishments were incorporated in 1904, they produced more than 70 percent of the national output as measured by value. Fifteen years later, more than 31 percent of all manufacturing establishments in America were owned by corporations, and their proportion of the national output had increased to 87.7 percent.[10] Firms such as the California Fruit Canners Association, Royal Baking Powder, the National Biscuit Company, and the National Candy Company had achieved 40 to 70 percent dominance in their individual industries, while the American Can Company, Du Pont, and Eastman Kodak enjoyed significant control over their individual markets due to controlling more than 70 percent of total production.[11]

The rise of oligopoly was the gasoline that fueled modern advertising. In oligopolistic markets, the dominant firms are hesitant to engage in cutthroat price competition. Firms are not price *takers,* as are firms in competitive markets; instead they are price *makers*, with considerable control over industry output and pricing. Each firm is large enough to survive a price war, so price competition would only reduce the size of the revenue pie over which they are fighting. They tend to be more profitable, with pricing and output levels closer to those in a pure monopoly than to those in a purely competitive market. The key to having a stable oligopolistic market is creating barriers to entry that make it difficult for new firms to crash the party, force down prices, and open the field to competition. Firms instead tend to gravitate toward a pricing structure that maximizes the total revenue coming into the industry, similar to the way that monopolies set prices and determine output in economic theory.

When advertising is viewed in this context, it understandably becomes a mandatory business expense: in an oligopolistic market, every firm must protect its market shares from attack. To large corporations, advertising represents a competitive weapon superior to cutthroat price competition in the battle to expand and protect market shares. It creates an aura of prestige or desirability around a given product or service, thereby making it less susceptible to price competition. Once consumer preference for brand-name products has been established, firms can increase their relative market share without lowering their prices, thereby maintaining a healthy profit margin and enjoying an additional mechanism for keeping envious entrepreneurs away.

In the early twentieth century, not only did advertising become an adjunct to the "real business" of manufacturing, but it also became as vital as the steel, the workers, and the machinery because it created its own byproduct: the loyal consumer. Instead of representing a competitive selling of goods and services, advertising came to represent the competitive creation of consumer habits. Because the products offered by these oligopolistic firms tended to vary little in terms of price and quality—one brand of cigarette, shaving cream, or toothpaste was pretty much like any other—merely stating a product's physical attributes and price did not give consumers a reason to purchase that particular brand instead of one of its competitors. Advertising copywriters, therefore, had to come up with creative ways—often related indirectly at best to actual product attributes or to a genuine difference from prospective competitors—to make consumers prefer one brand over another. Ironically, the more similar the products, the more their manufacturers tended to spend on advertising to convince consumers that there was a real difference. Unable to cite tangible product information to differentiate themselves from their competitors, advertisers often employed strategies designed to appeal to and exploit consumers' emotions.[12] The purest representation of this phenomenon is what are called *parity* products, meaning products between which there are no meaningful differences other than those ascribed to packaging, marketing, and advertising.

In the late 1930s, it was this understanding that propelled the consumer movement in its campaign to regulate advertising as a way to promote more competitive markets and to ensure that ads provided information of actual value to consumers.[13] A 1941 experiment conducted by a Yale psychologist and the nonprofit organization Consumers' Research yielded telling evidence about how advertising worked in at least some oligopolistic markets.[14] The research examined the extent to which heavy advertising campaigns left consumers with the impression that a particular brand of cigarettes was qualitatively different from its competitors. In testing loyal smokers to see whether they could tell cigarette brands apart, the study found that only 5 of the 44 admitted Chesterfield smokers were able to identify "their" brand in a blindfold test. Likewise, only 3 out of 37 Lucky Strike smokers, 4 out of 55 Camel smokers, 6 out of 49 Philip Morris smokers, 8 out of 56 Avalon smokers, and 5 out of 52 devoted Domino smokers were able to do the same. Old Gold smokers had the highest level of brand recognition, yet of the 55 smokers who claimed to prefer that brand, only 11 could identify it.[15] These findings demonstrated not only that the association between brands and consumer satisfaction was largely psychological, but also that there in fact were no real differences between the various cigarettes, and perhaps between brands and generics.

Economists in the 1920s and 1930s grappled with the shift from competitive to more concentrated markets. Under economic theory, there was pure competition and there was pure monopoly, and every market structure between the two poles was regarded with suspicion as being insufficiently competitive. How rational, fair, and efficient were markets if they did not operate under the competitive model? This was not a question that many economists had much interest in pursuing. They continued to insist—or, better put, assumed—that it was still appropriate to regard the economy as being based on competitive markets. Consequently, because advertising played no role in this economic model, there was scarcely any mention of this promotional device in the economics textbooks of the time.

Contrast this view with business owners who viewed anything short of a pure monopoly as quintessentially competitive. A firm in an oligopolistic market regarded itself as in direct and deadly competition with the other firms in its industry; they could hardly be suspected of colluding.

Advertising, far from protecting and promoting monopoly power and market inefficiency, was a primary competitive weapon. In 1952 John Kenneth Galbraith, who had been a New Deal economist in the early 1940s, contended that this ambiguity concerning competition led to

> an endless amount of misunderstanding between businessmen and economists. After spending the day contemplating the sales force, advertising agency, engineers, and research men of his rivals the businessman is likely to go home feeling considerably harassed by competition. Yet if it happens that he has measurable control over his prices he obviously falls short of being competitive in the foregoing sense. No one should be surprised if he feels some annoyance toward scholars who appropriate words in common

> English usage and, for their own purposes, give them what seems to be an inordinately restricted meaning.[16]

Nor is this necessarily a liberal or left-wing observation. The economist Milton Friedman, in his conservative classic *Capitalism and Freedom* (1962), described competition as having

> two very different meanings. In ordinary discourse, competition means personal rivalry, with one individual seeking to outdo his known competitor. In the economic world, competition means almost the opposite. There is no personal rivalry in the competitive market place. There is no personal higgling. The wheat farmer in a free market does not feel himself in personal rivalry with, or threatened by, his neighbor, who is, in fact, his competitor. No one participant can determine the terms on which other participants shall have access to goods or jobs. All take prices as given by the market and no individual can by himself have more than a negligible influence on price though all participants together determine the price by the combined effect of their separate actions.[17]

This definitional slippage concerning *competition* and *monopoly* would mark governmental hearings on monopoly power, and all other deliberations on advertising, in the late 1930s and early 1940s.[18] The confusion would ultimately muddy the case of advertising's critics and provide a successful means for the industry to advance its own case while downplaying or marginalizing substantive criticism of its practices.

The situation came to a head between the 1920s and the 1940s. During this period the existence of advertising was not taken for granted by millions of Americans or, perhaps most important, by the core components of the advertising industry. The industry saw serious existential political threats in every direction and acted accordingly.

The 1930s Consumer Movement

A breakthrough of singular importance came in 1927 with a book titled *Your Money's Worth: A Study in the Waste of the Consumer's Dollars*.[19] Written by Stuart Chase and F. J. Schlink, it gave impetus to what is commonly referred to as the 1930s consumer movement. The authors exposed fraud and manipulation by American manufacturers and argued that advertisements failed to provide consumers with sufficient product information. As a result, people were wasting money. Inefficiency in buying, the authors contended, increased in inverse proportion to consumers' knowledge.

Whereas industrial and government buyers bought efficiently because they possessed the necessary knowledge to deflate and disregard advertising, the average consumer was forced to rely on advertising propaganda that provided almost no factual information. Warning consumers against the perils of such marketing methods, the authors called for reform. In 1929 they created Consumers' Research to serve as a "watchdog" group by looking out for consumers' interests, testing products, and publishing the results in a newsletter called the *Consumers' Club Commodity List*. The modern consumer movement was born, and its defining issue was to greatly regulate advertising and reform it into something that would serve consumers rather than big business.

Consumers' Research employed technical experts and had its own laboratory for product testing. By 1932, the newsletter had been renamed *Consumers' Research General Bulletin* (further simplified later to *Consumers' Research Bulletin*) and boasted an impressive forty-two thousand subscribers.[20] Before long, the group had attracted a number of prolific authors who wrote articles and bestselling books on consumer-related issues. It received support from a range of professional organizations, including the General Federation of Women's Clubs, the American Home Economics Association, and the National League of Women Voters. Also important was encouragement from politically connected individuals with a commitment to federal regulation of advertising. In 1935 the group split over internal labor issues, leading to the creation of a second organization, Consumers Union, in early 1936. Whereas both groups defined their mission as protecting consumers, Consumers' Research turned politically conservative, whereas Consumers Union thrived on activist work.

There was considerable momentum for stricter regulation of advertising by the time of Franklin D. Roosevelt's inauguration in 1933. In June of that year, a bill to amend the 1906 Food and Drugs Act was introduced in Congress. Commonly referred to as the Tugwell bill after Assistant Secretary of Agriculture Rexford Tugwell, who was a strong supporter of the legislation, the measure called for improved labeling laws and mandatory grading of consumer goods. It also sought to empower the Food and Drug Administration (FDA) to prohibit false advertising of any food, drug, or cosmetic. Catching advertisers' immediate attention was a stipulation defining a false ad as one that used "ambiguity or inference" to create a misleading impression.[21] Few of the major manufacturers objected to a ban on blatantly false advertising, but their reaction to the proposed ban on "ambiguity and inference" was strong and adverse. The clever use of advertising to create enough ambiguity for consumers to infer the advantages of one product over another, even if none existed, was precisely what drove much of the consumer industry, and it was therefore a significant component of capitalism at large. The members of the business community were fully aware that their rationale for advertising might sound hollow, especially to consumers affected by a severe economic depression, so they tried their best to avert direct discussion of the issue. Their common response was that people should be grateful to advertisers for bringing them products that were convenient and cheaply mass-produced. They also objected to the bill's requirement of a grading system for consumer products, arguing that not only would uniform standards be impossible to establish, but they were unnecessary because advertisements provided sufficient product information.[22]

The stage was set for a five-year legislative battle over several revised versions of the Tugwell bill. The advertising industry's cause was aided by a series of well-developed public relations and lobbying strategies and considerable influence over the commercial mass media. Beyond the immediate goal of preventing passage of the bill, the long-term strategy was to stop the consumer movement's momentum and prevent similar measures from being proposed in the future. By the mid-1930s, the advertising industry had launched a string of campaigns aimed at convincing the public that advertising had "benign" and "useful" functions. Speakers' bureaus, motion pictures, radio broadcasts, and front groups were used to spread the industry's message. Editors and publishers were impressed by claims that advertising revenues would decrease drastically should the Tugwell bill become law. As a result, the press generally neglected to inform the public about the proposed measure or else presented it in a negative light. With each new version of the bill, industry concerns took greater priority, and the issue of consumer protection, which had been the initial impetus for the legislation, gradually faded from the spotlight.

Despite demands from consumer groups, New Dealers, and government regulatory agencies, advertisers survived the battle with surprising ease. When the Wheeler-Lea Amendment to the Federal Trade Commission Act was passed in 1938, it reflected the advertising industry's successful effort to render such protection painless for business interests. Nor did the consumer movement's demand for mandatory grading of goods become law.[23] The Wheeler-Lea Amendment is still the law of the land concerning advertising regulation; Congress has never revisited the matter in anything close to a fundamental or structural way.

There are good reasons for recent scholarship to have identified the 1930s as the defining moment for the advertising industry. In my 2006 book *Advertising on Trial: Consumer Activism and Corporate Public Relations in the 1930s*, I supported the prevailing view that the major debate over advertising in the U.S. economy and American society ended in 1938.[24] Now, based on additional research, I qualify this notion and argue that the battle over the role of advertising in our political economy ended not in the late 1930s but during World War II. Advertising was still a political issue at the end of the 1930s, if only because corporate capitalism was arguably at its low ebb in popularity and advertising was a defining and controversial feature of the economic system. More importantly, the war elevated the seeming contradictions of advertising and allowed its critics one final chance to corral and regulate it. It was the war experience, every bit as much as the legislative battles of the 1930s, that defined the role of advertising in both our postwar political economy and our cultural firmament. *Advertising at War* shows how the war experience helped advertising to solidify its position as a cornerstone institution in the United States—and an indispensable one at that.

Defense, War, and Advertising

In the late 1930s, and in spite of recent victories, the advertising industry was nowhere close to being out of the proverbial woods. In the summer of 1938, right after the passage of the Wheeler-Lea Amendment, the economy lapsed into a new depression. This prompted the formation of the Temporary National Economic Committee (TNEC), an unprecedented government body created to determine the extent to which the existing capitalist system was a structural drag on the economy and society. As part of its mission, the TNEC singled out advertising and marketing for evaluation as suspect institutions. Always on the alert and hoping to avoid a public debate over advertising's economic function, the advertising industry did not respond favorably to the TNEC's basic questions about the use of advertising to restrict competition. Although advertising was used primarily for this purpose, the industry was less than forthcoming in admitting as much, especially because the committee had strong evidence that such practices could ultimately hurt consumers and at times hinder new investments and economic growth.

Just as the TNEC's investigations were hitting full stride, the preparations for war added to the industry's problems. How could the role of advertising be justified in a dramatically altered war economy? During the Great Depression, manufacturers had defended advertising as a tool for creating consumer demand and as a strategy for economic recovery. But in 1940, with war on the near horizon, that argument was quickly unraveling. Raw materials for domestic consumer goods were in short supply, forcing the government to impose rationing and price controls. Thus, if advertisers promoted products that were scarce or unavailable, it might have an inflationary effect and possibly cause black markets. Advertisers were desperate to keep their brand names before the public, but they worried that promoting their products might be viewed as problematic, if not unpatriotic, by the American public.

Directly related to this concern was the government's quest for revenue to finance defense spending. Since World War I, businesses had been allowed to claim a large portion of their advertising as a tax-deductible expense, which meant that they could spend lavishly on ads and deduct most of the cost. Now, however, with advertising seeming less essential to the economy, and with some viewing it as downright destructive, industry leaders feared that Congress would put an end to the practice, not just for the war's duration, but possibly even beyond. In their view, the three years following the passage of the Wheeler-Lea Amendment, far from being a time of triumph and social approval, had instead found them continually in crisis and in a downward spiral.

Something had to be done, and in November 1941, a few weeks before the Japanese attacked Pearl Harbor, key members of the advertising community met with a number of high-ranking government officials to discuss the dire situation. They eventually produced the outline of an industry-wide program to protect advertising. Within weeks, America was embroiled in all-out war. Soon thereafter, to the advertising industry's surprise, the government contacted some of its leaders with a request for help in mobilizing its home front campaigns.[25] By early 1942, the Association of National Advertisers and the American Association of Advertising Agencies had taken the official initiative to create the Advertising Council, Inc., which positioned itself as a private adjunct to the government's war information efforts.[26]

Soon Washington and the Advertising Council were working in tandem, reminding the American public of the need to salvage scrap metal, conserve fats, buy war bonds, and enlist in the armed services.[27] The strategy of incorporating war-related messages into regular product advertising enabled advertisers to accommodate the government's need for publicity while keeping their brand names alive during wartime, when some of their products were frequently not available. Nevertheless, the council had to work diligently in order to gain cooperation from its members, keep the politicians, especially suspect New Dealers, in line, and curry public support for its efforts. To this end, it had the crucial and unflagging support of the commercial news media, which were effectively a branch of the advertising industry.

In contrast to the 1930s, when public debate over advertising regulation had developed into a wide-ranging dispute, with lawmakers taking challenges to the commercial dominance over society quite seriously, there was little in the way of controversy evident during the war. Most of the important decisions affecting advertising were made behind closed doors by appointed government officials with little public accountability. For some of the consumer advocates who remained focused on advertising, most notably Consumers Union president and Amherst College economics professor Colston E. Warne, this was a source of tremendous frustration. In their eyes, if advertising's economic purpose had been dubious in the 1930s, the war had only magnified its apparent asininity. And if grading and standardization had seemed like a good idea during the Great Depression, they made even more sense during a period in which rationing and restrictions on consumer durables had become the norm. While those practices caught the wartime attention of a somewhat dispersed consumer activist community, the direct fight against the advertising industry's political gains was left almost singularly to the energetic president of CU.

Also hampering the galvanizing effort was a lack of public transparency. Whereas consumer advocates in the previous decade had come face to face with a community of vocal adversaries, the latter had moved their wartime political battles to the inside corridors of Washington, leaving opponents with a less tangible target. Warne challenged the newfound partnership between government and business, calling the arrangement a public relations ploy by the advertising industry and "one of the major scandals in American life."[28] He counseled close scrutiny of advertisers' wartime activities and bravely questioned the somewhat dubious advantages they were receiving in exchange for their wartime services. Warne knew as well as industry representatives that the outcome of wartime policy debates might extend into the postwar era, so important issues were at stake. In retrospect, it may appear as though the industry was holding all the cards, and it was not really much of a battle. But in the early 1940s, with the nation fighting for its very survival and public enthusiasm toward advertising far from certain, such an outcome was not a foregone conclusion.[29]

Unlike the advertising industry, which had a natural ally in the commercial press, critics found themselves waging an ongoing battle just to be seen and heard by politicians and the general public. An important factor in the lack of critical media discourse was the recognition by newspapers, magazines, and radio that a reduction in the Advertising Council's activities might translate into diminished revenues for them. As a public relations vehicle for business, the Advertising Council functioned in several capacities. Its immediate objective was to secure businesses' right to advertise throughout the war. An important secondary goal was to secure the status of advertising as a tax-deductible business expense by claiming that it was playing an indispensable patriotic role. The unstated but overarching goal was to gain a solid foothold in Washington and help the American public in fighting the Axis Powers. The purpose of the Advertising Council was to sell advertising as part of the system of free enterprise.[30]

As World War II came to an end in 1945, the advertising industry found itself in an enviable position. The stage was being set for a postwar society dominated by commercialism and a political climate in which criticism of the institution of advertising and commercial values would be considered suspect, even "un-American." The Advertising Council deserved a large share of the credit for its long-term vision, steadfast course, and constant encouragement. Thus advertisers had good reason to face the postwar era with renewed enthusiasm. Largely as a result of the council's relentless work, the industry enjoyed improved relations with the public as the war faded from view. Moreover, and just as important, the intimate working relationship among business, industry, and government leaders continued into the postwar era, growing ever more congenial.[31] Whereas the advertising industry's prewar victory had been fraught with uncertainties, war-related events had turned the government into a supporter of advertising and the industry it represented. This, in turn, would help to facilitate a close and mutually beneficial postwar relationship and create a symbiotic relationship between Cold War policies and private consumption in what Lizabeth Cohen has termed the "Consumers' Republic."[32] Advertising's institutional role, including its claim to be a pillar of a free society and therefore of democracy, was soon off-limits to fundamental debate.[33] This was the advertising industry's ultimate triumph.

Chapter Outline

The title of this book is intentionally ambiguous, as it tells the story not only of how advertisers supported the war effort but also of how the industry used its position of power to advance its self-interests in ways that were not necessarily beneficial to the American public, during either wartime or peacetime.

I connect the period from the passage of the Wheeler-Lea Amendment in 1938 to the conclusion of World War II and the establishment of advertising as part of the postwar political economy.

The first chapter takes us to 1938, right after the battle over federal regulation of advertising had ended. It explores the significance to advertising of the TNEC's investigations and discusses the ongoing government investigations into advertising's economic role. Chapter 1 also discusses the shift from a consumer to a defense economy and how the changes affected the advertising industry's raison d'être. Demands for advertising restrictions combined with renewed government interest in consumer conditions kicked industry leaders into a state of high defense. They were desperately searching for solutions to what they perceived as a deepening quagmire.

Chapter 2 explores the advertising industry's response to the prewar challenges outlined in chapter 1. It discusses industry strategies for "educating the public" to a view of advertising as socially and economically useful. More specifically, it shows the use of institutional advertising for this purpose and discusses how industry leaders worked behind the scenes to prepare a solid defense of advertising. The chapter concludes with the creation of the Advertising Council, Inc., an organization that would come to define the advertising industry's public relations efforts during World War II and beyond.

Chapter 3 looks specifically at the strategizing and planning efforts that went into the Advertising Council. It delineates the council's organizational setup and its working relationship with the government's Office of War Information during its first year of existence. It discusses the council's criteria for accepting the government's domestic information campaigns and how individual campaigns were prepared and implemented in actual advertisements. The chapter concludes with a discussion of advertisers' victory in the battle to keep advertising a tax-deductible expense for business.

Chapter 4 details the concerns of Consumers Union, and particularly of Colston Warne, about the mutually beneficial relationship between advertisers and Washington, including Warne's frustrations as he attempted to gain publicity and public traction for his crusade. It also explores the renewed interest in grading and standardization of consumer goods due to war conditions and how the measure was as welcomed in activist circles as it was opposed in the advertising community.

Chapter 5 explores the debate over payment for the government's home front promotions, which pitted the media's desire for increased advertising revenues against concerns about government encroachment on the First Amendment. The government's decision to rely on the advertising industry's volunteer contributions through the Advertising Council was clearly a vote of approval for the organization, but it also imposed a huge responsibility on the business community, demanding a large and well-orchestrated effort. The chapter concludes with a discussion of how internal struggles within the Office of War Information helped to further solidify the advertising industry's role in the war effort and led the council to change its name to the War Advertising Council.

Chapter 6 chronicles the council's activities throughout 1944. It discusses how individual advertisers were coached to stay on course, sacrificing money, resources, and some of their creative independence to streamline the government's campaigns and make the council a success. This was not always easy, especially when commercial concerns clashed with patriotic goals—a fact driven home by a highly controversial anti–venereal disease campaign. With this campaign, the council found itself awkwardly in the middle between its obligations to the Office of War Information and the need to protect individual advertisers' self-interest. The chapter discusses the situation and how the problem was eventually solved.

Chapter 7 follows the council through the last months of the war and into the reconversion period, when it worked diligently with leaders of the advertising industry, business, and government to determine its role in postwar America. The chapter discusses the nature of these deliberations and explores the newly elevated role of advertising as a public relations tool for the business community at large. No longer satisfied with taking directives from the government, the postwar council, once again called the Advertising Council, assumed a more independent role in regard to campaign selections. Its campaigns over the next few years included programs that were more explicitly designed to educate the public about the superiority of the American system of free enterprise and the virtues of corporate capitalism.

The epilogue brings the story up-to-date, suggesting the impact of wartime events on advertising and consumer activism after World War II and exploring their reverse trajectories in the 1950s. With a few notable exceptions, it was not until the later 1960s that advertising came under new scrutiny by a nascent consumer movement.[34]

1

Prelude to War

The advertising industry concluded the turbulent decade of the 1930s with some sense of accomplishment. Its public relations campaigns appeared to have marginalized the consumer movement's most radical demands, and the five-year battle over federal regulation of advertising had culminated in the Wheeler-Lea Amendment, a law that for all practical purposes sanctioned existing advertising practices. Nonetheless, the years from 1938 through 1941 were fraught with danger in the minds of industry leaders, who perceived the notorious New Dealers to have intensified their critical stance toward advertising as the decade drew to a close. Many were of the opinion that the federal government was determined to crack down on advertising, or even destroy it.[1]

A series of events reinforced this notion. One was the formation of the Temporary National Economic Committee (TNEC) in 1938. Although the committee's objective was not specifically to investigate advertising practices, its focus on monopoly building cast advertising as a tool used in the creation of uncompetitive markets and as an impediment to economic recovery. Subsequent investigations by the Federal Trade Commission (FTC) were more explicit in this regard and put the advertising industry in a defensive stance. While the industry worked frantically to debunk the claim that it was fostering monopolistic tendencies, the escalating war in Europe generated additional concerns. Raw materials were becoming increasingly scarce as production shifted from consumer to military markets, causing critics to question the need for advertising of consumer goods. Promotion of products that were in short supply might have an inflationary effect and could lead to the emergence of black markets. A series of bills were proposed in Congress that would have effectively halted advertising during the war, leaving advertisers to fear that the public might not be eager to return to an advertising-laden society once the fighting was over. The industry was faced with a formidable challenge in attempting to justify its role in the economy and fight back.

Advertising, Business Concentration, and Antitrust

Problems surrounding economic concentration and monopolistic tendencies had been an ongoing concern in the United States since the latter part of the nineteenth century. Congress had responded by passing the Sherman Antitrust Act in 1890, which prevented monopolies and cartels from obstructing competition and harming consumers in the marketplace. Enforced primarily by the Antitrust Division of the Justice Department, the law prohibited contracts, combinations, and conspiracies in restraint of trade, as well as monopolization, and it prescribed substantial fines, even prison terms, for violators. But the legislation was far from perfect. If a corporation violated the law, it could simply dissolve and reorganize as a new corporate entity. And because corporations had traditionally been created by state governments, they were not subject to federal control and oversight.[2]

Concerns about corporate dominance of markets continued into the twentieth century, becoming a cornerstone of Theodore Roosevelt's presidency. In 1914, Congress augmented the Sherman Antitrust Act with the Clayton Antitrust Act, which addressed specific types of restraints not covered by the 1890 measure, including exclusive dealing arrangements, tie-in sales, price discrimination, mergers and acquisitions, and interlocking directorates. With the Justice Department's Antitrust Division and the Federal Trade Commission jointly overseeing compliance, it was quickly apparent that the new law would not be vigorously enforced.

Business consolidation continued to strengthen after World War I and had become a problem by the time the nation plunged into the Great Depression in the 1930s. Many blamed the economic stagnation on monopolistic pricing structures and production restraints.[3] Between 1930 and 1938, the per capita U.S. income was $397 a year, down from $606 in the previous decade. The decrease was shared by all segments of the population.[4] By 1937 the economy had finally returned to 1929 output levels, and unemployment had been reduced from a peak of 25 percent to 14 percent. The Depression appeared to be over. Then the economy unexpectedly went into a tailspin: by early 1938, manufacturing had fallen 30 percent from its 1937 high, five million additional Americans were out of work, and the unemployment rate was nearing 20 percent.[5] The economic crisis, now approaching a decade in length, began to look as if it might never end.

Some liberal economists, joined by Thurman Arnold, the assistant attorney general in charge of the Antitrust Division, saw this as an opportune moment to turn their attention to the question of monopoly and stagnation.[6] They wanted to explore how concentration and market control were contributing to the sluggish economy, which had left factory capacity unused and millions of workers unemployed. They argued that firms in highly concentrated industries had gained the power to control prices, in terms not only of what to charge for their products but also what they were willing to pay their suppliers. This meant that a few large firms enjoyed immense power over their individual markets, thereby preventing the economy from becoming efficient. These giant firms in largely noncompetitive markets could use their economic leverage to force suppliers to sell raw materials at low prices. But because they had a large reserve of capital, they were not forced to sell their own products at low market prices; they were able to hold on to their inventory until higher prices could be commanded. This upset the economy. With few people buying products, production was cut to limit the accumulation of surpluses, which resulted in a vicious cycle of unemployment and weakened purchasing power.[7] Monopolistic (or what we today would refer to as oligopolistic) markets, Arnold suspected, might well be exacerbating the economic stagnation and depression.

Seeking to get the economy back on track, Arnold and other influential members of the Roosevelt administration argued that stricter enforcement of the antitrust laws was the best strategy for securing free markets and policing monopolistic tendencies. If individual markets could be opened to a larger number of players, suppliers of raw materials would be able to sell at a fair market price instead of being limited to the artificial price ceilings set by a few powerful firms. Similarly, if producers had to compete for consumers on the basis of the price and quality of their products rather than trademarks developed through advertising, prices would come down and consumers would trickle back into the marketplace, gradually increasing the demand for goods and effectively bringing the economy back on track. Economic inequality would be lessened as workers' incomes rose, and that money would be spent, thereby spurring more investment and economic growth. The key to economic recovery was to move back toward market freedom and away from monopoly.[8] This, however, was easier said than done, because even business interests acknowledged that "the corporate form has a tendency toward concentration."[9]

The Temporary National Economic Committee

In the late 1930s, the country found itself at a rare political moment. It was then that American corporate capitalism was subject to the most intense level of scrutiny in the nation's history, accompanied by fundamental questioning about its suitability. Economists and New Dealers were increasingly gravitating toward the conclusion that monopoly (and its resulting inequality) was the explanation for the stagnation in the nation's economy. Frustrated by not gaining traction for a serious antimonopoly program at the Department of Justice, Arnold was pleased to offer his blessing and promise of cooperation when Congress decided to pursue the matter.

After a series of legislative deliberations, the Temporary National Economic Committee—commonly referred to as the Monopoly Committee—was established by a joint congressional resolution on June 25, 1938, with a mandate to study the "concentration of economic power in American industry and the effect of that concentration upon the decline of competition." Noting that "concentration of private power had escalated to unparalleled historical levels with the result of seriously impacting the economic effectiveness of private enterprise," President Roosevelt expressed hope that an investigation into these practices might reveal strategies that could "make the American way of living work more effectively" and lead to a "more equitable distribution of income and earnings among American people."[10] While advertising was never the specific focus of any TNEC investigation, its role in protecting markets and preventing competition reappeared in hearing after hearing, leaving many industry leaders ill at ease.

Congress initially allocated $100,000 for the committee and an additional $400,000 for the government departments and agencies that were expected to work closely with the TNEC, including the Department of Justice's Antitrust Division, the Federal Trade Commission, the Securities and Exchange Commission, the Treasury Department, the Commerce Department, and the Labor Department.[11] In an effort to show that there was broad support for the effort, members were drawn from the administration and from both houses of Congress. Joseph O'Mahoney, a Democratic senator from Wyoming, was tapped as the TNEC's first chairman, while Leon Henderson, the chief economist of the Public Works Administration, served as executive secretary.[12]

The Twentieth Century Fund, a philanthropic foundation started by the liberal businessman Edward Filene, had begun a study on "big business" in the United States as early as 1934, but a few years later the organization found itself overwhelmed by the scope of this undertaking. Thus its researchers were happy to transfer their records and findings to the TNEC, a government outfit with far more resources at its disposal.[13] The committee's first task was to review the existing federal economic policies in order to formulate a plan for better distribution of national income and full employment of "men, materials, machines, and money."[14] Working at breakneck speed during the fall of 1938, the group established the groundwork for public hearings on monopoly-related issues. In spite of loud grumbling from some business circles, in which the committee was viewed as yet another New Deal strategy for "putting the blame on business," the National Association of Manufacturers, the American Bar Association, and the United States Chamber of Commerce lent their support.[15] The time was not right for a business attack on government, and the government's public pronouncements were all conciliatory toward free enterprise. "No one," promised Chairman O'Mahoney, "will gain more than business from whatever steps are taken to define and clarify the role of Government as traffic officer in enforcing the rules of fair competition."[16] This meant taking stock of what individual companies and industries were doing to meet their social responsibilities.[17]

One year after the committee's inception, more than twenty experts were at work writing and supervising the preparation of monographs on various aspects of concentrated economic power. The publications fell into three general categories. One group produced historical, analytical, and statistical surveys of the status of competition and the nature and extent of concentration of economic control. Another analyzed data and made recommendations on how to deal with problematic issues. The third group evaluated the applicability of available devices for freeing the economy from the effects of monopoly control.[18] The TNEC's intention, explained Leon Henderson, was to present through reports and hearings "a series of typical situations, drawn from different industries, and illustrating different problems," and to analyze the significance of the varied situations for the "complicated and dynamic process which constitutes American industry."[19] If an investigation disclosed the existence of a harmful monopolistic condition, the corrective process under the antitrust laws would be set in motion, with the violator facing either criminal or civil prosecution or a combination of the two.[20]

The committee was quick to point out, however, that its purpose was not to single out businesses as bad, or to frighten anyone, but merely to apply antitrust regulations to determine whether an industry had gone so far along the path of monopoly control that competition was being hampered. The TNEC asked two basic questions in its detailed case study of American business. First, it asked whether a particular business combination had gone beyond the necessities of efficient mass production and become an instrument of arbitrary price control. Second, it asked whether the marketing practices in an industry—of which advertising was generally far and away the largest expense—tended merely to create orderly marketing conditions in which competitors could exist, or whether they were used to prop up rigid prices and maintain market control.[21] The stakes were high. Unless the government was willing to close the door on the arbitrary power exercised by private organizations and give the free enterprise system a chance, warned O'Mahoney, "we shall have a terrible time preventing the exercise of arbitrary power by the Government."[22]

Between 1939 and 1941, the TNEC spent more than $1 million, had a staff that included 182 experts, fully examined 95 different industries, and took testimony from 552 witnesses. It left a permanent record consisting of 37 volumes of printed testimony and 43 exhaustive monographs on various phases of its study. "There never was before, and may never be again, quite such an economic study as the committee closed its books on," *Time* magazine wrote in 1941. "It made headlines month after month with sensational charges of patent monopoly in the glass-container industry, of international patent combines which put Germany's finger in the U.S. magnesium and optical-glass industries, etc."[23] The publicity helped the TNEC generate large numbers of letters from citizens urging the government "to pursue the good work more vigorously and to take off the back of consumers the enormous spending of advertising."[24] One of the committee's rather disturbing conclusions was that out of the hundreds of American industries, only four or five firms controlled between 50 and 75 percent of the output, which effectively gave them control over the smaller firms in their fields.[25] And as manufacturers were soon to discover, advertising emerged as one of the culprits responsible for keeping markets noncompetitive. "Advertising," reported a writer for the *Christian Science Monitor*, "appears to be under both political and economic attack, and advertising men are becoming increasingly concerned." The ideological raw material for a number of blows to the industry could be traced to the first TNEC monograph, *Price Behavior and Business Policy*, especially the chapter titled "Advertising Brands, and Trade-Marks," with its expressed distrust in the economic usefulness of advertising and its particular disdain for brand names.[26]

Special TNEC hearings to investigate "Problems of the Consumer" were held in May of 1939, putting advertisers on further alert. Some of the testimony went to the heart of parity advertising as a noncompetitive force. One of the most damaging witnesses was Jerome W. Ephraim, a New York City cosmetics manufacturer. After carefully researching the medical literature on oral hygiene, Ephraim had developed a toothpaste of such good quality that the American Dental Association recommended it to their patients. Ephraim had sent samples to major drugstore chains, mail-order houses, and department stores, but he was unable to break into the market. The story was the always the same: he was complimented on the quality of his product, and manufacturers found his price to be fair, but nobody wanted to carry his toothpaste unless he would agree to a massive advertising campaign, at a start-up cost of $100,000, to build up demand. With ten brands of toothpaste controlling 90 percent of the market and those manufacturers able to lay out millions of dollars to tout the superiority of their brand over one that was nearly identical in quality, Ephraim was up against a stone wall of monopolistic competition. "If I go into the open market today," he stated, "I can't do that at all, because the basis of competition there isn't the basis of quality and price, it is the artificial basis of brand competition."[27]

In a response that clearly reflected the "endless misunderstanding between businessmen and economists," Chairman O'Mahoney chastised Ephraim for not understanding advertising's economic function. The primary purpose of advertising, said the senator reprovingly, was to create greater demand and increase production, a process that eventually translated into lower commodity prices for consumers. "All discussion of advertising, it seems to me," he argued, "is totally irrelevant unless you can show that by the abolition of advertising and therefore the admission into the field of a large number of producers you would bring about an improvement of quality and a reduction of price."[28]

TNEC member Donald E. Montgomery, from the Consumers Counsel division of the Agricultural Adjustment Administration, came to Ephraim's defense, producing a letter from the South Shore Consumers' Society in Chicago, which sold Ephraim's toothpaste in addition to several heavily advertised brands. Purchased wholesale at a price of $1.20 a dozen, Ephraim's toothpaste retailed for 20 cents per tube. Identically sized products by Colgate and Squibb were obtained by the retailer at a price of $3.20 and $3.40 per dozen respectively and sold for 35 and 40 cents a tube. Thus, the heavily advertised brands were sold wholesale at nearly three times the cost and retailed at approximately twice the cost of Ephraim's non-advertised brand. Unable to rebut the argument, O'Mahoney reacted defensively, suggesting that Montgomery believed that "advertising ought to be abolished."[29]

Montgomery denied the charge, and Ephraim objected to it as well, stating that he had no problem with advertising as long as those unable to afford such promotional expenditures were not prevented from entering the market and introducing higher-quality products to consumers at a lower price. "If the Government will step in and say here is a toothpaste which meets minimum or high-grade standards for health, the amount of money which tooth-paste makers could then spend on advertising wouldn't be nearly as much and that then the appeal of low price will enter very materially into the picture and give a new small competitor who can produce cheaply a chance," added Willis J. Ballinger, economic adviser to the Federal Trade Commission. This was the same demand that consumer advocates had been making since the early part of the decade, and that had been raised earlier in the TNEC hearings by Consumers Union's Dexter Masters and Dr. Ruth W. Ayres, a well-known economist and consumer activist. Standardization and grading of consumer products, they all argued, was the key to creating a more competitive consumer market. Vehemently denying his opposition to advertising in general, Ephraim assured the committee that he did not want to prevent his competitors from charging more for each tube as long as consumers could check the properties of competing toothpastes according to established government standards.[30]

While lauding O'Mahoney as advertising's "champion," the trade press did not have much patience with certain government economists, including Leon Henderson, and it mourned the "unfortunate publicity" given to the monopoly aspect of advertising, a topic that, according to *Printers' Ink*, had not been intended as part of the hearings. *Business Week* accused Montgomery of having put Ephraim on the stand for the "sole purpose of attacking 'legitimate business,'" arguing that the hearing, which it dismissed as a dramatic show featuring "four housewives, a manufacturer of toothpaste, a purchasing agent, and the director of Consumers Union joining a Sears Roebucks executive in indicting misleading advertising and in demanding government standards," found an appreciative audience among TNEC members and government economists.[31]

In early 1940, the FTC conducted its own study on the cost of distribution. The objective was to ascertain whether advertising, especially national advertising, was costing the consumer too much. FTC commissioner Robert

E. Freer assured the industry that the probe into advertising was only a small part of a much larger study of distribution costs, but that was not enough to satisfy advertisers, who suspected that its real purpose was to attack advertising.[32] The FTC expressed confusion about why members of the advertising community would fear "a fair survey of the place of advertising in the distributive system" and repeatedly told them that there were no hostile or hidden intentions behind the study.[33]

Far from all were reassured, including congressman and former advertising executive Bruce Barton, who viewed the study as an assault on advertising by people who wanted it destroyed. Although he was careful not to accuse the FTC itself of being anti-advertising, he viewed the probe as a warning of worse government attacks to follow.[34] "The danger to the whole country from Government control of advertising," agreed Senator Robert A. Taft (R-OH), "is much greater than the danger that any considerable number of people is going to be defrauded by advertising."[35] Freer was at a loss to explain this reaction. The FTC had conducted more than one hundred general economic inquiries into almost every phase of business activity in the United States. Not once could he recall an instance when one of those surveys had led to such extravagant charges or smear tactics.

The industry's suspicions intensified when Thurman Arnold, who had been both active and successful since being put in charge of the Justice Department's Antitrust Division in 1938, suggested that advertising could be used as a tool for building monopolies, a practice in clear violation of the Sherman Antitrust Act. In one prominent TNEC case, five of America's leading cigarette manufacturers were found guilty of using "several specified means including advertising" to fix, regulate, control, and tamper with the wholesale and retail prices of their own and other tobacco manufacturers' products in order to illegally suppress, restrain, and eliminate competition in the cigarette-manufacturing field.[36] This, however, emphasized Arnold, who served as a TNEC committee member, did not mean that advertising itself was to blame. The problem was not that advertising was a violation of the law, he said, because "no fair-minded, intelligent persons reading the charges could possibly come to the conclusion that it is"; but when advertising was used for the wrong purpose, it could easily come to play an important role in a monopoly scheme.[37] The Antitrust Division was not concerned with whether advertising was wasteful or ineffective in and of itself, but it took a keen interest in uses of advertising that were designed to destroy market competition.[38]

In a grander version of the toothpaste example that had emerged during the TNEC hearings, tobacco companies had successfully used advertising and a variety of national promotional schemes to create and maintain public acceptance of their products, to the point where the public now demanded those particular brands. By all accounts, this forced retailers to either carry these brands or risk going out of business. In and of itself, this was not against the law, but Arnold claimed that the defendants had used their brands' popularity as a means to impose "full-line forcing," a practice he illustrated with an example from the liquor industry. "Suppose you are a liquor manufacturer," he said.

> You spend millions advertising White Smoke whiskey until the nationwide demand is so great that every retailer must carry White Smoke whiskey or lose his customers. There is no possible illegality about building up a nationwide demand through advertising. . . . But suppose that after you have created this nationwide demand you go to the retailer and say . . . "You cannot have my White Smoke whiskey, unless you carry all my other unadvertised whiskeys because I want to hinder my competitor from building up a stock in your store." This the Antitrust Division calls an unreasonable use of power which has been acquired by a legitimate method.[39]

It was this "unreasonable use" of advertising that was illegal. Advertising was not problematic when it was used to sell or increase competition, but only when it was used to eliminate competition.[40] "Many of us have felt, at times, that National advertising campaigns may lead to over-competition, but hardly to restraint of trade," reflected William L. Ransom, trustee of the Academy of Political Science and former president of the American Bar Association.[41]

Acknowledging that the use of brand names itself was "old in our law" and had a legitimate function, and making it clear that he was not "anti-advertising," Arnold stressed that it was only when advertising was used for illegitimate purposes such as gaining monopolistic or semi-monopolistic control that it became a problem.[42] He assured a jittery advertising community that the government had no plans to increase the existing regulation of advertising, and that his only mission was to make sure that advertising was not used in violation of the Sherman Act. Arnold viewed that law as guaranteeing everyone a free market in which to start a new business enterprise in accordance with "the American competitive way"; the idea of the legislation was "to protect the man who advertises his wares, and not to prevent him from advertising." Thus the government's fight against monopolies was being conducted with advertisers' best interests in mind.[43]

Most of the conciliatory attempts were lost on the advertising industry, which was furious with the assistant attorney general, claiming that his antimonopoly crusade was yet another government attack on advertising, a promotional device that played no role in, and shared no blame for, the practice of full-line forcing. If the courts were to decide that excessive advertising was a monopolistic practice, warned *Advertising Age*, "American business will have lost one of its most precious freedoms."[44] It accused Arnold of fabricating the existence of a dark conspiracy where none existed.[45] *Advertising Age* was not alone. "The attitude of this school of thinkers towards advertising strikes far deeper than a mere hate of unethical advertising practices," complained the trade publication *Printers' Ink*. "At the basis is the belief that advertising itself is uneconomic as well as anti-social."[46] While *Editor and Publisher* was careful to establish its opposition to full-line forcing and any practice that threatened to shut out competitors, it was unable to see how extensive advertising behind a meritorious product, "with the aim of pre-empting for the product the largest possible market that can be had," could be considered a violation of business morality.[47]

Smarting from the perceived attack, advertisers completely lost patience when the Justice Department sent questionnaires to twenty-two major oil companies in mid-1941 demanding complete data on their advertising expenditures. The Justice Department wanted even the most minor details about advertising costs and media placements, samples of actual advertising copy, names of agencies, and amounts spent in each media category.[48] The purpose, according to the government, was to determine the extent to which advertising was used to compel retail gasoline stations to carry only one line of products. The assistant attorney general suspected that large oil companies, much like cigarette manufacturers, intended to crush their competition through the use of full-line forcing—and that advertising played an important part in this conspiracy to restrain trade.[49]

Why, wondered industry leaders, would Arnold send out a questionnaire—which on its face was designed to bolster a predetermined inclination to consider all advertising a wasted effort—if he was interested only in full-line forcing?[50] They reminded him that only three years earlier he had accused advertising of functioning merely to push consumer preferences from manufacturer A to manufacturer B—what he had termed "a wasteful system of distribution."[51] This seemed to prove that he was on a wild-goose chase, determined to carry out a vendetta against advertising. "He is not concerned with waste, for 'in a free market waste cures itself,'" contended *Printers' Ink*. "Only as he has said on many occasions, ours is not a free market, but ridden by monopoly, which crushes new enterprise. What he gives with one hand he takes away with the other."[52]

Fearing the practical implications of possible new advertising regulations, the commercial mass media rushed to advertising's defense. The *Chicago Tribune* went so far as to accuse the Department of Justice of trying "to repeal the first amendment by consent decree," while the *Herald* in Lexington, Kentucky, lauded the importance of "uncontrolled advertising" as "the basis of free speech and a powerful force in lifting the American standard of living." Senator Taft shared these sentiments, warning that the Roosevelt administration was "yearning for government control and regulation of advertising," and that giving the government the "power to tell every newspaper what it shall put in its advertising columns" was "only a short step before it will be telling every newspaper what it shall put in its news and editorial columns." He slyly suggested that the antimonopoly probe might be government retaliation against critical press treatment of the government's policies.[53]

The threat posed by the TNEC to business in general, and advertising in particular, was that it would lead to recommendations for sweeping reforms of the economy and take dead aim at large corporations and their antimonopolistic practices. But when the committee submitted its final report in the spring of 1941, its recommendations were rather vague, basically calling for a strengthening of antitrust enforcement at the Department of Justice and the FTC. "With all the ammunition the committee had stored up, a terrific broadside might have been expected," *Time* magazine observed. "Instead, the committee rolled a rusty BB gun into place."[54] By this time the economy was experiencing rapid growth, due entirely to war preparation. Everyone's attention was turning to war, and for advertisers this loomed as an even greater threat to their modus operandi than the investigations had posed.

Advertising in a Defense Economy

By 1940, the need for funds to cover the nation's defense spending had become dire. The first step toward collecting the approximately $3.5 billion that was required was an increase in federal income taxes, followed by a bill that proposed a war excess profits tax on corporations with a net income of more than $10,000.[55] The absence of such a tax during World War I had enabled some manufacturers to grow rich and prosperous on what many characterized as the government's dime. Congressman Jerry Voorhis (D-CA) was determined not to see that happen again. Just as the American people shared the crisis, they should share its expenses in a fair manner. If the proposed measure could be properly drafted, the congressman estimated that it might raise upward of $500 million in additional government revenues.[56] While careful to emphasize that the proposed tax applied not to normal profits, but only to the portion of a company's earnings that resulted from war trade, Voorhis was confident that many business owners would be more than eager to pay their share, especially when they were asked to consider the brutal contrast between "the slaughters of soldiers" and "the reaping of exorbitant profits by a few favored individuals." He was right: Congress passed HR 10413 in 1940 and effectively subjected "excess profits" by American businesses to a tax rate of between 25 and 50 percent.[57]

It was not long, however, before accountants discovered a loophole, pointing out that a manufacturer could avoid these taxes simply by spending any excess earnings on advertising. That expenditure could then be charged as a business expense and would effectively reduce the amount of excess profits subject to taxation. Thus, a large portion of the extra advertising would cost the manufacturer nothing. The idea was first discussed in small private circles, but in November 1940 an article in *Advertising and Selling* explained in detail how a firm could avoid paying taxes by spending its money on advertising.[58] Major advertising executives immediately denounced the strategy, concerned that it would seriously hurt the industry's standing.[59] Ad agencies were quick to proclaim their objection to the use of advertising for the purpose of skipping taxes, and they denied that they urged clients to do so.[60] "Our agency," said Bruce Barton, "would never recommend that a client increase his advertising appropriations on the ground that a major part of the expenditure otherwise would go for taxes."[61]

Voorhis's next move was to put forward a bill designed to put a stop to the new practice.[62] HR 10720, often referred to as the "Advertising Tax Bill," called for a cap on the amount that manufacturers were allowed to declare as an investment in advertising. The measure sought to limit tax-deductible advertising expenditures to $100,000, and in a move that seemed highly aggressive to advertising industry interests, it proposed separate taxes on outdoor advertising and sought to control, even prohibit, the advertising of liquor, tobacco, and certain luxury articles.[63] Manufacturers in those fields happened to be among the relatively few industries that spent more than $100,000 a year on promotions.[64]

The law that allowed businesses to declare a large portion of their advertising costs as a tax-deductible expense had existed almost without interruption since World War I, and its repeal would almost double the amount that businesses were required to pay in federal taxes.[65] Thus the proposed bill, according to the trade journal *Tide*, reflected "the first official statement of an attitude toward advertising which has long given the trade the creeps."[66] *Advertising Age* concurred, warning that the "extreme proposals contained in the bill are typical of the sort of attacks on advertising which may be expected in Congress and the state legislature in 1941" and calling for a united action against the measure.[67]

Some industry defenders suspected that the legislation's true purpose was not to raise revenues but rather to bring about "the ultimate destruction of business and industrial enterprise." The *L.A. Examiner* went so far as to call it "entirely a Communistic devise, based on false and vicious philosophy that advertising is a wasteful and costly burden on the consumer and is unproductive of economic gains."[68] Others accused its supporters of lacking even the most rudimentary knowledge of business and the role of advertising in the economic system, claiming that the measure discriminated against large advertisers.[69] "The proposed law is just as unfair and illogical as a law that might put a special tax on companies hiring more than 100 salesmen," argued *Advertising and Selling*.[70] "Advertising is like payroll, it is neither large nor small in amount, except in relation to the size of operation," agreed the president of the American Association of Advertising Agencies, John Benson.[71] Some even called Voorhis's patriotism into question, contending that a ban on the advertising of certain items was similar to what was happening in totalitarian countries.[72]

Although advertisers were outraged by the proposal, they feared that an open fight might be viewed as unpatriotic, that it would reflect poorly on advertising and leave it exposed to public attacks. As a result, the trade press urged extreme caution. Yet something had to be done. *P.M.*, the only daily newspaper at the time that refused to accept advertising—and, not coincidentally, one of the few dailies that frequently reported on the advertising industry—painted a mocking but fairly accurate picture of advertising trade spokesmen, describing them as "always nervous about the prospective of restrictive legislation," and as pushed into "a hysterical condition in which they see statutory spooks under every bed, and dread a possible Congressional investigation of advertising."[73] But, said *Advertising Age*, unless the advertising industry could come up with a way to deal with the tax issue, it could find itself in a difficult situation.[74]

Thus, the industry decided to fight the measure by pointing to advertising's social utility. It argued that American manufacturers could make a far more patriotic contribution if they invested their money in advertising than if they paid those funds directly to the government in the form of taxes. Because advertising flowed through a maze of taxable channels—advertising agencies, printing houses, lithographers, paper manufacturers, and the mass media—it actually boosted Washington's tax revenues. Moreover, it contributed to increased production and higher employment, which ultimately translated into a broader tax base for the government.[75]

Drafted late in the session, the Advertising Tax Bill did not get a hearing in Congress, let alone a vote on the floor. Evidence suggests that Voorhis dropped the bill as a result of the industry's heavy lobbying efforts: he had a quick and somewhat mysterious change of heart after a private conversation with Charles M. Murphy, general counsel for the Advertising Federation of America (AFA), and the measure was not reintroduced. The congressman subsequently argued that his sole purpose had been to defeat the few companies that spent large sums on advertising merely for the purpose of avoiding taxes, and he used the opportunity to praise advertising as an essential element in free and open competition and a useful weapon against monopoly. The Department of Justice, which denied having any connection to the bill, promised the AFA that "some important advertising group" would be given a chance to review drafts of any new legislation that would affect advertising.[76]

This, however, was not enough to put the industry at ease. By late 1941, the Association of National Advertisers (ANA) was up in arms over the 1941 Revenue Act (HR 5417) and a stipulation in the bill that would tax radio and outdoor advertising in order to raise $3 billion for defense expenses. The fact that this was presented as a tax on entertainment had the ANA ready for a fight. Amusement taxes, according to the association, were usually paid by those enjoying the entertainment, not by the producers of such fare. Moreover, because the tax would be imposed only on radio time sales and not on sustaining programs, it constituted, in effect, a tax on advertising. "To tax advertising," stated the association, "would be to impose a burden on a business function which helps to make sales and thus helps to make taxes."[77] The ANA urged advertisers, agencies, and media to register their objections with their elected representatives, with the result that these groups lobbied intensively and very successfully to remove this clause from the bill.[78]

The legislative victory did not mean that the advertising industry could let its guard down. In the fall of 1941, Representative Carl Vinson (D-GA) introduced HR 5781, a bill to restrict war profiteering. If passed, the measure would prevent businesses that were selling goods to the government under national defense contracts from deducting the costs of advertising and other promotions for these products as tax-exempt expenses.[79] The industry was once again on full alert, defending its prerogatives. "When a national advertiser leaves his regular product to manufacture tanks or guns, he cuts ties with both his dealers and the consuming public," explained *Advertising and Selling*. "In lieu of normal business transactions, he must at least keep alive latent awareness of his peace time operation through advertising. And, although his current copy may not be the means by which he obtained the defense business, the obligation 'to keep his name before the public' which the disarrangement of his normal business entailed, should definitely be allowed as a business expense in figuring the cost of the defense contract." Still, the trade journal warned the industry against "the familiar outcries of rage," arguing that it would be "the wrong way to tell Congress of the bill's inequity," and it accurately predicted that the measure would not pass.[80]

The fight over manufacturers' right to deduct the cost of advertising continued as America entered the war a month later. Now, with an even larger share of the nation's raw material being used to fill government contracts, a good argument could be made that advertising was less beneficial, even unnecessary and counterproductive to the war effort. Even a few members of the advertising industry advocated that advertising be curbed for the war's duration, and that businesses should pay for their ads out of pocket and not be subsidized by American taxpayers.[81]

On the other hand, there were some government officials who continued to side with the industry majority. The business-friendly New Dealer Raymond Moley, for example, argued that government contractors should have a right to claim advertising as a tax-deductible expense because many businesses were rapidly approaching the point at which the government would be their only customer. In order to compete with noncontracting competitors, therefore, those businesses needed to keep their brand names in front of the public for the war's duration. "Suppose company A, which has always sold its entire product to the public, is now turning in 100 percent of its production to the government. Meanwhile company B is still making essential goods for the public," Moley reasoned in an attempt to illustrate the potential unfairness of the situation. "Shall we deny A the right to keep its millions of friends aware of its existence while B proceeds as usual? After the war, A and B will once more be competing for the consumer's dollar. Shall A be handicapped because it put on a uniform for the duration? Clearly, justice requires that a way be found to keep good names alive."[82]

Adding to the industry's worries was the creation in August 1941 of two new defense agencies, the Office of Product Management (OPM) and the Office of Price Administration and Civilian Supply (OPA). Established to manage the wartime economy, they were met with a great deal of industry skepticism. Advertising, the industry feared, would be a low priority for the agencies and might be seen as a barrier by the newly charged government officials. Before long, however, the advertising community discovered that it had little to fear from the OPM because of its business-loyal staffers. The OPA, on the other hand, was seen as more of a problem because it attracted individuals with less apparent devotion to the needs of business.[83]

In order to keep inflation under control, the OPA imposed price ceilings, determining the maximum amount that a manufacturer could charge for a product or service, thus making the need for standardization and grading more pressing.[84] The possibility that a company's advertising costs might not be factored into these maximum prices added to the advertising industry's worries. Thurman Arnold offered little reassurance. "Whether the price ceiling law will allow you to add the advertising as an additional cost is a different thing from stopping your advertising," he told manufacturers. "In other words, a shortage may not be considered justifiable to add the advertising as an additional cost; but those are all problems which you must face in this emergency."[85] The concerns intensified when Leon Henderson, now the chief price administrator for the OPA, suggested that manufacturers could offset the rising cost of raw materials by cutting back on advertising.[86]

"There is a time for all things," declared the trade journal *Broadcasting*, but "this is not the time for a witch hunt against advertising as an institution, operated by the praetorian guard of the Administration's most radical left wing."[87] It questioned how a government that had its hands so full because of the war was spending time and effort to go after advertising. "One thing . . . is evident," concluded the trade journal. "The attack is coming from all imaginable sources, with a trial balloon here and an incidental statement there. It's a job of shooting at a moving target. There's no legislation to attack. Advertising is being discouraged by suasion and innuendo."[88] The opinion in advertising circles was that government officials viewed the ongoing crisis as "an excellent opportunity for idealists to make a long-desired frontal attack on advertising, not on the true basis of their disbelief in its economic justification—but in the guise of 'emergency.'"[89] After taking stock of the situation, industry observers painted a bleak picture. Advertising was being attacked on several fronts, and with the defense program playing an increasingly large part in Washington's strategy, the industry was getting ready to wage a battle of its own.[90]

Conclusion

Although the five-year battle over federal regulation of advertising had been resolved to the advertising industry's general satisfaction by 1938, the legislative victory offered little reprieve. New economic conditions, brought on first by the economic crash of 1938, which provoked a series of government investigations that touched on advertising's economic function, combined with war in Europe to put the industry on high alert. Aware that a full-fledged opposition to TNEC investigations and new taxes might draw unwanted attention, the advertising industry chose another tack. Attempting to divert public attention from the looming issues, it used its promotional skills to "educate" politicians and the public about advertising and its usefulness during a period of national defense while hatching a comprehensive program to allay any doubts about the economic role of advertising.

2

Advertising Navigates
the Defense Economy

Industry leaders, their misgivings fueled by constant alarms, failed to recognize that New Deal actions against advertising had been relatively mild. They continued to monitor influential government officials, worried that a single critical comment might escalate into a crisis demanding the industry's full attention. America's response to the war in Europe and the gradual shift from a consumer to a defense economy raised new questions about advertising's role and function in society. Now, on the eve of the nation's own entry into the war, industry leaders were, in the words of one trade journal, trying "frantically to prepare a sound argument" for advertising's usefulness in the new economic environment.[1]

Advertisers understood the importance of building and maintaining good relationships with their audiences, and the industry wisely launched several forms of public relations aimed at educating the public, with the hope that the mass of American consumers would not merely tolerate advertising but acknowledge it as a beneficial social and economic force. This chapter explores the challenges faced by the advertising community in the period leading up to the attack on Pearl Harbor and immediately thereafter. It discusses how the industry dealt with new forms of criticism, how it viewed its role in the war economy, and how it eventually embarked upon a highly successful public relations venture: the Advertising Council.

Advertising's Role in the Defense Economy

The advertising industry had always been sensitive, even defensive, about its contribution to the national economy. And now, in early 1940, with war-related production demanding a disproportionate share of the nation's raw materials, production for the consumer market was suffering, and the possibility of inflation was causing the government to consider price controls.[2] To encourage consumption when commodities were scarce and few new products were needed might lend credence to the argument that advertising was wasteful, if not downright unpatriotic.[3] The claim that advertising performed a valuable economic function by introducing new products, encouraging competition, and ultimately leading to mass production, thereby allowing consumers to enjoy better and more competitively priced goods, had not been entirely convincing during the 1930s and was even less so in the changing economic situation brought on by the war.

Thus industry spokesmen began to take another tack, declaring that the new economy had not diminished advertising's usefulness but in fact had elevated its importance. Advertising could play an educational role, guiding consumers toward products that did not compete with defense production for supplies and raw materials. This, according to industry leaders, not only would help slow down inflation, but also would increase the level of business activity and employment. The result would be a healthy economy and higher tax revenues for the government, which could be used to support defense expenditures. This new rationale for advertising sounded both plausible and upbeat and seemed a far cry from the unpatriotic tendencies that some of the TNEC investigations had suggested.[4]

Moreover, and perhaps even more important, the business community envisioned an instrumental postwar role for advertising. Even before the United States entered World War II, there was serious concern that the private sector would not be able to immediately absorb the returning citizen-soldiers and the workers who had been employed in wartime production, and that the nation would fall back into a depression as a result. The solution, according to advertisers, was to maintain the visibility of brands such as Ford, Chrysler, and General Motors during the emergency and help secure a demand for the old familiar products once the war was over. The result would be continuously high industrial production and low unemployment, reducing the possibility of a depression. Some even predicted that advertising might help push postwar production beyond anything previously dreamed of.[5]

This argument was supported by experiences with advertising during World War I. Manufacturers that had maintained their advertising budgets during this period had managed to regain their leadership positions in the postwar era. Large companies that had discontinued or greatly reduced their advertising appropriations during the war had fared much worse. A study tracing seventeen manufacturers from the latter category concluded that six were absorbed by competitors after the war, one failed and went out of business, one went into receivership, one was forced to cut its workforce in half, and one lost nearly half its sales volume and all but two of its customers. Three other companies lost leadership in their fields, one was operated by the banks for five successive years, and two lost serious ground to competitors.[6] The clear lesson was that in order to prosper in a postwar environment, manufacturers needed to advertise during wartime. The purpose of wartime or emergency advertising, suggested one industry spokesperson, was "primarily to preserve present markets, maybe even enlarge them, for the time when Uncle Sam may not be the biggest customer. . . . Then a company will be well off if, by good advertising, it finds that it still has loyal dealers and a public that has not forgotten, but is just waiting to buy again."[7]

While stressing their commitment to the immediate defense effort, however, the advertising community admitted openly that selling the American public on the value of free enterprise was still their highest priority. One high-ranking advertising executive proposed that the American Association of Advertising Agencies (AAAA) establish a mechanism for convincing the country that the American way of life must be protected and preserved. "By selling America to Americans," claimed Roy F. Irvin, "we can sell advertising as the power that worked when everything else failed. And that, after all, is quite a plug for advertising."[8] Paul Garrett, who in addition to his high-level involvement with the Advertising Federation of America (AFA) was held in high esteem as a public relations practitioner, agreed. "Years ago we strove for more honesty in advertising," he said. "I would like to see us fight now for more understanding through advertising." The use of advertising for unity building and patriotic ends could effectively demonstrate its usefulness and increase its stature. "What a power for good it would be if this most powerful of public relations instruments could turn its great talent to the creation of a better understanding among our people of their own institutions."[9] Together, these goals provided ample justification for an extensive use of institutional advertising in the period leading up to the war. It was important, however, that advertisers not be seen as taking advantage of the situation.[10]

Advertising in a Defense Economy

The shift to a defense-oriented economy was evident by the late 1930s, although the full impact of the change was not widely felt until the early 1940s. Significantly, this was also a period when advertisers were increasingly attracted to so-called "institutional" advertising. The practice of highlighting the industry behind the product, as opposed to the product itself, became increasingly appealing as regular consumer goods disappeared from store shelves and manufacturers scrambled for ways to keep their brand names viable and build goodwill for the future.[11] In order to divert attention from what might be perceived as an excessive use of advertising during a period of product shortages, advertisers attempted to convey the idea that they were helping consumers by guiding their spending and preparing them for the ultimate return to a postwar economy. Moreover, and just as important, associations and individual industry leaders encouraged corporations to publicize their own sacrifices and to tell consumers how their businesses had adapted to the war situation—how, in effect, "we're all in this together."[12] A survey conducted by *Printers' Ink* in July 1940 found that 89 of 112 prominent advertisers planned no changes in their advertising appropriations, while 15 were considering an increase in such spending for the following year.[13] By the late summer of 1940, more than 50 of the nation's leading advertisers had used defense themes in their product advertising, and others were following suit.[14]

Manufacturers of heavy goods with direct links to the war led the effort to invoke defense themes in their ads. Airplane and automotive manufacturers, steelmakers, and machine tool producers were among the first to find themselves with the government as their only customer. Although immediate sales were not a problem, companies worried about maintaining their relationship with the consuming public. Thus, institutional advertising telling consumers about a manufacturer's role in the national defense effort seemed an "ideal way" to approach these problems. Of course, some products lent themselves more easily to defense tie-ins than others. Manufacturers of chemicals, airplanes, and machinery could easily promote the importance of their products in the preparedness program, whereas producers of consumer-oriented products were forced to use war themes more for illustrative purposes.[15]

Some manufacturers of factory equipment went a step further, blatantly aligning themselves with the war effort and imbuing their products and services with an aura of patriotism even when the link between product and defense was weak at best. The argument was simple, and the ad copy was blunt:

automobile assembly lines were now turning out Sherman tanks and B-24 Liberators. Without those tanks and bombers, the Axis might win the war.[16] Companies that produced items for sale to soldiers were especially eager to say so in their advertisements. Gillette and Mennen stressed soldiers' use of their shaving supplies; Wrigley did the same for its chewing gum. Camel and Chesterfield, Lucky Strike and Pall Mall, Raleigh and Webster advertised the preference of America's soldiers and sailors for their tobacco products. Makers of Alligator rainwear and Fortune shoes as well as pen companies such as Parker and Wahl also used their army contracts for promotional purposes. Companies that were only indirectly affected by the war-preparedness situation used defense themes as attention-getters. For example, ads for both the Bank of Manhattan and Hammermill Paper included tanks; Best Foods promoted their new margarine, Nucoa, by depicting a lunching aircraft worker with the caption "Defense workers eat hearty."[17]

Figure 1. "It's Chesterfield." This ad shows how defense themes were used in prewar cigarette advertisements. *Life*, June 30, 1941, 31.

Figure 2. "I Torture Tanks." This action-packed prewar ad bragged of the military's preference for Camels over other cigarette brands. *Life*, November 11, 1943 (back cover).

Defense-theme advertising made frequent use of the American flag and other patriotic symbols. Scores of companies, acting individually and on their own initiative, devoted substantial amounts of advertising space and time to messages highlighting American ideals and institutions. Other major trends were new products and models that were claimed by their manufacturers to embody special features of distinctively American character and the incorporation of American colors and atmosphere into sales and advertising appeals: an "Americanism crusade" that, according to one observer, went far beyond the scope of "promoting American-made goods to the home folks."[18] By 1941, several advertisers had begun to incorporate the selling of U.S. savings bonds and stamps—universally recognized as a gauge of citizen participation in the war effort—into their sales efforts.[19]

Patriotic themes became so popular, in fact, that the government was forced to issue guidelines regarding when and how flags and military uniforms could be used in advertising copy. Both the U.S. Army and Navy extended help to advertisers who submitted material to them for review.[20] Some industry observers worried that excessive flag waving and use of patriotic associations might backfire. "The cold-blooded truth," warned one public relations expert, "is that words, promises, arguments have taken on new implications and no longer convey simple, direct meanings because they have been used so often in making statements that didn't pan out."[21]

A sixty-page red, white, and blue manual issued by the Crowell-Collier Publishing Company represented yet another attempt at aiding advertisers in their public relations efforts. *John Doe Looks at Industry in War* suggested ways in which manufacturers could use advertising to tell average Americans about product shortages, product substitutions, and their own role in the national defense market. Not surprisingly, given Crowell-Collier's dependence on advertising revenues, the brochure included a strong pitch to manufacturers, encouraging them to continue advertising in order to maintain their companies' visibility while saving "prestige in a competitive market."[22] Johns-Manville and General Electric were among the national advertisers that experimented with lower-keyed "goodwill" advertising. General Electric, for example, sponsored a weekly radio program called *The Week in Defense* in order to keep the public informed about the defense effort and what corporate America was doing to help. In keeping with the softer approach, commercial breaks were kept modestly brief. Johns-Manville's efforts included a series of magazine insertions in the *New York Post* describing various industries and their contributions to national defense, which were accompanied by a coordinated advertising campaign in the home cities of the featured industries.

The brief advertisements were tailored to each industry and declared Johns-Manville's pride in serving as a supplier.[23]

These and similar promotions answered *Printers' Ink*'s call for using the "war flavor" without dragging in too much of the "sob sister flavor." The secret behind good war advertising, argued the trade publication, was to play on patriotism without becoming overly sentimental. Advertisers were encouraged to give their advertising a "strong he-man" flavor. Successful war advertising maintained the competitive standing of a manufacturer's branded products—whether automobiles or electric ovens—even though the production of such consumer goods was temporarily curtailed. It also acquainted the public with the manufacturer's role in national defense and built good relations with the public in anticipation of the day when the troops would come home and business could return to normal.[24]

Defense themes became increasingly popular throughout the first part of 1941. By July, however—about five months before Pearl Harbor—the trend showed signs of receding. A study based on advertisements placed in major American magazines suggested that consumers' interest in defense-theme advertising had leveled off. An examination of 386 issues of eighteen consumer magazines revealed that only 498 (3.6 percent) of their 13,741 advertisements used defense as a theme, and that a relatively small group of 119 manufacturers were responsible for this form of promotion. Topping the list of manufacturers using such themes was an unnamed cigarette company, followed by the U.S. Army. While the level of interest among men seemed to be little changed from the year prior, women's enthusiasm had declined by between 10 and 15 percent. Thus, researchers found that magazines with a predominantly female readership carried only a small amount (0.7 percent) of defense-theme advertising, while such promotions characterized between 6.3 and 8 percent of all advertising in *Time*, *Look*, and *Liberty*. One explanation for this trend was that fewer goods were being produced that were logically suited for defense-theme promotions. Another possibility was that manufacturers had begun to question the efficacy of using defense themes in their ads.[25]

Printers' Ink invited the industry to rethink its traditional public relations methods, stressing that the use of advertising could not be justified "solely by a series of free advertisements 'interpreting advertising to the American people.'" Defense of advertising was "a long, difficult and continuous job," the trade journal warned, one that would require advertisers' full commitment and that could not be "entrusted to stooges, miracle mongers or yes-men."[26] Having come to the realization that using advertising copy to forge connections between products, patriotism, and "Americanism" addressed only part of its credibility issue, the advertising industry began to seek out other strategies.

Advertising: An Organized Defense

The advertising industry had spent the better part of the 1930s defending itself against growing consumer resentment, which had resulted in a series of business-sponsored educational efforts designed to overwhelm the opposition's messages. Part of the strategy had been the creation of industry front groups (also called third-party groups) to help spread the industry's own message.[27] One example was the Committee on Consumer Relations in Advertising, which was formed by the AAAA in 1938 to research economic aspects of advertising and consumption and was sponsored by its members to the tune of a million dollars. Its main objective was to sway public opinion in its favor.[28] In 1936, the ANA and the AAAA created the Advertising Research Foundation for the same purpose, and two years later that group received support from the Harvard Business School and a $30,000 grant from advertising agency owner A. W. Erickson's widow for a massive research project to map the economic and social effects of advertising. Written by Harvard economics professor Neil Borden and promoted by representatives of the advertising industry as an "academic study, impartial and unbiased," *The Economic Effects of Advertising* offered a strong defense of advertising strategies and principles.[29] Warning that anti-advertising forces had been "moving in on the advertising process in a manner not unlike that of the Hitler strategy of divide and rule," industry leaders, including ANA president Paul West, stressed the importance of getting the findings out to a wide audience, including high-ranking Washington officials, members of Congress, top business executives, consumer leaders, and groups in which "legislation or regulations affecting advertising" were being considered.[30] He expressed grave concerns about the kind of advertising criticism that that he saw "manifesting itself daily in many quarters" and reminded his colleagues of

> the talk by high officials in Government of curbing advertising as a means of controlling inflation and restricting it as a means of controlling production, the recent last-minute incorporation of a tax on radio and outdoor advertising and electric advertising signs and devices in the tax bill now before Congress, the thinly veiled attacks on trademarks and brands, the push for mandatory standardization and Government grade labeling of all consumer goods, the continued charges that advertising is a waste, that it fosters a monopoly, that

it is an added cost to the consumer—all these and more are causing growing alarm that advertising is going to be throttled by whatever method, for
whatever purpose and with whatever motive."[31]

At the same time, the president of the ANA acknowledged that there was
room for industry improvement, and he urged his colleagues to adapt to "the
basic changes which are surely coming."[32] By the summer of 1941, the AAAA
and the ANA had formed a joint committee to help the advertising industry
find common ground and design strategies for a united defense.[33] Still worried
that too much talk about war-related issues might come across as unpatriotic,
however, the group decided to focus primarily on the economic critiques of
advertising that had emerged over the past three years. Using a nonconfrontational approach, and consciously avoiding language that might evoke the idea
that the advertising industry was trying to evade defense-related problems,
the committee stressed advertising's economic importance, arguing that it
was not an "appendage to be lopped off" but rather an integrated part of the
overall economic system.[34] Careful not to be seen as criticizing individual
government officials for their views, the committee planned to demonstrate
the similarity between the assault on advertising and the "general attack on
individual freedom throughout the world" at the time.[35]

The sentiments were shared by the advertising community at large. "If private enterprise is paralyzed and destroyed, through widespread destruction
of public confidence in its efficiency and its motives," noted Ralph K. Strassman, vice-president of the Ward Wheelock Company, "it is but a short step
to the suppression of personal rights."[36] It would be no small feat, however,
to "effectively counterbalance the government's attempts to smear advertising
in the eyes of the public."[37] It would require vision, management, and cour-
age along with sound thinking by advertising men and could not, as Everett
R. Smith, director of marketing and research at McFadden Publications, so
aptly put it, be "merely 'agin' the government."[38] Thus, the committee stressed
the need to prepare a proper case for advertising that would marshal all the
facts, demonstrating advertising's function and its important role in the war-
oriented economy.[39]

Hot Springs, November 1941

In November, the joint AAAA-ANA committee called a meeting in Hot
Springs, Virginia, at which some seven hundred representatives from the
advertising and media industries were joined by people from the business

community to discuss national advertising and its role in the economy.[40] The attendees came from a wide variety of backgrounds, making for an unusual and highly interesting conference. Many of the sessions were filled beyond capacity. The delegates tended to share the organizers' view that the consumer movement's radical element, which only a few years earlier had been considered business's worst enemy, no longer represented the largest threat. They were far more concerned about the federal government's attitudes toward advertising. "The danger lies not so much in what extremist, alarmist elements in the anti-advertising forces are trying to do, but the fact that the more moderate elements, among those in charge of the nation's machinery and in Congress, simply do not realize what is taking place because they don't fully understand what advertising is and how it functions," explained the ANA-AAAA committee in charge of the summit.[41]

"If we honestly believe that the system of free enterprise has made this country great, has made its people better off than the people of any other nation in the world," said advertising agency president C. R. Palmer, "then we must support and if necessary *fight* for that system."[42] Because advertising was so closely connected to free enterprise, a strategy for defending its use would need to encompass a larger battle to secure free enterprise for the postwar period as well. James Webb Young, a senior consultant at the J. Walter Thompson agency, who was one of the elite group of industry representatives in charge of the Hot Springs meeting, warned the advertising community against trying to win this battle while ignoring business's fight for survival: "Let us ask ourselves whether we, as an industry, do not have a great contribution to make in this effort to regain for business the leadership of our economy. We have within our hands the greatest aggregate means of mass education and persuasion the world has ever seen, namely the channels of advertising communication. We have the masters of the techniques of using these channels. We have power. Why do we not use it?"[43] Young suggested that a soft-sell approach would yield the best results. "John D. Rockefeller did not escape the charges of being a robber baron until he became a philanthropist," he said. "Is this a tip on public relations for us?"[44]

In spite of the volatile political situation during the fall of 1941, talks at the Hot Springs meeting largely ignored world events. Most of the delegates were interested in the war only to the extent to which it encroached on "business as usual," and they viewed advertising's role within the larger context of national defense and preparedness. This did not escape the government's attention. Both Leon Henderson, the director of the Office of Price Administration, and William L. Blatt, who served as director of the Materials Division of the Office of Product Management, criticized the advertising community on these grounds. Henderson chided advertising interests for being too preoccupied with their own problems, asserting that they had an obligation to discuss advertising's role in the defense effort.[45] He did, however, surprise the Hot Springs delegates by denying that he personally held anti-advertising attitudes. Some forms of advertising, he acknowledged, were socially useful and played an important economic role. "If I have a point of view about advertising, it is that under the sort of expanding economy I would like to see, *there should be more of it.* That is, more of the right kind," said Henderson, adding that he found institutional advertising to be of particular merit.[46] He also urged advertisers to rethink their strategies in light of the general defense situation and envision new opportunities.[47]

The delegates were pleased with Henderson's speech, which *Printers' Ink* editor C. B. Larrabee characterized as "at least a minor miracle."[48] Not only did Blatt and Henderson move the defense issue to the foreground of the debate, but their words were the last to make an impression on the participants before they left Hot Springs.[49] The organizers were similarly affected. They realized that a big flag-waving committee would not take care of advertising's problems, and that a more organized approach was called for. "We need deeds, not words," urged the president of the Centaur Company, Harold B. Thomas. When he called for a rising vote on whether all present were willing to give their time, energy, and money for the task ahead, the audience reportedly "arose as one man."[50]

War in America

If the delegates could have peeked into the near future, they would have realized that the talks by Henderson and Blatt constituted an outline for the advertising community's most effective public relations campaign to date— one that would combine the use of patriotic copy with a strategic campaign to legitimize advertising in the minds of the American public and Washington officials. But none of that was evident at the close of the meeting. If anything, industry observers were slightly disappointed about the outcome of the conference. "Santa Claus did not ride through the lobby at the Homestead. Nor did those who attended the special joint meeting of the Association of National Advertisers and the American Association of Advertising Agencies among the Virginia mountains last week take home with them, wrapped in a neat bundle, the answers to the problems besetting their businesses," concluded Larrabee.[51] Others expressed much the same sentiment: "This year's convention and its plans for a pro-advertising campaign would have been fine—three years ago," wrote the editors of *Advertising and Selling*. "If advertising wants to raise, rather than further hurt its professional prestige, it would do better to impress the public with efforts in behalf of the country, rather than efforts in behalf of itself."[52] Subjects that should have been suggested and discussed, said the editors, included cooperating with the government in efforts to aid military enlistment, disseminating defense information, conserving defense materials, and improving national morale. They also warned that any trace of selfish behavior on the part of advertisers might backfire: "Whatever is done for *its own*, advertising had also better avoid leaving itself open to criticisms of the Blatt variety. . . . The 'war record' of advertising after the emergency will be scrutinized just as carefully as that of any 'fit' individual."[53]

The Hot Springs talks were not immediately forgotten, however. Many advertising executives were inspired by the meeting and left it eager to transform the ideas they had heard into more practical forms. A follow-up meeting to discuss how "the governing group of the Advertising Council or whatever it is to be called" should be organized and funded took place a few weeks after the November conference.[54] Paul B. West and the president of the Young and Rubicam advertising agency, Chester LaRoche, who had been instrumental in organizing the original meeting, took charge of the new venture. West was the instigator, but it was not long before the highly enthusiastic and motivated LaRoche emerged as the leader of the informal group.[55] Then came the Japanese attack on Pearl Harbor, which effectively advanced the group and forced it to define its purpose.

Within a few days after the United States entered World War II, Donald M. Nelson, the OPM's director of priorities, contacted West, asking for advertisers' assistance in fighting the war and stressing the government's need to be supported by their creative talents and to be given access to their channels of communication.[56] Washington's invitation could not have come at a more opportune time. The Hot Springs meeting had illustrated the advertising industry's need for a new public relations approach aimed at protecting the free enterprise system and advancing advertising's role within it. The meeting had made it obvious, however, that the industry needed to move cautiously and diplomatically, taking the utmost care not to represent advertising in a self-serving or unpatriotic manner.

Nelson's call suggested that the industry would be given a chance to improve its relationship with the government. To the extent that this cooperation took place in order to benefit the war effort, it held the promise of improved relations with the public as well. The advertising community reacted to the proposal with enthusiasm. They would do a great job at stimulating enlistment in the war effort; they would help sell war bonds; they would help build up the nation's morale—all in a generous and selfless spirit. Advertising, the industry leaders assured, would serve "primarily as a public information service."[57] Advertisers were "ready and willing to do their share in behalf of the national war effort through promotion of defense bonds and stamps and other government activities in their advertisements and on their radio programs" and hoped that the government would decide to "make full use of advertising in all its forms to accelerate accomplishment."[58]

Washington's request spurred cautious optimism as industry leaders hoped that a more organized undertaking might result in an increased (and improved) use of advertising to inform the public about war-related issues. It was a heaven-sent opportunity that would give the industry a starring role in the greatest promotional endeavor yet undertaken by the United States.[59] "The advertising office's greatest skeleton, fear of federal interference, will crumble into dust with Uncle Sam himself turning to advertising to gain defense program results," predicted one industry observer. "Mr. Advertising himself will walk jauntily down Main Street, publicly recognized as a tried and true defender of the American Way."[60]

The main concern now was to develop a plan for mobilizing advertising on a national scale. Moving at a breakneck pace, a handful of key figures, representing national advertisers, ad agencies, and media, met on January 5, 1942, and formed a tentative organization, naming Chester LaRoche chairman, Paul B. West secretary, and Frederic R. Gamble assistant to the chairman. This small group, convened at a defining moment in the nation's history, marked the unofficial founding of the Advertising Council, Inc.[61]

The idea of an industry-run agency to help the government with its program was not entirely novel. In 1917, President Woodrow Wilson had created the Committee on Public Information (CPI)—commonly known as the Creel Commission after its leader, George Creel—to mobilize American support for World War I. Advertising practitioners had begun assisting the CPI almost from the outset, and in early 1918 Creel established a separate Division of Advertising. With solid backing from organized advertising interests, the division became a clearinghouse for the distribution of $5 million in space and services donated by the advertising industry to the CPI and created a series of successful campaigns to sell Liberty Bonds and promote a host of other war-related projects that the government deemed important, including support for the Red Cross. In exchange for buying newspaper or magazine space for this purpose, individual advertisers were allowed to put their name in the ad's credit line.

Initially, the government's appeals for support could not be incorporated into regular product advertising. While they might have been paid for by advertisers, produced by advertising creatives, and carried for free by the commercial mass media, they were not yet mixed with appeals for the public to buy consumer products or keep brand names in mind for the war's duration. That changed in the spring of 1918, when the Advertising Division devised a "duplex plan," permitting corporate advertisers to promote the war effort and their own products at the same time. This, according to the U.S. Rubber Company, allowed for "the possibilities of impressing the public with the idea that business and Government are one and inseparable," a notion that appealed to the many American corporations seeking moral legitimacy and public acceptance. The division became a crossroads for everyone who worked in advertising during World War I and was given credit not only for knitting "widely scattered and decentralized groups and individual practitioners into an occupational community" but for helping to formalize advertising as an industry.[62]

The industry had also assisted the National Recovery Administration's "Buy Now" campaign in the early 1930s, and in the spring of 1941 the AFA had established a National Defense Committee for the purpose of matching donated advertising services such as creative talent and media space to the government's publicity needs. The first assignment was a recruitment poster for the Selective Service System, which was distributed to local advertising clubs across the country for display in government buildings and draft board offices and posted in every Pullman car in the country during June of 1941. Subsequent posters emphasizing similar aspects of the national defense program were produced and promoted in a similar way.[63]

Now, with war a reality, Donald Nelson and Robert Horton, director of information for the Office of Emergency Management, were strongly in favor of giving advertising an important role to play in the government's information strategy. The Office of Facts and Figures, which served as the government's information office at the time, admitted that it had been planning to ask the AAAA and the ANA to form a small committee to help the government, and said that the Advertising Council had exceeded its highest hopes and expectations.[64]

The Advertising Council: Early Considerations

The Advertising Council was not officially announced until March 1942. With a stated mission to "provide a means for marshaling the forces of advertising so that they may be of maximum aid in the successful prosecution of the war," the council set up offices in Washington and New York and appointed Miller McClintock as executive director at a salary of $33,000.[65] McClintock was not selected from the ranks of influential advertising executives, but he had a clear notion of the council's mission and viewed its objective as interpreting the government's advertising needs and passing them on to business. McClintock had a doctorate from Harvard and had worked as a reporter for the *San Francisco Bulletin*. As the former director of the Advertising Research Foundation, he had also worked in close cooperation with the ANA. At the time of his appointment, he was director of the Bureau of Street Traffic Research at Yale University. He was also employed as the chief executive of the federal government's Traffic Audit Bureau, which evaluated outdoor advertising displays. Other members of the council's executive committee included Chester LaRoche, chairman; Harold B. Thomas, vice-chairman; Paul B. West, secretary; and Frederic R. Gamble, treasurer.[66]

McClintock made it clear that the council's intent was to involve practically every organized advertising group and that careful consideration had gone into selecting representatives from small as well as large agencies, advertisers, mass media, and related groups. Ten of the thirty-one officers came from the ranks of national advertisers. Advertising agencies were represented by ten members. There were three representatives from the newspaper industry and two from national magazines. The radio, outdoor advertising, and retail industries were each represented by one person. National advertisers, agencies, and major media industries contributed a total of $100,000 toward the first year's operating budget.[67] With the exception of the executive director and a few staff members, the council was dependent upon volunteer labor and donated services.[68]

The council's official purpose was to serve as a clearinghouse. It developed a system whereby advertising needs and skills for a specific campaign or program could be quickly assessed, and it helped to clarify the government's promotional goals to advertisers. Many government agencies were enthusiastic, and several began using these services even before the council was officially announced.[69] Much to the Advertising Council's delight, the Treasury Department, which ultimately held the power to rule on advertising's tax-deductible status, was among the early adopters.

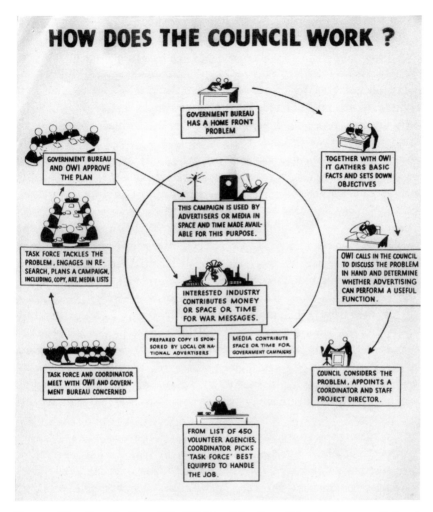

HOW DOES THE COUNCIL WORK ?

GOVERNMENT BUREAU HAS A HOME FRONT PROBLEM

GOVERNMENT BUREAU AND OWI APPROVE THE PLAN

TOGETHER WITH OWI IT GATHERS BASIC FACTS AND SETS DOWN OBJECTIVES

THIS CAMPAIGN IS USED BY ADVERTISERS OR MEDIA IN SPACE AND TIME MADE AVAILABLE FOR THIS PURPOSE.

TASK FORCE TACKLES THE PROBLEM, ENGAGES IN RESEARCH, PLANS A CAMPAIGN, INCLUDING, COPY, ART, MEDIA LISTS

OWI CALLS IN THE COUNCIL TO DISCUSS THE PROBLEM IN HAND AND DETERMINE WHETHER ADVERTISING CAN PERFORM A USEFUL FUNCTION.

INTERESTED INDUSTRY CONTRIBUTES MONEY OR SPACE OR TIME FOR WAR MESSAGES.

PREPARED COPY IS SPONSORED BY LOCAL OR NATIONAL ADVERTISERS

MEDIA CONTRIBUTE SPACE OR TIME FOR GOVERNMENT CAMPAIGNS

TASK FORCE AND COORDINATOR MEET WITH OWI AND GOVERNMENT BUREAU CONCERNED

COUNCIL CONSIDERS THE PROBLEM, APPOINTS A COORDINATOR AND STAFF PROJECT DIRECTOR.

FROM LIST OF 450 VOLUNTEER AGENCIES, COORDINATOR PICKS 'TASK FORCE' BEST EQUIPPED TO HANDLE THE JOB.

Figure 3. "How Does the Council Work?" Advertising Council flowchart, 1942 or first part of 1943. Courtesy Ad Council Archives, University of Illinois Archives, RS 13/2/305.

The Tax Issue—in Wartime

With America's entry into the war, advertising's role in the distributive system became even more suspect. Many manufacturers produced strictly to fill government contracts, with the result that consumer products had become even scarcer. Even a few dissidents within the advertising community itself advocated that advertising be curbed for the war's duration, and others believed that such promotions should be paid for out of each business's pocket rather than being heavily subsidized by American taxpayers.[70] But for the lion's share of the industry, and all of the trade organizations that coordinated its political, lobbying, and public relations efforts, this was a clear battle for survival. Hence the advertising industry waged an all-out effort to combat the tax measure, making monitoring of lawmakers' stand on the issue a high priority. As part of the lobbying effort, industry representatives compiled a list of congressional members who were to be "investigated" with regard to their position on the proposed tax.[71]

Attempts to disallow all advertisers' right to this tax break were fought ferociously. "Advertising is not a finished product," contended the ANA before the Senate Finance Committee in early 1942. "It is a business process." Rather than crippling "the most vital tool of business" and harming the mass media in their role as "substantial taxpayers and employers of labor," the association suggested more aggressive taxation of business profits.[72] Much to the industry's relief, however, attempts to tax advertising were met with substantial resistance in Washington.

In the spring and summer of 1942, reports James J. Kimble, the Treasury was facing a serious problem with the sale of war bonds. Treasury Secretary Henry Morgenthau Jr. had promised to sell a billion dollars' worth of bonds per month, but actual sales were nowhere near that amount. Embarrassed by an angry President Roosevelt and growing public criticism, Morgenthau began to doubt his ability to reach the set goal. Although sales picked up throughout the war, the income was not enough to offset the escalating war expenses, and the fact that one-third of the population did not know "what the U.S. was fighting for" did not do much to ignite the effort.[73]

Morgenthau's solution was to shift to the use of periodic war bond drives, as opposed to maintaining an ongoing effort.[74] It was toward this end that he was one of the first government officials to ask for promotional help from the Ad Council. His request was received with great enthusiasm, and soon the Treasury was relying almost entirely on the council's help in promoting its sale of war bonds and stamps to the American people. The income from these securities allowed the nation to borrow money for the war effort from its citizens and relieved some of the pressure for new tax revenues. The Advertising Council treated this task with the utmost consideration. It designed an elaborate campaign plan and instructed individual advertisers on how to incorporate the Treasury's purchase pleas with their institutional or consumer-oriented advertising. Both the Treasury and the advertising industry knew, however, that a new tax law prohibiting or severely restricting advertisers' ability to deduct promotional expenses from their income taxes would mean the end to much of their cooperation. The result would be a much smaller venue for the Treasury's campaign.

This may have been a factor in the Treasury Department's final decision to side with advertisers in the debate over advertising as a tax-deductible business expense. Morgenthau emerged as a driving force, asserting that both his department and the Bureau of Internal Revenue fully appreciated advertising's importance in the national economy and declaring that "ordinary and necessary" advertising with "a reasonable relation to the business activities in which the enterprise is engaged" would remain a deductible business expense. This did not exclude institutional advertising in reasonable amounts or goodwill advertising calculated to influence the buying habits of the public.[75] Advertising met these criteria so long as it was not carried to an "unreasonable extent" and did not constitute an obvious attempt to avoid tax payments. Under the existing tax laws, this meant that the government sponsored advertising at an average effective rate of 80 percent. Companies in the top 95 percent excess profits bracket got away with paying only 5 percent of their advertising costs.[76] The Treasury Department objected only to expenditures that were seemingly "extravagant" and out of proportion to a company's size or its past advertising budgets. Paul West congratulated the Treasury on "a fine understanding of the true functions of advertising and its place in business."[77] Not only did Secretary Morgenthau understand advertisers' need to maintain brand name loyalty, but his decision was also seen as an indication that government officials had become more friendly toward advertising after seeing that "the promotion world" could be put to work to help win the war.[78]

Exactly how the government would come to interpret the Treasury's directives on advertising was not clear, however. With an adversarial New Deal administration fresh in their memory, advertisers were apprehensive. They wanted to know if all advertising, including the promotion of products being sold through government contracts, would fall under the ruling. A meeting between representatives from the ANA, the Treasury Department, and the Bureau of Internal Revenue clarified the issue. Both the Treasury Department and the Bureau of Internal Revenue recognized advertising's role in the national economy and had no intention of restricting reasonable and normal advertising through taxation. The latter agency was also willing to approve normal expenditures for new types of advertising that had emerged as a result of the war and to acknowledge that advertising costs might have risen.[79]

"In clarifying its stand governing the allowability of advertising expenses," *Advertising Age* said, "advertising men agree that the Internal Revenue Bureau of the Treasury Department has made an outstanding and noteworthy contribution to American business."[80] *Printers' Ink* assured readers that the advertising industry had nothing to fear from the government and told them to "perk up and become a little more realistic and trusting." Moreover, argued the trade publication, "with the attitude of government officials so friendly and helpful, it naturally follows that 'reasonable' will be just that and if it is what more can anybody ask?"[81] This, however, did not mean that advertisers could throw caution to the wind. The president of the ANA warned them against violating the spirit of the tax ruling and stressed the law's call for "reasonable, ordinary, and necessary" advertising expenses, not, as had been suspected in the past, for increased advertising expenditures as a means of avoiding taxes. The latter, according to one trade publication, constituted nothing less than "a prostitution of advertising" and had to be avoided at any cost.[82]

Concerned that their promotional strategies might not meet the government's criteria, many advertisers began submitting their campaign plans to the Bureau of Internal Revenue for prior approval to make sure that their ads would be covered under the tax-exemption rule. Most proposals were favorably, but not automatically, approved.[83] The International Latex Corporation, for example, was not allowed to deduct expenses for a series of ads consisting largely of reprinted, and well-known, newspaper columns. McGraw-Hill Publications was denied the same privilege after running an ad to influence tax legislation before Congress titled "Our Present Tax System Will Kill Post-War Jobs." The Bureau of Internal Revenue decided that these advertisements were "political" and not a reasonable, ordinary, and necessary part of the companies' activities. The fact that product and institutional ads carried their own, albeit more subtle, political overtones did not seem to register with the appropriate authorities.[84]

The average citizen, however, was hit harder by the Treasury's new tax rules. In 1943, most American workers saw their taxes go up sharply. The progressive personal income tax rose to 94 percent of top income, but most of the new revenue came from lower personal exemptions. Whereas only four million Americans had filed an income tax return in 1939, that number tripled by 1942.[85] Consumers Union (CU) questioned the fairness of having consumers pay a disproportionate share of the money needed for the war effort through increased taxes, especially during a time when corporate profits were on the increase. While corporate earnings had risen 25 percent from 1939 to 1940 and continued to rise in 1941, a worker making $500 a year was forced to pay $110 in taxes.[86] The fair solution, according to

CU, was to change the rules so that any corporate profits above 6 percent would be taxed at a rate of 100 percent, and to close all loopholes for business and individual taxpayers. As an emergency measure, Congress should also set a maximum amount of net income that an individual could retain after paying taxes. The result would be an additional $5.5 billion in federal revenues, which would eliminate the need for a general sales tax and relieve low- and middle-income people from having to shoulder a disproportionate tax burden.[87]

Although advertisers had strenuously fought their own tax burdens only a few months earlier, they now stressed private citizens' obligation to support the war effort through higher taxes. "All have to be sold the idea that war-work, war-taxes, war-self denial, war-giving, and war-spending are the personal business and responsibility of each man and woman in the whole continent," preached an industry observer. "No exceptions can be made, and no omissions in groups allowed."[88] The hypocrisy was carried to an extreme by the Stewart-Warner Corporation, which argued that instead of using tax day as an occasion to grouse about income taxes, American taxpayers should treat it as "another American Thanksgiving" and celebrate their patriotic contributions.[89] The advertising industry, on the other hand, argued that its own sacrificial contribution to the war effort would come through the Advertising Council's work for the government.[90]

Conclusion

The escalating European conflict and America's gradual involvement in the war effort brought a new set of challenges for the advertising industry. Attempting to justify their usefulness to the war effort, individual advertisers began to incorporate war-related messages into their product and institutional advertising. But industry leaders were still searching for a better public relations strategy, one that could improve their relationship with Washington and help secure markets for postwar prosperity. Thus they were delighted when the government approached them with a request for promotional assistance. The result was the formation of the Advertising Council in early 1942. The council's involvement in war-related information campaigns more than answered the industry's need for a perfect public relations vehicle, and its first victory was helping to secure advertising as a tax-deductible expense for business.

3

The Initial Year of the Advertising Council

In certain key respects, advertising and advertisers themselves underwent major changes in 1942. This chapter explores the first month of the Advertising Council's existence. It discusses the industry's challenges in adhering to a common goal and probes the relationship between Madison Avenue and Washington, D.C., during the first year of World War II—a relationship that for the first few months was fraught with communication problems and a certain degree of mistrust on both sides.

The situation was greatly helped by the creation of the Office of War Information (OWI) in June of 1942, followed by the establishment of an Advertising Division in the Bureau of Campaigns in August of that same year. Tasked with advising agencies "on the most appropriate and effective means of keeping the public adequately and appropriately informed about the war effort" and with the responsibility to "review, clear and approve all proposed radio and motion picture programs sponsored by federal departments and agencies," the OWI consolidated the functions of several former government agencies, a move that helped facilitate the Advertising Council's activities. By providing their services to the government through the council at no charge, advertisers hoped to impress upon the American people that theirs was a patriotic institution helping the war effort. The ultimate goal, however, was to elevate the public's perception of advertising and secure for the industry a "place at the council tables in the great task of reconstruction after the war."[1]

The Ad Council would be put through its paces in the months to come. In order to win the government's trust, it would have to demonstrate that it represented the advertising industry at large, and in order to win the industry's confidence, it would have to show that its public relations activities were producing tangible results. It was through the skillful juggling of these various tasks and priorities that the council would demonstrate its relevance, indeed its pivotal importance, to the industry as a whole. At the first commemoration of the attack on Pearl Harbor in December 1942, the advertising industry was well on its way to achieving these goals.

Initial Problems

Internal disagreements about the Advertising Council's role and strategies were evident right from the beginning and would prove to be an ongoing theme throughout the war. The advertising professionals in charge of the council came from large and well-known institutions, causing many of the smaller advertisers and agencies to feel that they had been left out. Some viewed the council with a great deal of suspicion, accusing it of being an exclusive organization that shamelessly presented itself as the united voice of American advertising while caring only about the big players.[2] Bruce Barton, who had been an advertising executive before entering politics, issued a warning: "The self-appointed men of the Advertising Council," he said, had "established a contact with Government" that might "prove the undoing of the business."[3]

The council was in fact highly attentive to the problem and also highly concerned about how to most effectively involve the several hundred smaller advertising agencies that had volunteered their services. It quickly established branch offices in Los Angeles, Detroit, and Boston to build broader support in local advertising communities.[4] This was a good beginning, but the task of coaching advertisers would present a continuing challenge.[5] During the first months of 1942, the media were full of war-theme advertisements, but only a small percentage of them followed the Advertising Council's guidelines. Eager to do the best job possible, the council launched what would become an ongoing attempt to streamline the national advertising effort, including a study of public reaction to various war themes.[6]

The working relationship between the Ad Council and various government agencies was somewhat disorganized, which posed another problem. The absence of guidance regarding what kind of advertising support Washington needed and wanted was a constant source of frustration for the newly created council. Directions and true facts were in short supply, and communication was often lacking. Many government agencies chose to approach leading advertisers on an independent basis with requests for space and time for their particular story or problem, which disrupted the council's coordination of the overall effort.[7] Expressing some concern, the trade publication *Printers' Ink* advised the government to take full advantage of the Advertising Council lest the nation be denied the benefits of "the greatest system of mass communication ever developed in the history of this earth."[8]

Before the OWI was established in the summer of 1942, there were three agencies under the War Information Board that dealt with different aspects of providing information to the public. The Office of Emergency Management had a Division of Information to coordinate information to be sent to its various agencies. The task of conducting public opinion polls and maintaining the many offices for public inquiry throughout the country was assigned to the Office of Government Reports, established in 1939. The Office of Civil Defense was created in the spring of 1941 for the purpose of analyzing public attitudes and the appropriateness of government propaganda. By October of that year, the latter had been renamed the Office of Facts and Figures (OFF).[9]

The OFF was designated as the clearinghouse for all federal advertising, but as the newly established Advertising Council soon found out, it was slow to exercise its authority. "One of the first jobs to be done in making official advertising and publicity work successfully in the interest of the war effort is to get effective coordination and centralization of all activities in this category," urged *Advertising Age*, pointing to the advertising community's dissatisfaction with the issue.[10] Advertisers called for the appointment of an "advertising manager" to help coordinate the government's various needs for publicity with the talent, space, and time offered through the council in hopes that this would help get more campaigns off the ground.[11] As the former advertising manager for the Colgate-Palmolive-Peet Company and a past head of the ANA, Ken R. Dyke was fully aware of the situation when he accepted the job as director of the OFF's Advertising Division. Arriving at the OFF from a position with the National Broadcasting Corporation (NBC), Dyke immediately recognized that many government representatives failed to appreciate advertising's role in the war effort, and this he found problematic. "The present situation as it applies to effective utilization of advertising space which is potentially available to the government is appalling, wasteful, ineffectual, and unnecessary," he complained. "Advertisers do not know what is desired of them—and many of their self-guided advertising efforts have undoubtedly done more harm than good."[12]

Many government officials remained unconvinced of the benefits of working with the Advertising Council, but supporters forcefully pushed their agenda. The OFF's assistant director, Allen Grover, for example, asked the heads of the office's Radio and Graphics divisions, Vaughn Flannery and William Lewis, to set up a meeting with Ad Council executive director McClintock in order to clear their minds of "a great many suspicions about the present objectives of the Council."[13] In spite of feeling ignored and misunderstood by some Washington officials, the council benefited greatly from having Dyke in charge of the Advertising Division. By the late spring of 1942, he had designed a plan for stronger cooperation and devised a strategy for achieving better use of war themes in advertisements.[14] It included the publication of periodic "citation sheets" suggesting areas where advertising tie-ins could be beneficial to the war effort. These included explanations and background information as a means of encouraging advertisers toward more effective war-theme advertising. Issued in separate magazine, outdoor, and radio advertising editions, the citation sheets also provided what the Advertising Division, in cooperation with the Ad Council, considered to be "outstanding examples" of war-theme advertising, giving advertisers, who often did not have a clear sense of the government's preferences, some idea about what it was looking for.[15] A few months later, the Bureau of Campaigns created a "Wartime Advertising Exhibit" in the lobby of the Commerce Building in Washington, D.C., featuring bureau-approved ads so that the public and prospective advertisers could see examples of successful home front promotions.[16]

Six months into the war, the government had become increasingly reliant on the Advertising Council's help, and the Council was working closely with several government departments on a wide range of war-related publicity projects.[17] While the working relationship between Washington and Madison Avenue was a long way from being fully synchronized, it was improving. The Ad Council was becoming more adept at interpreting the government's publicity needs and suggesting ways for advertising to reflect those concerns. Its skills in directing advertisers toward more effective use of media for promoting the sale of war bonds, the planting of victory gardens, enlistment in the war effort, and salvage of commodities that were in short wartime supply were improving in tandem.[18]

In spite of strong support from several government leaders, however, including President Roosevelt, who praised advertising for its "splendid spirit of cooperation" and patriotic place in the nation's total war effort, industry leaders were not fully convinced of Washington's commitment.[19] "The important thing to remember," reflected one agency man in the late spring of 1942, "is that Government isn't sure it likes Advertising, even yet." He wondered why amateurs rather than advertising experts had been given the job of running the government's advertising programs. Why was there not a designated advertising bureau with competent advertising personnel to give direction, instead of department heads who knew nothing about advertising? While acknowledging that a few government departments appreciated what the Ad Council was trying to do, he expressed frustration with the fact that so many others did not know how to take advantage of its services. "The best advertising is produced by a team consisting of a good advertising agency plus a sophisticated client. The government has the best agency talent in the world: the Advertising Council, which represents all the agencies of America, but the other half of the agency is lacking. . . . Doesn't it seem odd that, with all the alphabet divisions Washington has spawned, an advertising bureau has not been conceived for the emergency? . . . It will take all of Advertising's leadership—all its winning persuasiveness—to sell an administration hostile to advertising." He envisioned a government agency that would take over all advertising functions and provide the Ad Council with a contact man in every department that requested its help. "This is a hell of a time to have to learn but the government is going to have to do it," he added. "And Advertising, at this late date, is going to have to teach it."[20]

The OWI and the Bureau of Campaigns

The Advertising Council worked with the OFF's Advertising Division on an entirely unofficial basis for the first few months, but in June 1942 the Office of War Information replaced the combined services of the OFF and the Office of Government Reports and officially recognized the Ad Council as its major liaison with the advertising industry.[21] Put in charge of coordinating the flow of war-related information from the government to the public was OWI director Elmer Davis, a respected radio commentator for the Columbia Broadcasting System (CBS). Unlike George Creel, who had been able to build his Committee on Public Information from the ground up during World War I, Davis had to piece the OWI together from a number of existing agencies that lacked the authority to handle the war effort in a satisfactory manner.[22] This would become a recurring problem, making it a favorite target for the OWI's opponents during the months and years to come.[23] Refusing to join the critics and relieved to have a person with media knowledge in charge, the Ad Council expressed great satisfaction with Davis's appointment, stating that there was "good authority for the belief that in Mr. Davis the Advertising Council has a very good friend."[24]

The OWI was organized into a Foreign Branch and a Domestic Branch, the latter under the leadership of Gardner Cowles Jr., a Republican and a prominent publisher.[25] The Domestic Branch was made up of seven smaller bureaus. One was the Bureau of Campaigns, established in August 1942. It was responsible for the central planning and control of all major information programs directed toward the public by government departments, bureaus, and agencies, including the News, Radio, Publications, and Graphics bureaus, the Bureau of Motion Pictures, and the Bureau of Campaigns. Success was monitored through public opinion surveys conducted by the OWI Bureau of Intelligence, which employed several people with experience in the emerging field of advertising research.[26]

Motivated by the need to eliminate "wasteful publicity practices," the OWI decided not to set up its own advertising department, choosing instead to rely on the council's services in solving the government's advertising problems.[27] The newly created Bureau of Campaigns was given the important task of planning and timing all government information campaigns and coordinating the intercommunication between government agencies in need of promotional help and advertisers, agencies, and media that could provide such assistance through the Ad Council. It was also responsible for monitoring the subjects and illustrations used in manufacturers' war-theme copy.[28]

By November 1942, only three months after it had gotten off the ground, the bureau was already managing an overwhelming sixty-six campaigns.[29] A priority system that ranged the projects in terms of their individual importance to the war effort was quickly established, and Dyke stressed the need for government agencies to make their initial contact for assistance with the Bureau of Campaigns. "You can readily realize the chaos that would result in our relationships with the Council if everyone in the government could go to the Council direct with their problems," he said.[30]

In an attempt to streamline the bureaucratic process, each government department or agency that requested help was asked to delegate a representative to serve as campaign manager. That person would deal directly with the Bureau of Campaigns, making sure that all projects were conducted in accordance with OWI policies, and would facilitate cooperation between his unit and the Advertising Council. The council's task, in turn, was to offer concrete advice to government agencies in search of promotional help and to make sure that only projects with a direct connection to the war effort were approved.[31]

Elmer Davis chose top advertising men to lead the Bureau of Campaigns. Ken Dyke, director of the Advertising Division in the former OFF, was selected to head the bureau, while Andrew Dudley, former sales manager of the Wrigley Company, was hired as his deputy chief. Again, and much to the

Advertising Council's relief, both men were familiar with the inner workings of Madison Avenue, where they were widely respected.[32] "No high-pressure glamor boy, Dyke is a practical advertising man," observed *Time*. "He is more concerned with 'the advertising approach' than with advertisements, with the orderly definition of the problem, the basic research and the step-by-step planning which have made advertising the machine tool for selling the products of mass production. He sees the job to be done as an advertising job, but with this big difference: in peace, advertising sold the people plenty and pleasure; in war, advertising must sell them understanding of sacrifice and harsh restriction."[33]

Although Dyke was technically representing the government's interests, he clearly viewed it as his responsibility to aid the advertising industry in its quest for a prominent role in the government's promotional planning.[34] The ANA congratulated the government on the move to coordinate wartime advertising and applauded the choice of Dyke and Dudley, whom the organization considered "well versed in advertising and in the problems of handling an advertising appropriation."[35] But Paul B. West, who was both president of the ANA and a member of the Advertising Council's Executive Committee, sounded a warning in a letter to Dyke. "Your difficulty," he wrote, "will be to preserve the objective viewpoint and the practical touch that you now have. If you will let me, I shall hope to have sufficient frequent contact with you to help you all I can on that score. . . . One has to be *practical* to run an association of this kind these days."[36]

The Advertising Council—Summer 1942

With the government's increasing reliance on advertising methods and techniques, its close cooperation with the Advertising Council, and the appointment of individuals with close ties to the advertising industry to important positions in the federal information program, advertisers now had a say in government activities. Dyke was pleased. "Practically each day sees more men from advertising ranks fitting into key positions in and around the Washington picture," he observed. "In addition to those fellows who are actually on full-time down here, we have the continual guidance and assistance of the National Advertising Council [*sic*]. This group is being of invaluable assistance in helping us accomplish important objectives."[37] Others noticed the trend as well. "It is becoming more and more evident to men at the wheel in Washington," observed *Editor and Publisher*, "that the job of financing this war and of mobilizing every ounce of public energy behind the war effort cannot be effected without controlled display advertising."[38]

The trade publication was especially encouraged by what it saw as a trend toward educating people through advertising. Much of "the best advertising" did not try to sell people anything. Neither did it play on their desires. It did not whet their appetites, making them want to spend money they did not have on things they might not need. Instead, it taught them how to conserve and how to make things last longer. "Advertising of this kind is going to give advertising's critics, in and out of the Government, a new conception of the role of advertising in our whole social and economic system," promised the trade publication, adding that this was exactly the type of advertising the government wanted. "It needs this kind of advertising in its all-out prosecution of the war on the home as well as on the fighting front." *Editor and Publisher* hailed advertising for doing its part to bring the country together as "one united fighting machine." But advertising's job was far from done, and the trade publication urged advertisers to step up their efforts.[39] The Ad Council's response came in the form of "A Plan for Business to Use One of Its Principal Tools to Help Win the War," a pamphlet that promoted advertising as a "powerful tool of democracy" and explained how industry-sponsored "war information advertising" could strengthen morale and ensure action on many vital home fronts.[40] Advertising, promised *Advertising Age*, was a force that could "make Goebbels' propaganda machine look like a peanut whistle—an art and science developed in the United States to a point unapproached anywhere else in the world."[41]

The OWI was far more willing than its predecessor the OFF to leave promotional tasks in the hands of private industry, and the Advertising Council thrived on the close and frequent contact with important government officials. It regarded simplifying relationships between Washington and its 441 volunteer agencies (with a workforce of approximately twelve thousand people) as one of its most important tasks.[42] "The best lobbying for advertising is a good job well done," stated an industry observer. "The growing use of advertising methods to sell the war to the people will be an education in sound practice for both the government and the business."[43] The council appreciated the improved working relationship with Washington, praising the government's cooperation with the Bureau of Campaigns and its director, Ken Dyke, as especially satisfactory.[44] Sharing these sentiments, the OWI sought to make the partnership even stronger—to achieve what Coles termed "a complete marriage between the Advertising Council and the Bureau of Campaigns"—in order to better coordinate the government's promotional efforts. Part of the deal entailed the placement of a competent full-time council representative in the Bureau of Campaigns in exchange for an OWI representative working full-time in New York, where the Ad Council's headquarters was located. Reflected in this arrangement was an interesting overlap between advertising interests and government needs, a trend that would intensify as the war proceeded.[45]

Although there was nothing "typical" about the Ad Council's work, a basic pattern soon emerged. All council projects were initiated through the Bureau of Campaigns. The bureau was the focal point for government drives as well as the agency; it was where various other federal agencies made their promotional needs known. In setting up a typical campaign, Dyke first met with representatives from the appropriate government departments and agencies. After a proposed campaign had been analyzed and approved by the bureau, the Advertising Council was invited to participate. The next step was for the council's executive committee to discuss the proposal, evaluating its usefulness in the overall war effort and determining whether it merited advertising support. Once a project had been approved, the council's board of directors designated one of its members as project coordinator; in addition to assuming full responsibility for carrying out that particular campaign, the coordinator also served as advertising manager for it.[46] The next step was to select one or more of the more than four hundred advertising agencies that had volunteered their services to the council, and campaign plans were then developed in cooperation with the designated ad agency or agencies, a project director from the council's paid staff, and the government department that had requested the promotional help. Preliminary plans, usually copy suggestions, layouts, and miscellaneous material, were worked out and submitted to the Advertising Council's board for approval.[47] Advertisers were asked to underwrite the various campaigns, and they used the finished materials in their advertising. In other words, the council coordinated campaigns for the government in the same way that an ad agency worked for any large commercial client.[48]

Advertisements prepared by McCann-Erickson and paid for by the American Iron and Steel Institute encouraged people to salvage scrap metals. Kenyon and Eckhardt's campaigns asked people to conserve fats and found a willing sponsor in the glycerin-producing industries. Newell-Emmett made posters and pamphlets for the army, navy, and FBI. Young and Rubicam promoted the government's war bonds.[49] Advertisers, in turn, incorporated campaign messages into their many advertisements. All of the council's services were donated to the government free of charge.[50]

The Ad Council's first major task was to organize a large salvage campaign. Initiated by the Bureau of Industrial Conservation of the War Production Board in April 1942, it aimed at reclaiming rubber, metals, fats, and oils for the manufacture of various war materials. Advertisers in the steel, soap, and automobile industries emerged as natural underwriters in this undertaking. In one case, the council designed a nationwide campaign directed at housewives, asking them to save fats and grease for soap production and thereby "help beat the Axis." The task of coordinating the effort was handed off to one of the large agencies that had volunteered their services to the Ad Council, Kenyon and Eckhardt, which in turn called for newspaper ads, radio announcements, posters, and a Disney movie short to promote the effort. A group of top-notch copywriters, working on a purely voluntary basis, turned out layouts and sample radio scripts for the campaign. After being approved by the War Production Board, the entire project was turned over to the Association of American Soap and Glycerine Producers, which represented almost all of the big manufacturers. Within two months, soap and glycerin producers had pledged $500,000 for the campaign.[51] The food industries sponsored a national nutrition campaign under the slogan "U.S. Needs Us Strong. Eat Nutritional Food." Advertisers could combine their sales objectives with council promotions. Typical was a Kraft promotion for Miracle Whip salad dressing that featured a nutritional table and a large color photo of fresh fruits and vegetables (see fig. 12 on p. 130).[52]

As 1942 came to an end, the Ad Council was actively involved in several major government campaigns. One was focused on the food situation, using promotional material to explain the government's agricultural goals and problems associated with the shortage of farm labor. Another provided information to the public about nutrition-related issues, including the importance of starting "victory gardens" for the individual household table. A conservation campaign aimed at automobile owners promoted the importance of carpooling, tire preservation, efficient driving, and conservation of gasoline (tires and gasoline, of course, were rationed), and a campaign sponsored by the U.S. Treasury Department urged everyone to invest at least 10 percent of their earnings in war bonds and stamps.[53] A key challenge for the council was helping advertisers explain the role of war bonds when they used this appeal in their product ads. Many Americans were unaware that these bonds would eventually pay interest, and some viewed them as a donation to the war effort much like a donation to the Red Cross or the United Service Organizations (USO). Thus it was up to the council (through the use of words such as *lend* and *invest*) to convey the difference and increase sales.[54]

Unlike the ANA and the American Association of Advertising Agencies (AAAA), which had been the driving force behind the Advertising Council, the Advertising Federation of American (AFA) had kept a low profile. As the central organization for advertising clubs across the country, the federation had developed a set of guidelines, outlined in the thirty-nine-point *Guide for Wartime Advertising Policies*, to assist its local members in the production of ads that promoted the government's war objectives.[55] This, of course, sounded very similar to what the Advertising Council was doing on a much larger scale, but America had been at war for nearly a year before the AFA recognized the importance of a unified advertising response and gave up on its solo project. Cooperating with the council, it now called on local advertising clubs to serve as "War Advertising Committees" for local civilian defense agencies, much as the Ad Council worked for the OWI on a national level.[56] "If professional advertising men and women would work actively to sell the Advertising Council's projects to people in their own communities, we would be well on our way to achieving that kind of local understanding which is essential to our war effort," promised the AFA.[57]

During its first seven months, the Advertising Council helped create more than four thousand advertisements. In addition to several hundred posters and scores of leaflets, it also produced portfolios for each individual campaign to inform and encourage participation from individual advertisers. One agency wrote and produced more than twenty-five hundred radio shows and spots for the government during the same period. By November 1942, the Department of Commerce estimated that the advertising community, acting through the council, had donated $3 million in payroll time and $60 million in advertising space and time to the government.[58] Several hundred advertising agencies had volunteered their services for a long list of projects.[59] Keeping advertisers up to date was the *Guide to War-Time Advertising*, which replaced the old citation sheets. Prepared by the Ad Council for the OWI, the monthly publication kept advertisers, agencies, publishers, and broadcasters apprised of new and ongoing campaigns and told them how to help.[60]

Changing Government Attitudes toward Advertising

Government agencies that had once been considered hostile to advertising were gradually becoming convinced of its usefulness in promoting the war effort. Even the Office of Price Administration, traditionally viewed as a hotbed of anti-advertising sentiments, began to recognize the value of advertising as a way of conveying war-related information to consumers in a positive, effective manner. "The bond of mutual confidence between advertising and government has been strengthened by the influx of business and advertising men into war agencies," noted *Broadcasting*. "The only question is whether this represents a complete conversion or merely a marriage of convenience." In any case, concluded the trade journal, Washington's new attitude was advertising's "first real break in years from the Government."[61] Additional praise came from the Bureau of Foreign and Domestic Commerce, which declared that advertising was "indispensable to the functioning of free enterprise and the creation of a high standard of living." There was no denying that the attitude of wartime Washington was different from that of peacetime Washington in the heyday of the New Deal.[62]

This friendly, even grateful, government attitude toward the industry was visible at the annual AFA convention in June 1942. Several government speakers thanked advertisers for their wartime contributions.[63] "Washington, often suspicious and lacking in the understanding of business functions, is beginning to see that through advertising the urgent needs of the nation can be simplified, dramatized and sold to the American people," observed *Advertising Age*. At the same time, and much to the advertising industry's delight, "the purpose, function and justification of advertising" was being demonstrated "to the men who determine the policies of the administration."[64]

However, and in spite of the recent changes and a broader public acceptance of its activities, the Ad Council needed all the help it could get. Many individual advertisers showed little interest in the council and what it was trying to achieve, and this greatly worried McClintock.[65] Thus, in the fall of 1942, the ANA convened a meeting between advertisers and government officials, a reunion of sorts of the Hot Springs meeting that had been held a year prior. The conference, which received enthusiastic support from Elmer Davis, focused on the ongoing need for improved communication between advertisers and the OWI.[66] "The great forces inherent in this group are not being utilized as effectively as they should because of the lack of knowledge and understanding of these government programs now unfolding which affect so vitally our ways of living and doing business," wrote Paul B. West in a letter inviting Vice-President Henry Wallace to speak at the conference.

> I know that our members are willing and anxious to be of the utmost aid in winning the war. This aid can be used not only in the form of increased production of war goods, but also the efficient use of mass communication in giving the public the information it needs and in promoting the voluntary cooperation of all Americans. . . . By bringing the proper representatives of the government together with this group in the type of meeting we have planned, the needed understanding can be achieved and with it the cooperative effort which is so essential to the success of the war program.[67]

Wallace declined for reasons unknown, but key individuals from government and industry were in attendance at the event, which Ken Dyke character-ized as "the most constructive, informative and stimulating meeting of that sort which we have ever attended."[68] The noticeable difference between this conference and others was the shift in focus from production to distribution, marketing, and advertising.[69]

While most representatives from the advertising community described the industry's contributions in selfless and patriotic terms, claiming that the Advertising Council was "not a propaganda agency for business . . . not a lobbying organization for advertising," some dared to hint at postwar re-wards.[70] "Increased governmental control of business," noted one industry observer, "can be avoided if business does its own job so well that the public will not tolerate future interference."[71] Thus, in addition to creating success-ful campaigns, the Ad Council persevered in its effort to establish better relations with the public, even forming a separate public relations commit-tee for this purpose.[72] The best PR, according to council president LaRoche, would come from the successful handling of individual projects, providing the American public with a positive view of the industry behind the ads and giving advertising credit for "an important war job well done."[73]

The trade press expressed high hopes for productive cooperation, con-sidering it an excellent opportunity "to clarify in the minds of government regulatory and legislative authorities the proper functions of advertising during this war."[74] Also, and with a feisty 1930s consumer movement and fre-quent attacks on advertising fresh in memory, it was hoped that the council would serve as a diffuser, providing the advertising industry with a chance to improve its standing with the consuming public.[75] "The war has dumped into the lap of consumer advertising the biggest job it has ever had—and the biggest opportunity," *Printers' Ink* observed. "Not an opportunity for more profits to the advertiser and technician; but a chance to exert a greater influence over the consuming public than ever before. There will be profits later—after the war is over—arising out of greater consumer acceptance."[76]

The industry hung on every word of the government's praise and encour-agement. It was especially gratifying when Treasury Secretary Henry Mor-genthau Jr. thanked the Advertising Council for its "truly wonderful" help in promoting the sale of war bonds and credited the council with record-break-ing sales during the first bond drive in December 1942.[77] The Department of Commerce, headed by John H. Morse and characterized by *Advertising and Selling* as having "championed Advertising's cause with as much gusto as though it was politically expedient," also seized the opportunity to praise advertising.[78] Morse claimed not to recall "any period of similar length" when so many government officials had expressed appreciation for advertising.[79] The trade publication suggested that advertising had become a semi-official government enterprise, claiming that there was a noticeable trend toward "more intelligent use of advertising" in government circles.[80]

The Ad Council received full credit for these developments. Not only had it enabled advertising to play an important part in the war effort, but it had also helped the industry build a creditable record that promised to pay dividends in the postwar period. "When [the war] ends," predicted Donald Nelson, "our American free enterprise system is going to face the most magnificent opportunity any man could ask. If we have wisely preserved the basic structure of our economy during the war, we can then move on to a higher level of useful activity than we have ever known before. We are fighting this war to make possible the continuation and the constant improvement of that complex set of economic, social and political privileges which we fondly refer to as 'the American Way.'"[81]

Such recognition had been the Advertising Council's goal from the outset. A major part of its strategy had been to develop close relationships with government sources. While it encouraged government contacts to attend council meetings and to schedule frequent appointments with council members, it emphasized that the best cooperation resulted from frequent informal meetings with people such as Ken Dyke and his associates at the Bureau of Campaigns. In July 1942, the Advertising Council directed its chief to prepare plans for an "informal smoker type of gathering" between the council's board of directors and those engaged in promotional activities for various government departments.[82] It also recommended that three of its associate directors spend several days each week in Washington in order to expand their network of contacts and widen the scope of the council's operations. Presumably this would lead to a better understanding of the governmental machinery and also give the government an even deeper appreciation of business and advertising. "We must not only understand the function of government as it relates to business," stressed the council, but "we must also build an organization that knows not only the temporary personnel in Washington, but also the permanent personnel,—the career men who will be in Washington after the war."[83]

Conclusion

The Advertising Council enjoyed a successful first year. By the end of 1942, it had notably helped to improve the status of advertising in Washington, D.C. The crucial development was the government's increasing reliance on the council's services, culminating in the OWI's official recognition of the organization in August 1942. But the Ad Council still had much ground to cover before its mission could be accomplished. It had to maneuver through the myriad of wartime government agencies, which were often mired in political controversy. It also had to continually work with leading advertisers and agencies to convince them to cooperate with its long-term vision of the industry's needs. And the wartime economy always threatened to expose the irrelevance of advertising, hence fanning the flames for a resurgence of the moribund consumer movement that the advertising industry had worked so hard to demolish in the 1930s. The following months would put the council to the test on several occasions, the first involving a set of poignant criticisms led by an old foe in the consumer movement.

4

The Consumer Movement's Return

Just when things were going well for advertisers in Washington, an old arch-nemesis reentered the scene. After being so active in the 1930s, the consumer movement had kept a low profile throughout the defense period. A few groups, however, including Consumers Union, had done their best to keep the momentum going. Officially formed in 1936, CU had been created after an intense and at times violent struggle over labor practices in Consumers' Research. It branched out into lobbying and educational efforts and became a stealth defender of consumers' rights in the ongoing public hearings leading to the 1938 Wheeler-Lea Amendment. Emerging as the main consumer group, CU was most responsible for holding the advertising industry's feet to the fire. It called for advertising that stressed facts and information over slogans and brand names, and it joined other consumer organizations in demanding a grading system for consumer products to provide consumers with a level playing field.[1]

These demands were reflected in the five-year battle over advertising regulation in the 1930s. Largely due to heavy industry lobbying and massive media resistance, however, the resulting law did nothing to change existing advertising practices. The consumer defeat was followed by a vicious attack from right-wing media and business interests, and the congressional investigations looking into communist activities in the consumer movement that followed in 1939–40 left many consumer advocates severely disillusioned. The investigation, which was the first by the committee that would come to be known as the House Un-American Activities Committee (HUAC), was unable to prove anything. This, however, did not prevent certain business interests from wanting to keep the association between communism and consumer advocacy alive by frequently hinting that the opposition was communist-inspired or out to destroy the American system of free enterprise. Even though the attacks were discredited, CU had expended a great deal of its limited resources on defending itself, and the charges alone were enough to damage the group's standing. Its staff size was reduced, and its budget shrank.[2]

But circumstances surrounding the defense and war economies raised some of the consumer movement's concerns to a new level of importance. Its core idea for grading and standardization of consumer goods had been rekindled as part of the government's TNEC investigation and continued to linger as an issue throughout the war. Likewise, the changed economic situation brought on by the war again called the economic function of advertising into question and gave its critics new credence.

The fighting spirit of CU cofounder and president Colston Warne also helped to bring the organization back into the political limelight. After receiving a doctoral degree in economics from the University of Chicago in 1925, Warne had accepted a series of temporary appointments before he landed a tenured position at Amherst College in 1930. Inspired by Thorstein Veblen and Consumers' Research cofounder Stuart Chase, Warne became involved with the new group and emerged as an outspoken defender of consumers' rights. Later, when labor disagreements erupted within the organization, he sided with the striking workers and left to help establish CU. As the organization's first president—a position he would hold for thirty-three years—Warne was given a public, and very prominent, platform for his relentless work on consumers' behalf.[3] The war situation in the early 1940s further reinforced his opinion of advertising as a wasteful institution, antithetical to consumers' and the public's interests. Wartime advertising, or what he considered the advertising industry's exploitation of the war emergency for public relations purposes, had him further enraged.[4]

As powerful and sophisticated as the advertising industry was as a lobbying force, the consumer movement was weak and ineffectual, even inept. Its strength was in the power of its ideas, and the belief that those ideas would resonate with the vast majority of Americans if they were exposed to them, a concern that was shared by the advertising industry. But whereas a few years earlier an invigorated consumer movement had been easily galvanized, the war had now brought other concerns, leaving Warne to fight an important but frequently lonely fight. Adding to his challenges was a reluctance on the part of the advertising-supported mass media to draw attention to the issues.

Plotting a New Revolt

Even before the United States became an active participant in World War II, the issue of price control had risen to the top of the government's concerns. In May 1941, President Roosevelt had established the Office of Price Administration and Civilian Supply (later the OPA under the War Production Board), but it was not until the passage of the Emergency Price Control Act in January 1942 that rationing went into effect. Defining its mission as working to "expand supply, ration scarce commodities equitably, keep prices from soaring, and thereby aid the war, avoid hardship, reduce unemployment, promote morale, and diminish the amount of sacrifice necessary for the war effort," the agency kept plenty busy.[5] Soon products such as rubber, automobiles, and sugar required rationing books and stamps, followed by oil, coffee, shoes, and processed foods. Later that spring, the OPA issued the General Maximum Price Regulation, which set limits on what a merchant could charge for specific items. By the war's end, this law would cover nearly six thousand commodities—close to 90 percent of all goods sold. Rounding out the efforts to stabilize the economy and keep inflation in check was the OPA's authority under the Emergency Price Control Act to regulate wages.[6]

According to Roosevelt, civilians could support the men who were fighting overseas by adhering to the rules of inflation prevention, paying more in taxes, buying war bonds, and refraining from buying items on an installment plan.[7] Believing that advertising was a "wasteful and inflationary expenditure at a time when our energy should be devoted to war," Warne urged the OPA and other war agencies to scrutinize price ceilings to make sure that product prices did not contain allowances for unnecessary advertising. He agreed with those who had suggested an excise tax on all advertising of consumer goods. This, he argued, not only would bring in additional government revenues, but it might also help bring inflationary tendencies under control.[8]

Responding quickly to the war emergency, CU added a new publication to the existing *Consumers Union Reports*. First published in February 1941, *Bread and Butter* was designed to "help consumers protect their living standards by providing them with up-to-date, reliable information about what is happening to the prices and quality of consumer goods."[9] While most advertisers showed only minimal interest in the task of informing wartime consumers about pricing and product attributes, CU's publications explained the practical changes brought about by the war emergency. They discussed issues such as how to plan and grow victory gardens, how to care for products and make them last, and how to save money on home canning of fruits and vegetables.[10]

Now more than ever, CU viewed advertisers' established practice of stressing emotional satisfaction over product information as an obstacle for consumers rather than constructive assistance.[11] It urged the public to organize and put pressure on the government to make sure that their interests were represented while promising to exert its own "united pressure towards the job of maintaining a healthy, strong, alert America to win the war—building a greater, more prosperous America after the war has been won."[12] And while advertising might instill in consumers a certain desire for goods that were no longer readily available, *Bread and Butter* and *Consumers Union Reports* stressed the unpatriotic aspects of buying products on the black market. Unlike advertisers' contributions through the Advertising Council, CU's work on these issues was rarely acknowledged in the mainstream media.[13]

Less than a year after Pearl Harbor, total advertising volume had increased by 21 percent above its average 1935–39 levels, filling the mass media with patriotic affirmations and doing little to impress Colston Warne. The latter was up in arms over the enormous amounts of scarce resources, including paper and ink, that the industry commanded. The situation was especially troubling in light of the inflationary effect of encouraging consumers to buy during a time of general scarcity. How could government officials such as Henry Morgenthau Jr. of the Treasury Department and Donald Nelson of the War Production Board express support for the extensive deduction of advertising as a cost of doing business when they were fully cognizant of its detrimental effects? Warne suspected that the answer lay in the increasingly cozy relationship between advertisers and Washington. Not only had advertisers established "a conscience-fund of free space for Treasury campaigns," but the creation of the Advertising Council had solidified the industry's entrenchment by attaching its members to the Treasury staff, as well as to the Office of War Information.[14] CU's president scolded Nelson for not restricting the use of paper for advertising purposes, especially when 80 percent of all ads continued to promote the sale of goods as if no war were going on, and he accused Nelson of appointing men with strong ties to the paper business to the board's Newsprint and Newspaper Division.[15]

In the fall of 1942, Warne got the idea to organize educators from major U.S. colleges and universities in an effort to draw public attention to these issues. He sent a letter to potential supporters asking them to endorse the view that companies should be permitted to deduct for tax purposes only the amount of advertising that was essential to secure the sale of their actual current output. Under the existing rule, the federal government, in effect taxpayers, was paying advertising costs for companies that were trying to shelter earnings from high excess profits taxes, and this was exceedingly unfair. The fact that Warne's proposal might result in reduced income for the advertising-supported mass media was not a concern. In fact, he contended, less media reliance on advertising might actually be a good thing.[16]

Warne mailed 500 invitations to academics at 58 institutions and quickly received 224 signatures.[17] In a letter (later part of the *Congressional Record*) sent to Morgenthau, Nelson, Director of Economic Stabilization James F. Byrnes, and OPA head Leon Henderson in December 1942, the signers pilloried advertisers who were exploiting the war for personal gain. They questioned the use of advertising as a means to stimulate consumption at a time when raw materials were in such short supply, and they objected to manufacturers' habit of wrapping their copy in patriotism for the sole purpose of selling consumer products and preserving their brand names for the postwar era.[18] Stressing emphatically that they took no issue with advertising during times of peace, the professors worried that using advertising to stimulate consumption in wartime was working against government efforts to check inflation.[19]

Copies of the letter were sent to Washington on December 18, and an unembellished summary was submitted to the press for release on December 21. Warne was immediately deluged with telephone calls and telegrams from trade publications wanting copies of the letter. *Printers' Ink* was vigorous in its opposition, and *Tide* went so far as to portray Warne as a devil.[20] C. B. Larrabee, the editor of *Printers' Ink*, accused the letter writers of "indulging in sweeping criticisms" and claimed that the teaching profession was "honeycombed with pretty narrow-minded, selfish people."[21] *Editor and Publisher* reassured the American public that the letter in no way reflected the average educator's view of wartime advertising.[22] Coming to the industry's defense, New York University professor George Burton Hotchkiss, a loyal friend to the advertising fraternity, lambasted Warne and his cosigners for being "pathetically grotesque" in their denunciation of advertising and for not giving it sufficient credit for its patriotic contributions to the war effort.[23]

Although Warne's involvement was in his role as an Amherst professor, the Advertising Federation of America was quick to assure the public that the accusations were more reflective of CU than of educators in general. The organization accused those who had signed the letter of being "intellectually dishonest" and of trying to magnify its importance by describing themselves as economists, political scientists, psychologists, and the like without disclosing their lack of specialized knowledge in the particular field covered by the statement.[24] While acknowledging that a letter signed by 200 educators might seem impressive, the organization gleefully noted that none of the 3,600 members of the American Economic Association had signed the statement. Neither was it supported by any of the several thousand teachers in the schools of business administration across the country or the approximately one thousand members of the American Marketing Association. The real purpose behind the letter, the federation suspected, was not to help the war effort but to use it as "the occasion for advancing a cause that reflects a particular social point of view or theory." This charge was not to be taken lightly. "Advertising like all other parts of the free enterprise system," claimed the AFA, "must be prepared to defend itself."[25]

Although the "emotionally prejudiced" were beyond education, the federation recognized the need to inform the general public so as to "counteract the influence of irresponsible statements and appeals" and resolved to use renewed energy and resources to educate Americans about the functions of advertising in a war economy.[26] Other members of the advertising community chose a more confrontational approach, launching a strong attack on the letter writers, calling them "fellow travelers" and accusing them of lacking the most basic knowledge of how advertising worked.[27] The educators did have some supporters in advertising and business circles, but those individuals had a realistic fear of retaliation from employers, colleagues, and professional organizations should they decide to voice their opinions.[28] It was rumored that advertisers had contacted colleges and universities to complain about the professors on campus who had signed the statement.[29] The Ad Council wisely stayed out of the fray.[30]

Neither did Washington rush to engage. OWI head Elmer Davis shrugged off the proposal as the opinion of "the particular economists who endorsed it" and doubted that the plan would be sympathetically reviewed by his agency if it should be formally proposed.[31] Donald Nelson eventually sent a personal letter to Warne, while a more official statement from his office said that specific stipulations in the Emergency Price Control Act of 1942 prohibited the OPA from taking any direct action with respect to limitations on advertising. It was up to the Treasury to decide. While deputy head John Kenneth Galbraith agreed that limiting the tax-deductibility of advertising might direct additional funds to the federal treasury, he did not think the technique would help lower the prices of advertised products.[32] The Treasury Department could not pass the buck so easily, and Morgenthau's office was initially at a loss for an appropriate response. "The person to whom the letter was referred laughingly told me that he was stalling until an appropriate reply came to mind," reported Warne. "It is very apparent that the effect on the Treasury is quite marked."[33] Critics of the government's policies on wartime advertising were also alarmed to see OPA head Leon Henderson quoted as supporting a "full volume of advertising during wartime, irrespective of its absorption of paper and chemicals and the need for slowing down consumer demand."[34]

Advertisers heeded the call. The one-year period between August 1942 and August 1943 saw a huge increase in all forms of media advertising (with the exception of outdoor advertising). Newspaper advertising increased by 19.2 percent, and magazine advertising by 57.3 percent. The number of network and spot radio ads rose by 58.0 percent and 24.1 percent, respectively.[35] In 1943, the November 28 issue of the *New York Sunday Times* devoted no less than 470 of its 576 columns to ads for handbags, compacts, gloves, lamps, ties, oriental rugs, mink coats, and expensive perfumes; and even though scotch and rye were practically unobtainable in the city at the time, the December 2 issue of the *New York Times* carried eleven ads for liquor.[36] Warne's take was that the Treasury was fully cognizant of the problem but that it was too intimidated by business to act decisively in the public interest and declare a truce regarding the advertising of scarce and unavailable goods while the nation was attending to "the central business of winning the war."[37] A worsening paper shortage did little to stop the trend. In October 1943, the Department of Commerce estimated that advertising in all media had risen to 60 percent above prewar levels.[38]

In spite of their defensive attitudes, several members of the advertising community understood the problems associated with wartime advertising and why critics might have a difficult time accepting it. Speaking at a meeting of the Association of National Advertisers in May 1942, for example, Frederick L. Schuster, vice-president of the Lehman Corporation, said frankly that it was difficult to defend advertising as a means of stimulating consumption when $70 billion in purchasing power was fighting for $30 billion worth of consumer goods.[39] But because this was such a sensitive topic, advertisers had neither the luxury nor the inclination to engage in a public debate. Thus, as had been the pattern in the past, they elected to "spin" the issue, emphasizing the positive and patriotic aspects of wartime advertising in hopes that the public would be persuaded. American businesses were encouraged to use the press, the periodicals, the radio, and word of mouth to "create an alternative view" and tell people "just what it means to this country that we have at our disposal these great productive enterprises for producing the vast quantities of mechanical weapons which will make the defeat of Hitler possible." A study conducted by the National Association of Manufacturers found that 70 percent of respondents believed that American companies were making extravagant profits as a result of the war, which only underscored the need to build a better public image for business.[40]

Although there was some discussion about extending the letter-writing campaign, Warne and his fellow signers ended their efforts after the first round. A few months into 1943, the advertising community no longer seemed overly worried. The commercial mass media had carefully ignored the issue, thus preventing it from spilling into the sphere of public discussion. Warne, however, was determined to keep the subject alive. Before the letter campaign had run its course, the seemingly relentless consumer leader came up with the idea of a radio broadcast "in which the waste of material and inflationary effects of much war-time advertising would be brought home to the public." He somehow thought it possible that such a program could be broadcast over New York City station WMCA.[41] Given his knowledge of, and personal experience with, the broadcasting industry, this was a rather curious proposition.

Advertising Critique on Radio

An ongoing challenge for the consumer movement was how to reach that 59 percent of the population who favored increased regulation of advertising, as the advertising industry's own research had concluded in 1940.[42] But this was easier said than done. While advertisers commanded nearly unlimited resources and enjoyed a close relationship with the commercial mass media, consumer advocates were lacking on both fronts. CU, arguably the most well-organized consumer organization, had a wartime circulation of only around 55,000 for *Consumer Reports*, and *Bread and Butter* attracted even fewer readers.[43] Thus it needed to generate coverage of the problems associated with wartime advertising, ideally at least neutral if not sympathetic, in the press and on radio. Coverage of these issues was virtually nonexistent, and what little there was tended to be decontextualized or dismissive. The problem was compounded by the lavish coverage that the advertising industry received; the public was inundated with ads promoting the industry's patriotic contributions to the war effort.

Such press coverage was no surprise then, nor should it seem so in retrospect. The consumer movement had never had a friend in the commercial mass media, especially when it came to the topic of advertising. Most of its efforts, including its attempt to regulate advertising on the federal level during the 1930s, had not been given fair treatment in the mainstream press.[44] There was little doubt about the reason for this: nearly all the news media depended upon advertising for the lion's share of their revenues and profits. Journalists and editors were hardly encouraged to pursue stories critical of an industry of which the news media were, in effect, a key part. Whatever may have been the benefits of the newly emerging professional journalism with respect to protecting editorial content from the influence of media owners and advertisers, they did not extend to providing ample and balanced coverage of advertising policy debates in this period.

As far as can be determined, the daily press and news magazines included virtually no coverage of the debate over advertising regulation during the early 1940s and throughout the war.[45] In the minds of the commercial press, keeping the advertising industry thriving was essentially synonymous with the fight to preserve freedom of the press. It fueled a righteous indignation, especially as the nation was at war with fascism. Radio was a regulated industry and adhered to different rules. Unlike print media, broadcasters received valuable monopoly licenses to scarce channels at no charge from the government. In exchange, they were expected to serve the public interest and provide a balanced presentation of the important issues of the day. This came to assume a form of self-regulation in the National Association of Broadcasters Code of 1939.[46] But whereas commercial advertising accounted for approximately two thirds of the revenues of the newspaper industry, it accounted for 100 percent of the revenues of radio broadcasters. Their very existence depended upon a strong advertising industry.[47] The interests of advertisers and broadcasters frequently intertwined. So while advertising was routinely praised on commercial radio—where advertisers actually produced most of the entertainment programming—the consumer movement was only rarely deemed to be in the public interest.[48]

One such occasion came in December 1941, when CBS gave Warne a thirteen-minute slot in order to "balance" a pro-industry interview with the research director at the McCann-Erickson advertising agency, Dr. L. D. H. Weld. Unbeknownst to the listening audience, however, Warne had been forced to submit a copy of his manuscript prior to the broadcast and had been censored from mentioning specific advertisers (and likely CBS sponsors) who were involved in stipulations and cease-and-desist orders issued by the FTC. He was also prohibited from mentioning the Hearst Corporation, which owned *Good Housekeeping* magazine and had been subjected to some of the FTC investigations.[49] During the broadcast, Warne managed to make a case for his "10-point indictment of current advertising"; he attracted scores of letters from listeners, many of whom later contacted CU to learn more about the organization, its views on advertising, and its new publication, *Bread and*

Butter.[50] Upset not only that he had been censored but also that CBS had neglected to provide a proper introduction to his talk, Warne demanded that the network grant him another broadcast slot over its full network so that he could present his case, including advertising products affected by FTC orders. The president of CU also filed a formal complaint with the Federal Communications Commission (FCC), claiming unfair censorship. While the commission found the argument alarming, it did nothing to rectify the issue.[51] In spite of these circumstances, the industry trade press somewhat ironically applauded CBS's willingness to provide Warne with this opportunity, offering it as "proof" of the industry's tolerance of opposing views.[52]

This, along with the general lack of exposure, was a source of great frustration among consumer advocates. Thus they were quite excited a few months later when Warne got another opportunity to reach a large audience. The occasion was a published debate with Lee Brantly, the advertising director of the conservative Crowell-Collier Publishing Company—a firm with a long history of undermining consumer activism—about the merits of wartime advertising.[53] Sponsored by the American Economic Foundation, the interchange was featured in a weekly column called "Wake Up, America," which was normally published in some four hundred newspapers, typically reaching six million readers. Brantly opened the debate by arguing for the importance of advertising during wartime. Not only did advertising educate people about the war effort, he asserted, but it helped to build morale and preserved the mechanisms of the American economy for the postwar era. "Talk of employing ads to build morale is sheer nonsense," countered Warne. "Manpower and materials are needed for total war, not for disguising advertising ballyhoo." Wartime advertising was merely an excuse for companies to perpetuate their brand names while dodging excess profits taxes, because the war had made it possible to sell most products "without a nickel's worth of advertising." Responding to Warne's attacks and his claim that advertising wasted valuable resources such as paper, chemicals, and transportation, Brantly contended that advertising was as essential to the war effort as "planes and tanks, and ships." This did not sit well with Warne. "Just turn our advertising-laden Sunday papers loose on Hitler," he taunted. "He will run before the pulchritudinous females, armed with cosmetics and girdles. Beat Hitler with three color industrial ads saying 'forget-me-not.' Or, better still, loosen our pontifical radio announcers to do battle for company and country. Forget the cannon, bring on the advertisers!"[54] To the dismay of the consumer movement, only a handful of the newspapers that regularly carried "Wake Up, America" elected to publish the debate.[55]

CBS still showed no interest a year later when Warne offered to discuss the "Open Letter" campaign on the air. "The next time period which we allocate to a spokesman for one of the several consumer organizations should be allocated to a different spokesman than your own," stated the network. "This is because you were the last such spokesman on our network and all considerations of balance and variety of speakers, as well as our desire to reflect more than one facet of any movement, would argue against repetition."[56] Once again, a complaint to the FCC did not produce the desired result. The commission claimed that the licensing of individual stations was outside its jurisdiction, but it promised to keep the complaint on file and review it when CBS's license came up for renewal.[57]

Keeping critics in line and off the air was only part of the advertising industry's struggle. The spring of 1943 brought another, albeit not entirely new, challenge. The request for grading and standardization of consumer goods had been on consumer advocates' agenda since the early 1930s and had received ample attention during the TNEC hearings in 1939. Now, with the limitations on production and product quality caused by the war, these proposals seemed to make even more sense.

Grade Labeling versus Advertising

Although product labeling had been mandatory since the passage of the Pure Food and Drug Act in 1905, the label or tag attached to a commodity informed consumers only about its properties, not about its quality. For example, while two competing brands of canned peas might both carry labels listing their contents as peas, water, preservatives, and salt, there was no way for consumers to judge the size and quality of the peas or whether the can with the recognizable brand name might be worth more than its generic competitor. The 1930s consumer movement had lobbied heavily for a change in this practice, stressing the need for the government to establish standards for goods and to develop a ranking system that would make it possible for consumers to determine the quality of what they were buying. They argued that just like government and industrial buyers, consumers should be able to assess the qualities and specifics of a product and not be forced to rely on brand-name advertising for information. Much to consumer advocates' delight, their demands received considerable support in the Consumers Advisory Division of the National Recovery Administration before it was dissolved in 1935.

Not surprisingly, however, advertisers were strongly against the idea. They argued that the public had not demanded grading, that government had no business interfering with consumers' sovereignty, and that consumers should have the opportunity to judge products in accordance with their own standards rather than those of a third party, whose criteria might differ. For example, manufacturers deemed the idea of labeling canned goods solely as either A, B, or C quality to be particularly flawed. Because flavor depended to a certain degree on individual preference, this quality was particularly difficult to grade and could therefore unfairly affect a product's overall rating. Consumers, they argued, were better served by advertising than by paternalistic government information. The real fear for advertisers, of course, was that quality standards would go a long way toward reducing the significance and effectiveness of brand-name advertising.[58] Although a few manufacturers eventually adhered to a voluntary plan, most did not want the properties of their trademark to be known out of fear that customers would discover that heavy advertising did not guarantee high quality. The affected industries threw their weight behind a massive lobbying effort, and the measure to establish standards failed.[59]

Not long thereafter, the TNEC resurrected the idea. As part of its investigation into the concentration of corporate power, the committee devoted a 433-page monograph to "Consumer Standards" and highlighted the need for such measures in its hearings on consumer problems. Working from the theory that small, independent manufacturers were at a competitive disadvantage against national organizations, the TNEC viewed the grading and marking of lesser-known petroleum, textile, and other products as an effective strategy for letting people know what they were buying. Chances were that consumers might well prefer a less widely advertised but possibly superior product from a smaller manufacturer, thus fulfilling the committee's dual goal of assisting consumers and making markets more competitive.[60]

Testifying at a 1939 TNEC hearing dedicated to "Problems of the Consumer," Dr. Ruth Ayres, formerly a member of the National Recovery Administration's Consumers' Advisory Board and now with the Consumers' Counsel Division of the Department of Agriculture, lent her full support.[61] The absence of grading standards meant that shoppers were forced to negotiate a maze of confusing price and packaging terms, she said. As an example, she pointed to a study by the Bureau of Standards showing the wide variety in packaging and pricing for tomato juice available at one Washington, D.C., store. The twenty-one containers, representing eleven different brands, came in seventeen different sizes and contained fifteen different volumes, ranging from 19¼ to 99 fluid ounces. They were being sold at fifteen different prices, ranging from two containers for 9 cents to a single container for 39 cents; and there were sixteen different costs per fluid ounce, ranging from 3.3 cents to 6.7 cents for the cans and as much as 7.5 cents for one of the bottled juices. Packaging and pricing of cereals and cosmetics created the same level of consumer confusion.[62] Additional testimonials pointed in the same direction: advertising was not providing enough information to help consumers buy intelligently.[63] "Consumers want facts about the goods they buy," said Consumers' Counsel director Donald E. Montgomery. "They want to be able to compare one commodity with another so as to make an intelligent decision as to which one best serves their individual need."[64]

All this had made sense to consumer advocates in the 1930s, but now, with a war on the horizon, grading and standardization took on new pertinence. Without adding cost or destroying established product names, grading could ensure better quality and provide a more accurate purchasing guide than advertising alone and could perform a valuable function in the fight for wartime price controls.[65] Grading proponents looked with great interest to Canada, where such measures had become obligatory and where the government could close down a production facility if the owner failed to adhere.[66]

This was not an abstract notion; it was an idea that could resonate with a public wanting the most bang for its buck, and one that had the advertising industry on edge. Ignoring a Gallup poll showing that a slight majority of the public favored the standardization of goods, the advertising industry clung to the view that such measures were unnecessary and that consumers neither needed nor wanted this protection.[67] Still, the issue of grading and standardization was more closely linked to the ongoing government task of keeping prices and inflation under control than many advertisers were comfortable admitting. The war situation had elevated consumers' need for credible product information, and brand-name advertising was an even less credible indicator of value now that manufacturers were forced to use inferior raw materials for their products. While the government had ways of checking manufacturers' adherence to the OPA's price ceilings, it had no standards or procedures in place for assessing the quality of branded merchandise.[68] Consequently, some manufacturers sold inferior products containing lesser-quality raw materials under existing labels, while others tried to get around the price stipulations by decreasing the weight and quantity that consumers could reasonably expect.[69] Such cheating was prevalent in many industries, including canning. With the best-quality fruits and vegetables going to the armed services, canners were left with lesser goods for the consumer market, which some still sold at top-ceiling prices. A repetition of blindfold tests showed that many big and well-known brands were offering goods of inferior quality without reflecting this fact in their advertising claims.[70]

Adding to the advertising community's worries, especially as America was becoming an active participant in World War II, were the government's plans for the replacement of brand names with a generic "Victory" label based on government specifications and modeled after the British system.[71] The plan called for the War Production Board to work out specifications for all manufacturers in each industry. That, according to a concerned *Wall Street Journal*, meant "no special gadgets to exploit, no difference in price or quality to talk about in advertising." The unanswered question was whether the "Victory" products would be advertised at all.[72] ANA secretary George S. McMillan went so far as to caution manufacturers against placing their brand names on "Victory" models because the public might come to associate them with "inferior" merchandise.[73]

Attempting to create some calm around the situation, OPA administrator Leon Henderson outlined the government's key reasons for wanting to establish standards. First, he argued, they would enable the civilian population to get the most out of a limited supply of materials and labor. They would also reduce the actual costs of production, and they would aid in the determination, simplification, and enforcement of control and prices. The prices of "Victory" models were based on their production cost, and the ceiling price was set so that the producer could make a fair profit.[74] "By reducing the number of varieties, styles, fancy packaging and the like," said Director of Economic Stabilization James F. Byrnes, "we can clear the way for a fuller production of basic essentials."[75] This did not mean, however, that the road to standardization would be simple and straightforward. In addition to political disagreements, the project promised to be both time-consuming and costly.[76]

In contrast to advertisers' negative reactions, consumer advocates welcomed the plan for "Victory" brands with open arms precisely because they understood its radical implications for advertising. If the products in specific categories were effectively interchangeable, and their attributes were stated directly on the label, what sense did it make to spend a fortune on advertising? Would it not make more sense for producers in a presumably "competitive market" to see who could offer the lowest price on an item while meeting the required standards and forget emotional and patriotic appeals that had nothing to do with the actual product and only added to its cost? This clearly was Colston Warne's dream world, and it was a direction in which the advertising industry did not want to go. In fact, argued Warne, the best solution would be to establish a basic government brand for commodities in each essential field, with advertising "forgotten" and distribution costs cut "to the barest minimum." Although other classes of goods might still be available for those with higher incomes, the basic brands would give consumers the choice of buying the cheaper varieties that required a minimum of labor and production.[77]

The government was warming up to the idea, and a Standards Division was created in the early fall of 1942 to provide the OPA's operating divisions with technical assistance in developing specific standards for a variety of goods.[78] At the helm of the new office was Dexter Keezer, a well-known consumer advocate and former executive director of the Consumers' Advisory Board. Ruth Ayres, who had directed a consumer purchase study for the War Production Board in addition to other consumer-related involvements, was put in charge of the division's educational branch.[79] By January 1943, the OPA's Standards Division had reduced the sizes and styles of select consumer and industrial products from 12,000 to 3,400.[80]

To say that American manufacturers were annoyed would be a clear understatement. Not many supported the standardization efforts, and even fewer were in favor of grade labeling. Unlike most other producers, canners had been given special permission to compute their own ceiling price by calculating cost and adding a margin. In effect, this system guaranteed them a profit without providing any workable method to control retail prices.[81] Thus it should come as no surprise that canners, or at least those who sold most of their crops for buyers' labels, were the most aggressive grading opponents.[82] Criticizing the system as expensive and a waste of government resources, they argued that it would make products more expensive because the additional cost of labeling would have to be passed along to consumers. That claim was quickly denounced by the Department of Agriculture, which had been put in charge of creating the grade criteria, with individual price ceilings to match.[83]

Although the grading proposal contained no suggestions for wartime curtailment of trade names, manufacturers were resentful about what they saw as an attempt to accomplish this objective under the cloak of a drive to curb inflation.[84] They proceeded as if their demise were the government's goal and worried that the many millions of dollars they had spent to create "brand loyalties" would be largely wasted.[85] "This process of grading, with all its vast complexities and needless labors—and needless inspections—is made wholly unnecessary for the simple and obvious reason that the buying public is perfectly familiar with the names and brands of merchandise which meets every requirement," noted one critic. "Indeed, the assurance given by thousands of familiar labels, upon food products, clothing, refrigerators, tobacco, chewing gum, toilet articles, candies, household articles and so forth, are much more convincing than would be any number of 'grade labels' that might be pasted to such products by bureaucrats who know little or nothing about manufacturing problems or what actually constitutes good products."[86] Industry representatives argued that consumers were better served by the descriptive labels that manufacturers already used on their cans. The problem was that these labels were written by the producers themselves. They adhered to no particular standards; one manufacturer's "extra fancy" peaches could be of lesser quality than another's "fancy." Thus the labels resembled regular brand advertisements and provided little information about the price or the actual product.

Ignoring the fact that grade labeling would be required only if one manufacturer packed more than one grade of canned fruits under one brand, industry representatives continued to play up claims that mandatory labeling "would regiment consumer buying habits, kill the incentive for even better quality products at lower prices, destroy the consumer's freedom of choice, and restrict the natural American trend toward ever high standards of living."[87] The ANA commissioned George B. Hotchkiss for a study on the matter. Although the advertising organization was adamant that the final result was "entirely that of the author," it must have been very relieved that the professor's "findings" so perfectly matched its own opinions. The enthusiasm about standards and grade labeling, offered Hotchkiss, was "largely due to propaganda that emphasized the theoretical merits of the method without offering proof that official regulation of the quality of consumer goods [was] beneficial."[88]

Consumer advocates took a different tack. The Consumer Division of the Office of Product Management had expressed an early interest in grade labeling, and several professional women's groups had joined the fight.[89] Not only would such labeling assist the OPA in establishing price ceilings for products, but honestly graded products would help consumers know what they were paying for.[90] And because canned goods were being rationed, it was especially important for shoppers to be aware of what they were getting for their rationing points.[91] Consumer activists also viewed grade labeling as an important tool in the fight against the monopolistic tendencies that had been discussed as part of the TNEC hearings only a few years prior. If small producers were allowed to compete on the basis of quality instead of advertising volume, they might gain a competitive edge. Thus, they were encouraged by the OPA's decision to require grade labeling on most canned fruits and vegetables starting with the 1943 crop.[92]

Although many industries were affected by the requirements, the fight against grade labeling was fronted by the canning industry, which launched an all-out lobbying and public relations effort. A nonprofit educational organization, the Brand Names Foundation, supported by advertisers, advertising agencies, and advertising media, was inaugurated in 1943 to fight against "confused economic thinking." Seeking to convey a "clearer understanding" of how brand names and advertising helped people in their daily lives, the foundation used a whole range of promotional outlets, including print ads and radio, and sought a wide audience, including schools and voluntary organizations.[93]

The National Association of Canners followed suit by launching a million-dollar "education" campaign to sway opinion in its favor. It appeared as though the same ultraconservative forces that only a few years earlier had fueled the Dies Committee's attempts at framing the consumer movement as communistic were back at work. Pulling out an old trick, opponents claimed that the grading program was being designed by the "scores of hundreds of Communists and their Fellow Travelers and sympathizers" in key positions with federal agencies and bureaus. The people behind the proposal, they argued, had "the impairment and destruction of American Free Enterprise" as their sole objective and needed to be stopped.[94] The *Wall Street Journal* saw the program as the "first step towards standardization of everything else." And at the end of that road, it warned, is "the whole system which we like to call our American way of life."[95] According to newspaper mogul William Randolph Hearst, the idea of grade labeling could not have been worse if there had been criminal intent behind the proposal.[96] "Publisher Hearst," commented Donald Montgomery sarcastically, "says grade labeling is communism—original communism. Gosh, it's awful what a letter A, B, or C on a can of beans can mean if you think about it."[97]

As March gave way to April, the OPA was under mounting pressure to abandon the grade-labeling program. Prentiss Brown, a former Democratic senator from Michigan who had replaced Leon Henderson as the organization's head, was constantly being exhorted by the canning industry and its supporters to have the program dropped, while labor and consumer groups were eager to keep the system in place.[98] Abandoning the grading program, the latter warned, would be the same as taking a wrecking ball to the OPA's price control program.[99] "The issue is simple," said *Bread and Butter*. "Without grade labeling, price control cannot be fully effective."[100]

Canners and other opponents of grading could still count on the support of business-friendly politicians, however, including Democratic senator James Murray from Montana, Republican congresswoman Jessie Sumner from Illinois, and Republican congressman Charles A. Halleck from Indiana. Halleck emerged as a particularly staunch opponent of grading, going so far as to call for an official probe into the government's plans.[101] He quickly gained solid support from Republicans and anti-Roosevelt Democrats in Congress for his resolution to investigate the Office of Price Administration, the War Production Board, and any other agency that might be setting or planning to set standards for consumer goods.[102]

Manufacturers were also well-positioned to tackle their adversaries on mandatory grade labeling because they had some of their own people in key war agencies. Lou R. Maxon, for example, was the OPA's deputy administrator in charge of information and frequently advised Prentiss Brown on policy. He also happened to be the head of a large Detroit advertising agency that counted H. J. Heinz among its major clients. As a strong defender of industry interests, Maxon was dead set against grade labeling, fearing that it would spread to all fields of branded consumer goods, that all merchandise would eventually be regimented, and that a system of "state socialism" would be the result.[103] He described grade labeling as "the greatest threat to American industry and our way of life that ever existed" and rejected the idea that such a system was essential for price control. Why, he wondered, would Brown use the agency to "put across an idea that Congress has turned down six times?"—a reference to the various versions of the Tugwell bill introduced into Congress during every session from 1933 to 1938.[104]

Joining Maxon were Dan Gerber of the Gerber Baby Food Company and Norman Sorenson of the Coleman Canning Corporation, both recent additions to the OPA. Considering their financial ties with the canning industry, their appointments were a clear violation of official OPA policy, which prohibited any person with a financial interest in a particular field from being appointed to or retained in an agency position in which he or she would have to make price or rationing decisions involving that field. Not only did Gerber and Sorenson appear before the House Agricultural Committee to testify against grading, but it would later be revealed that the Food and Drug Administration had seized two hundred cases of Gerber's strained peaches for babies because they contained worms, and that the American Medical Association was reevaluating its endorsement of the company. This, according to critics, was evidence that the three high officials of the OPA who were leaders in the fight to remove quality restrictions from the price control program had acted in violation of long-standing OPA regulations. Brown did not protest Sorenson and Gerber's lobbying activities, however. Ignoring the recommendation to remove Maxon, Brown expressed faith in his deputy administrator's abilities and increased his powers by leaving him in charge of all communication regarding public opinion on grade labeling. Maxon was also authorized to fill in for Brown on final policy decisions when the latter was unable to attend. Only after massive protests from consumer and labor interests did Brown stop further expansions of his deputy's power, making him, in the words of *Bread and Butter*, a "virtual co-director of OPA."[105] These developments had a demoralizing effect on large sections of the OPA staff, and many considered resigning from the agency as a result.[106] Brown now found himself dogged by rumors that he might be ready to kill the measure.[107]

Upset with how things were unfolding, members of the Council of Organized Consumers, a New York–based organization representing a range of labor and consumer groups, traveled to Washington to remind the OPA head that there was no subject on which American consumers were more united than the need for grade labels for the effective enforcement of price controls. They returned unsuccessful when no such meeting could be arranged.[108]

In early April 1943, the business-friendly representative Halleck had organized a sweeping investigation into the OPA's activities under the pretense that federal authorities were trying to reform the nation's economy "along lines not authorized by Congress."[109] Testifying before a House subcommittee, Paul S. Willis, president of the Grocery Manufacturers of America, described the attempt by "professional consumers" to take advantage of the war emergency to impose "restrictive and unsound" measures upon the American food industry.[110] Later, in an open letter to Economic Director Byrnes and Price Administrator Brown, Willis argued that grade labeling would cause a deterioration of overall product quality because government grades would be far inferior to what manufacturers would produce in a more competitive environment. Grade labeling, he warned, would "place a ceiling on quality, rather than a floor under it."[111] Willis was joined by Charles Dunn, general counsel for the Grocery Manufacturers of America, who warned that the program would handicap the food industry and—an ironic claim considering the TNEC's investigation a few years earlier—function as a potential instrument for monopoly building.[112]

While treating Prentiss Brown with kid gloves, the subcommittee hearings administered some hard punches to economics professor John Kenneth Galbraith, another OPA deputy head who favored the grading proposal, even if he acknowledged that it might "have the effect of abolishing benefit of trade-marks."[113] Not surprisingly, Galbraith was generally disliked by the affected industries. "Why don't you take a sporting attitude and give us a chance to mix your theories with some sound advice from business men?" asked Lew Hahn, general manager and treasurer of the National Retail Dry Goods Association. "You know, when this war is over every business enterprise which manages to survive what you and your chaps are doing will be a national asset because it will provide employment."[114]

Feeling torn between consumers and canners and pressured by Byrnes to pass the measure, Brown tried to get off the hook by suggesting that the grading measure might be outside the OPA's jurisdiction and that congressional action was needed for its passage. This, according to legal staff, was not the case, leading the Council of Organized Consumers to accuse Brown of not wanting to alienate business. Pointing to the "vast" quantity of incoming mail from individuals and organizations, the group urged the OPA to keep its grading program.[115]

In May, Representative Clarence F. Lea (D-CA), who was the chairman of the House Committee on Interstate and Foreign Commerce, asked Brown to hold off on making a decision, informing him that a subcommittee of Lea's committee would be holding public hearings on "restrictions on brand names" later that month. Representative Lyle H. Boren (D-OK) was put in charge of the subcommittee, which met frequently during May and June of 1943. While awaiting the outcome, the OPA arrived at a temporary arrangement that allowed canners to omit government grades from their labels. The agency still required that such grades be marked on manufacturers' invoices and be made available to consumers on community price lists. The lists, posted in shopping centers throughout the country, showed canned brands by grade and their corresponding maximum price as set by the OPA.[116] To further assist consumers, the government printed a series of booklets containing information about the grading methods and procedures.[117]

Among those who were called to testify during the first week of the hearings in June 1943 were representatives from various industries who claimed that the OPA grading proposal had "nothing to do with the prosecution of war or maintaining production of goods" and was "aimed more at reform than at the control of inflation or the winning of the war." It should come as no surprise that CU president Colston Warne was not called to testify.[118] Representative Halleck had become convinced that the move for grade labeling was "a movement to exterminate brand names," an assessment seconded by Representative Boren, who characterized the proposal as the "whim and caprice of a few men" out to change the country's economic structure and threaten business and "our free press."[119] Boren used the hearing as an opportunity to attack the Washington bureaucracy, stressing the importance of keeping the economy "sound." In his view, anything that jeopardized the free and legitimate use of trademarks and brand names would endanger the economic welfare of the nation. And although national advertising, trademarks, and brand names might have their flaws, they were much preferable to "government control, standardization and any form of regimentation."[120] This was a bit much for Brown. Staging a comeback in defense of grading, he stated emphatically that its implementation would not cause established brand names to be discarded or impair their value.[121] Considering the program's goal of fighting inflation—so vital to production and morale during the war, and to the maintenance of free enterprise and democratic institutions after the war—Brown was befuddled by claims that such a system would undermine the American system of free enterprise.[122]

Grading opponents now pegged their hopes to a bill introduced by Senator Robert Taft (R-OH) that aimed to put an end to required grade labeling of all commodities and to any practice of setting price ceiling differentials that did not conform to established trade usage. Also, although this had never been among the OPA's goals or intentions, the bill prohibited any orders that restricted or eliminated the use of brand names and trademarks. It permitted OPA standardization orders only where the price administrator found "that no practicable alternative exists for securing effective price control." Much to consumer advocates' dismay, the Taft Amendment to the Emergency Price Control Act was passed by a Senate dominated by Democrats in July 1943, and in August Congress ordered the OPA to repeal grade-labeling requirements for a score of goods, complying with prohibitions that had been written into the Commodity Credit Corporation Act.[123]

In spite of the legislative victory, Lou Maxon resigned from his OPA position, unhappy with the clique of "professors and theorists" with "unworkable ideas" and a belief that the government should manufacture and distribute all commodities. "Our young lawyers have OPA so bound up in legalistic red tape, that Houdini himself couldn't entangle it," he said.[124] The grade-labeling measure might be dead for now, but Maxon warned business not to think that the battle had been won. Advertising was under attack. If grade labeling ever went into effect, the public might ask why one (widely advertised) Grade A product cost more than another (less advertised) Grade A product. Why should they pay more for a heavily promoted product when a lesser-known brand delivered the same quality and sold for less? The result would be a direct challenge to the practice of brand-name advertising and had to be stopped. He called on businesses to allocate at least 3 percent of their advertising budget to ongoing "education" of the public about the problematic aspects of grading.[125]

Consumer advocates were expectedly upset. Thanks to the "familiar coalition of Northern Republicans and anti–New Deal Democrats," reflected Colston Warne, and under pressure from manufacturers, publishers, and advertising agents, American consumers would now be paying fancy prices for the poorest grades of products, and the lack of effective quality oversight would make price control almost meaningless.[126] Representatives from leading consumer organizations contacted the new economic stabilization director, Fred M. Vinson, with pleas for help in reversing the decision. Consumer advocates explained that they had never been opposed to brand names; they simply wanted supplementary information in order to assist the OPA with the enforcement of its orders. In the absence of a grade-labeling system, consumers could not even hope to keep their home front pledge not to pay more than ceiling price for products.[127] An equally disappointed group of forty self-styled "fighting Congressmen" organized themselves into a "consumer committee" with the avowed objective of restoring the OPA's original grading program.[128]

By early 1944, and in line with what Alan Brinkley describes as "a massive shift of power within the federal government away from liberal administrators towards corporate interests," many of the principal officials responsible for the grade-labeling program, including John Kenneth Galbraith, had left the OPA, and more business-friendly individuals had been appointed to agency positions.[129] The industry was as delighted as consumer advocates were disappointed. The latter had not been entirely ineffective, however, and they continued to push for a repeal of the Taft Amendment. The possibility of a policy reversal kept the advertising industry on the alert throughout the war and beyond.[130]

Conclusion

In spite of damaging criticism, advertisers managed to keep their practices intact during the war. Discussions surrounding advertising's wartime function had exposed a number of shortcomings, and the industry had shown its true colors in the debate over standardization and grading of goods. The purpose of advertising was not to educate, inform, or help the public, but rather to make consumers believe that the more heavily advertised brands were better than store brands or less advertised products when, in fact, the opposite might be true. This practice, however dubious, represented the key promotional tool for America's major manufacturers, and there was no way, even during the worst of wartime conditions, that they could let it go. Chances were that consumers might prefer the grading system, or some of the reforms proposed by the industry's critics. Fearing that brand-name advertising might lose its luster after the war had ended and that any wartime concessions on their part might well continue into the postwar period and become permanent, advertisers saw it in their best interest to protect advertising as the consumer lingua franca for the war's duration.

5

Advertising, Washington, and the Renamed War Advertising Council

One of the first controversies to emerge in connection with war-theme advertising was the extent to which print media should be expected to provide free advertising space to the government. The discussion started early in the war, and the issue was not resolved until the end of 1943, after government sources, the commercial media, and the advertising industry had ironed out their differences and finally reached accord. While most large advertisers and media owners eventually came to the conclusion that private industry should provide space for free, the newspaper industry was split. Larger and more financially stable newspapers favored commercial donations of time, space, and talent, whereas local newspapers, weeklies, and independent radio stations wanted the government to pay for its own promotions. The issue dragged out for months, causing people on both sides to grow impatient with the government's hesitation in declaring an official policy.[1]

The eventual failure to secure paid government advertising and Washington's decision to rely on volunteer contributions from advertising and media interests played nicely into the Ad Council's hands and elevated its importance. It also brought new pressures on the advertising industry to coordinate its efforts. But the council's perseverance paid off. When an organizational shakeup in the Domestic Branch of the Office of War Information resulted in budget cuts for promotional activities in the middle of 1943, the Advertising Council was ready to pick up the slack, even renaming itself the War Advertising Council to reflect the government's increased reliance on the advertising industry for its promotional needs.

Paid Government Advertising: A Controversy

The government had looked to the private sector for help with advertising since the Civil War, when bankers and special government loan agents had been enlisted to advertise the sale of treasury bonds to the American public. The practice became more prevalent during World War I, when any suggestion that the advertising industry should be paid for these services was quickly dismissed by the Treasury Department.[2] This did not mean, however, that the government was categorically opposed to paid promotions. When U.S. savings bonds were first introduced in 1935, the Treasury bought full-page ads in national magazines such as *Collier's, Liberty, Time, Saturday Evening Post, Literary Digest,* and *Today* to promote its new securities. Three years later, it allocated $400,000 for this purpose, and in 1940 it fashioned an elaborate plan for the purchase of advertising space to promote the sale of war bonds and war savings stamps.[3] This approach to paid government advertising was in line with Canadian, English, and Australian practices on the eve of World War II.

In 1941, more than a year after it had declared war on Germany, the British government was spending an estimated $10 million on war-related advertising, and by the last quarter of the year it was responsible for 17 percent of all British newspaper ads. The ads provided information about issues such as food substitutions and product restrictions. They explained the rationing system that had been instituted and instructed the public on how to take care of their nutritional needs. The ads were credited with a great deal of success in the sale of British war bonds, including $800 million worth during the first Victory Loan Drive in February 1940.[4] And while it had taken the Ministry of Supply more than twelve months' worth of unlimited editorial space and speeches by cabinet ministers to secure twenty thousand pairs of binoculars, an advertising campaign for the same purpose produced three times as many binoculars in only eight weeks.[5]

Similarly, in Canada, according to the trade publication *Printers' Ink*, paid government promotions offered "a glowing testimonial" to advertising as "a vital instrument in the policy of a country at war."[6] Although individual advertisers assisted the government with its promotional needs and newspapers extended their editorial support of the war program, the Canadian government still recognized "the wisdom of stepping out as an advertiser on its own."[7] Thus, alongside individual advertisers, who, much like their American counterparts, used regular product advertising or institutional copy to help conserve gasoline and save scrap metal, the Canadian government would pay for its own ads. These were used to inform citizens about wartime labor strikes, how to feed a family during the war, and the use of corn syrup as a sweetener because of the strict rationing of sugar. As in England, paid government ads were also used to educate the population about nutritious eating and the importance of consuming the right amount of vitamins. At the same time, as U.S. advertising was dropping to an alarming 2 percent of national income—lower than at any time during the 1930s—Canadian advertising was getting a boost. The total Canadian advertising linage for the first eight months of 1941 was about 5.2 percent higher than in the comparable 1940 period.[8]

The U.S. government, however, was not as forthcoming as the Canadian, English, and Australian authorities in allocating advertising funds. If anything, congressional support for paid government advertising seemed to wane as the nation edged closer to war. In early 1941, the Treasury Department's request for $3 million to promote savings bonds had met with substantial resistance, and the $1.5 million eventually allocated for this purpose was enough to cover only part of the Treasury's promotional expenses, effectively forcing the department to depend on charity from advertisers and media owners.[9]

While the government was cognizant of its huge promotional needs, it hesitated to use its scarce financial resources for this purpose. There was also concern that appropriation of funds for advertising would lead to fierce media competition over the right to carry the government's ads, and that those who lost out might end up accusing the government of favoritism or collusion. Some federal officials even suggested that direct advertising was not the only, or even necessarily the best, means of presenting Washington's view to the public, claiming that speeches by government officials, especially President Roosevelt, might be just as effective in delivering war-related messages to the American people.[10] In fact, and in a move that may have wisely anticipated these issues, Henry Morgenthau Jr. had divested himself of his media holdings upon his appointment as Treasury secretary.[11]

Dwindling advertising income resulting from a contracting consumer market soon became a motivating factor in the call for paid government advertising. Small, local media pushed harder than their larger counterparts. The latter tended to attract major advertisers, who continued to promote their merchandise in order to keep their brand names before the public. The situation for local media was different. Most of their advertising came from smaller businesses with fewer products to sell, fewer resources, and less incentive to do institutional advertising. Even though advertising had flourished during World War I, one-eighth of all American newspapers, especially smaller publications, had folded after the war ended. Considering increased pressures such as the shortage of manpower and the prospect of a loss of advertising revenues in the present war, the future for many newspapers did not look bright.[12]

Newspaper publishers worried that a system for providing free publicity to the government could end up hurting those who refused to participate, and that Washington's demands for free space would cause the mass media to devote less editorial space to war-related issues. Individuals on both sides of the debate feared that the government, given its great advertising needs, would become one of the nation's largest advertisers, thereby dominating editorial rooms and threatening the freedom of the press.[13] Yet publishers' concerns about compromising their editorial integrity were more than offset by their worries over dwindling advertising revenues. Hence they often, at least initially, were in favor of paid government advertising, a position that had early support in advertising circles as well.[14]

Although many in the newspaper industry were happy to provide some free space and services for the sale of victory bonds, few wanted such donations to become standard practice, a point made even more forcefully after America's official entry into the war. Why, asked *Editor and Publisher*, should they sacrifice more than others?

> The Treasury does not call upon the paper manufacturers to give the government the paper upon which the stamps and bonds are printed. It does not ask the ink-makers to contribute their product. The Navy Department does not ask the steel mills to donate armor plate or shapes for battleships, cruisers, or cannons. The War Department pays full price, including profit, for every yard of cloth it buys for uniforms, every pound of nickel and copper for cartridges. That is as it should be. . . . respectfully, but empathetically, we must deny the right of the Treasury Department or any other branch of government to submit an advertising plate to a publisher with the request that he print it as a patriotic duty, free of charge.[15]

By paying for professionally prepared advertising, the government was not providing a subsidy to newspapers, but simply making appropriate use of their stock-in-trade.[16] Hence the American Newspaper Publishers Association (ANPA), at least in the early stages of what would become a lengthy debate, did its utmost to ensure that the government paid for its ads.[17] *Editor and Publisher*, which quickly assumed a leading role in the matter, argued that paid advertising served the government much better than donated services because it ensured that the messages, including wording and timing, were presented exactly as intended, thus preventing public confusion.[18] Many leading advertising professionals, who might have been concerned about their own job security, initially agreed. The American Association of Advertising Agencies, for example, stressed the importance of organizing the government's campaigns "with the same responsibility for results as in commercial use."[19]

Local newspaper interest groups, including the Washington Newspaper Publishers Association, the Kentucky Press Association, the Inland Daily Press Association, and the Louisiana Press Association, added their voices to the demand for paid government advertising, and some suggested that newspapers were getting the short end of the stick.[20] Why, for example, they asked, had the Treasury Department paid $80,000 in federal financing to Walt Disney for a motion picture to promote the government's home-front effort while asking the press to donate space on this issue for free? Attempting to inject a note of calm, the Treasury explained that Disney had been paid because the filming had forced the company to stop production on other projects; thus the money was reimbursement for time and labor. When it came to newspaper advertising, however, the Treasury was perfectly happy with the emerging practice among advertisers of working the government's home-front messages in as part of their commercial pitch.[21]

Several members of the American mass media thought likewise. The American Society of Newspaper Editors, for example, warned that paid government advertising might "gravely endanger the news and editorial integrity of American newspapers"; it declared its opposition to any governmental practice that resembled a wartime subsidy of the press. Taking a strong stand against pressuring the government to buy space, it argued that "the patriotic services of the American press never have been or never should be evaluated in terms of dollars."[22] That advertising might have a corrupting effect on news and information was by no means a novel idea. Critics had made this claim for decades, and now it seemed that the media were being backed into a corner. If government advertising was to be shunned because of its ability to influence editorial and news columns, what could be said about the corrupting effects of commercial advertising?[23] If public advertising corroded a free press, commented Colston Warne, who had long been a proponent of paid advertising, "the direct implication follows that private advertising also implies distortion of editorial opinion." This was an impression that he doubted the mass media wanted to foster.[24]

The mere mention of this inconsistency struck a raw nerve among supporters of paid government advertising, and they responded defensively. "To say that placement of paid advertising by the government would put newspapers under political control," stated one defender of the practice, "is to call against the American Press a pretty damaging indictment in an hour when the nation's life is in danger."[25] The maintenance of a free press, it was argued, was "fundamentally due to the multiplicity of the economic interests of the advertisers who furnish most of its financial support."[26]

The National Association of Broadcasters took a slightly different tack. Whereas newspapers eagerly accepted paid government advertising, the broadcasting industry had consistently provided the government with free airtime. Unlike the printed press, however, broadcasting was a regulated industry and was expected to carry important government messages gratis in exchange for the privilege of using the public airways free of charge. Still, broadcasters worried that government appropriations for the purchase of radio time would open a Pandora's box of problems, including higher taxes and increased control over the already regulated medium. In addition, it might lessen individual stations' control over programming and give a disproportionate advantage to those government agencies most able to lobby for an appropriation to secure radio time. And if Washington should adopt the most efficient advertising strategy, it might select large stations for its messages and put the smaller ones at a disadvantage. Last but not least, the association worried that members of Congress would apply tremendous political pressure upon government departments to secure allotments for stations in their home districts.[27]

Editor and Publisher was highly upset by the insinuation that newspapers and other media might use their political influence to extract money for advertising from the government. "The incessant harping on this thesis by temporary and permanent aids in the government is both annoying and illogical," it said. "It deprecates the patriotism of the newspaper fraternity. It disregards the wholly uncompensated efforts that the newspapers have put behind government's war projects, notably the recent drive for salvage and scrap. It assumes a condition which has not been proven—that newspapers would sabotage a government effort unless they received advertising as patronage."[28] A couple of closely related events helped to sway the outcome. One was a reorganization of the government's information agencies: the War Information Board and its Advertising Division were replaced by the Office of War Information and the new Bureau of Campaigns, which recognized the Advertising Council as an official component of the overall information strategy. Another factor was the decision by the Treasury Department to allow tax deductions for all "ordinary and reasonable" advertising.[29]

The Treasury Department was adamant that the government's proportional needs could best be addressed through the donation of space, time, and talent via the Ad Council, a view that soon gained support from other Washington officials.[30] Attempting to bring others around to the Treasury's view, Morgenthau's assistant, Peter Odegard, invited members of the newspaper industry to imagine a congressional allocation of $100 million to the Treasury for the promotion of war bonds the following year, with his office having also given large amounts to each of the other government agencies for promotional expenses, so that now they were all joined together in one super "Federal Advertising Bureau" to buy their way into the press. If this were the case, Odegard asked rhetorically, would "you, and your publishers, want to be dependent on the Government for the existence of the principal part of your revenue? Would you feel free to criticize when some government official could wipe out a half or a third of your revenue with a casual nod?" "I think," he added, "your liberty and your freedom are worth more to you than that, and I think you will also agree that, since the Government of the United States is no more and no less than the people of the United States, it is both inappropriate and unwise for the people to spend their own money to sell themselves their own Government securities."[31]

The Office of War Information (OWI) cited several reasons for its opposition to having the government pay for advertising. The first concern was cost. Judging by what the advertising industry was currently spending on war information ads, Washington was looking at a price of several hundred million or even a billion dollars to do the job right. Any smaller allocation, combined with the elimination of private contributions, might well result in fewer home-front promotions than the government was presently getting for free. Somewhat paradoxically, American taxpayers would have to pay more for what might be a lesser result. Operating a giant advertising fund and making decisions about proper media placement for the many different campaigns was not a task that the government wanted to take on. Last but not least, the OWI continued to worry that government allocations for advertising might be viewed as a media subsidy, thus posing a threat to freedom of the press.[32] OWI head Elmer Davis stressed that his agency had "always been and continued to be opposed to government-paid advertising," an opinion shared by his director of domestic operations, Gardner Cowles Jr., a newspaperman who was on loan to the government from the *Des Moines Register and Tribune*.[33] Cowles not only was convinced that commercially sponsored war-theme advertising was the way to go, but he was also concerned that the government's home-front campaigns might be doomed without the Advertising Council and individual advertisers.[34]

Many among the advertising community had initially agreed with the newspaper industry's position that the government should pay for some, if not all, of its campaign promotions, but they gradually changed their tune.[35] Ad Council president Chester LaRoche, for example, believed that advertisers had a "patriotic duty" to help the government, but he was unconvinced at first that private industry should be asked to carry the entire burden of government advertising. In a departure from the views of most Advertising Council members, he worried that Washington was taking advantage of the advertising community's generosity.[36] The discussion continued throughout 1942 and the early part of 1943, leading one trade publication to characterize it as "a war within a war."[37]

The Legislative Fight

With three bills that came before Congress in late 1942 and early 1943, the matter of whether the government should have to pay for advertising was finally settled. The Bankhead bill (S 1073), introduced by Senator John Bankhead (D-AL), and two bills introduced by Representative Clarence Cannon (D-MO) reflected the concerns of smaller newspapers that were facing financial difficulties and needed to be compensated for their government-sponsored ads. The measures met with strong resistance not only from large parts of the advertising industry—including the Advertising Council, which was now firmly against paid government advertising—but also, increasingly, from the mass media and the American Newspaper Publishers Association (ANPA), which had made a complete turnaround on this issue.[38] The ANPA was so appalled by the idea of having Congress appropriate $25–30 million to basically support a select group of newspapers that it abandoned all further demands for paid government advertising.[39]

By late summer, the Bankhead bill had hit a snag over growing concerns that the measure was not so much an effort to promote the government's home-front program as it was a strategy for local newspapers to recover advertising revenues that had been lost as a result of manufacturers' reconversion to war production. "If the Bankhead type of treasury advertising has smelled like a subsidy to a lot of papers before the bill passes," asked the chairman of the Allied Newspaper Council and the general manager of Gannett, Frank Tripp, "what odor ink will the president use to change the aroma after he signs it?"[40] Elmer Davis and Treasury Secretary Morgenthau were equally opposed. The latter made it very clear that he had no interest in exercising the kind of power over advertising that the Bankhead bill would give his agency. If anything, Morgenthau believed that the proposed measure would impede, rather than improve, promotional support for the sale of bonds and unfairly favor newspapers over other forms of media.[41] This view resonated with the owners of small, struggling radio stations, who questioned the wisdom behind a measure that would favor local newspapers but do nothing to help local radio.[42]

In spite of vocal opposition from consumer advocates and their supporters, the bill passed the Senate Committee on Banking and Currency in October 1943 by a vote of 11 to 5.[43] After being amended in two important particulars, it passed the Senate on a 40 to 35 vote the following month. The amended version (S 1457) reduced the total annual expenditure on paid advertising from $30 million to $15 million and stipulated that the entire amount should be spent on space in newspapers that were published in cities with a population of 10,000 or less.

At this point, the bill looked very much like a newspaper subsidy, a fact that even *Editor and Publisher* acknowledged.[44] Ted R. Gamble, the national director of the War Finance Division of the Treasury Department, testified before the Committee on Ways and Means of the House of Representatives that the bill put the government in a terrible bind. To advertise in some newspapers but not others would be greatly unfair, and to advertise in all of them would be economically prohibitive. And as much as he admired Canada's war effort, Gamble did not think the Canadian practice of paying for wartime advertising should be emulated in the United States because there was "no evidence whatsoever" that "the high productivity of the Canadian paid advertising plan in volume of sales to individuals and at low cost attest[ed] to the feasibility of the Government using its own resources and controlling its official messages."[45] Americans, he said, were lucky to benefit from an unparalleled volunteer effort that had produced amazing results, such as making 84 to 90 percent of the population aware of the Third War Loan in September of 1943.[46]

The House version of S 1457 was submitted by Representative Cannon in mid-December, but because of continued opposition and the high likelihood of a presidential veto, the House Ways and Means Committee decided to table the bill after an informal, but close, vote. The measure's opponents were as pleased as Senator Bankhead was disappointed. Consumers Union, which objected to the prominent role that private advertising was assuming in the war effort and had come out in support of paid government advertising from the get-go, asked that the issue be reconsidered.[47]

The defeat of the Bankhead bill effectively ended any talk of paid government advertising. The task of placing the government's home-front campaigns before the American public now rested solely with the nation's advertisers, and especially the Advertising Council. The organizational side was far and away the easiest aspect of the council's work. Actually implementing the various campaigns and making sure that advertisers adhered to its directives were far more challenging. Herding the advertising industry, arguably a strong-willed and independent group, was difficult. The council could only make recommendations to advertisers, not impose rules on them, and it lacked the power to stop even the most blatant war-theme abuses. Thus, if urging advertisers to donate space for the various council campaigns had been difficult, guiding their copywriting practices would prove equally, if not increasingly, problematic. Industry leaders worked hard to coach and convince the advertising industry at large, and their perseverance paid off. A major upheaval in the Domestic Branch of the OWI in the middle of 1943 helped to further solidify the Ad Council's role in the war effort.

Streamlining Wartime Advertising

The Treasury Department's decision to deem advertising a "reasonable, ordinary, and necessary" business expense led to a greater use of institutional advertising by manufacturers, but not all of them were squarely behind the Ad Council. Contributions to the war effort were purely voluntary, and it was clear to many in the industry that large groups of advertisers were not making a sufficient effort to comply with the council's objectives. Many advertisers preferred to design their own war-theme advertising, and often those ads boasted about the company's contribution to the war effort and neglected to tie in with council-sponsored campaigns. A lack of coherence thus continued to be a major concern. Not only was this hurting the various campaigns, but it also threatened to discredit the council and undermine its goals.

Ever since the early days of the war, the government officials in charge of home-front promotions had taken a keen interest in war-theme advertising, closely monitoring copy to ensure its congruence with their own agenda. Thus Associate Director Allen Grover of the Office of Facts and Figures was underwhelmed by one of the Southern Railway System's ads. "The headline is bad," he complained to the Ad Council's executive director, Miller McClintock, "and the phrases like 'a terrifying stillness,' 'the painful re-adjustment,' 'trying days for American industry,' 'Every industry that wills to live,' strike a note of gloom about post-war conditions which are certainly not calculated to make people fight the kind of fight we've gotten on our hands."[48] Other industry observers were equally concerned, causing C. B. Larrabee, the editor of *Printers' Ink*, to worry that "the bright glow" of advertising's achievements was being "dulled by the methods of a comparatively small group of unimaginative, unpatriotic men." Some, he observed in the spring of 1943, had stubbornly continued to use "themes and tricks that were unpleasant enough in pre-war days" but were downright outrageous during a war. "Others," he continued, "try to climb [on] the war-time bandwagon by using a war theme for products that are only remotely, if at all, related to our Victory effort. A few are still so unimaginative as to think that the public will believe that without their products the war might well be lost. To all these may be added the advertisers who insipidly congratulate themselves because they are doing no more and no less than what any other patriotic citizen should be doing. Advertising is running a grave risk of having the public turn on all because of the faults of a few."[49]

The concerns were echoed by Arthur Price, mail order sales manager for Sears, Roebuck and Company. "Every fat, overloaded war factory," he claimed in a speech before the Chicago Federated Advertising Club, "seems to be oozing glory and confidence, not so modestly reserving a great reward for its share in our unquestioned victory." He nominated the manufacturer of a "nationally famous" vacuum cleaner for the worst full-page color advertisement. "If homes are strong, the nation's foundation is impregnable," read the copy. "If there is high morale where we live, there is high morale where we work and where we fight. . . . A nationwide service organization, outstanding in the vacuum cleaner industry, is on the alert through this emergency to help you keep your _____ *vacuum cleaner* in apple pie running order." Neither did Price care for the following copy written for a rubber company: "Patriotism does not demand that you lay up your car. Just the opposite. Real conservation requires that you keep your car in service for the duration of war *as part of America's essential transportation system*. Don't think of it as a 'pleasure car,' it is a *war car* now."[50]

As a concerned member of the Ad Council, Stuart Peabody urged the advertising community to study current national weeklies, women's magazines, and radio programs. "You will find that perhaps a third of the ads in half-page size or larger are devoted to such slants as use of the Little Giant Widget on a tank or a plane or another engine of war," he said. "You will attend several

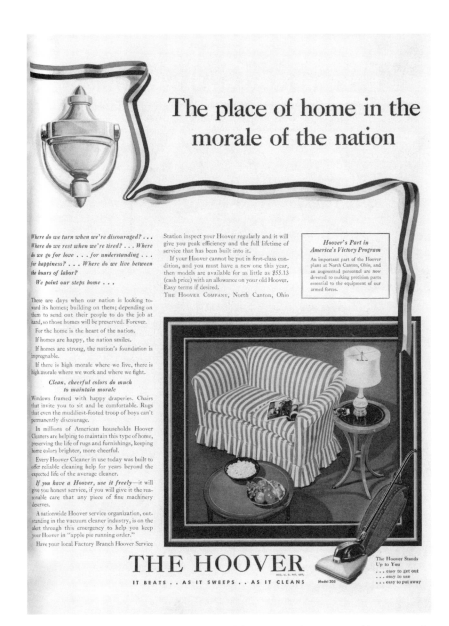

Figure 4. "The place of home in the morale of the nation." This Hoover ad is an example of manufacturers' early, and somewhat unfocused, attempts to tie their products in with the war effort. For a more streamlined effort by the same manufacturer, adhering to the Advertising Council's directives, see fig. 11 on p. 129. *Life*, March 2, 1943, 35.

Figure 5. "Do you ever look at your car this way?" This ad from the McQuay-Norris Manufacturing Company is the kind of promotion that was identified as problematic by the Advertising Council and concerned industry leaders. The text and illustration create an unrealistic association between the product and the war, and nowhere in the copy is there any mention of the Ad Council's campaigns. *Saturday Evening Post*, February 13, 1943, 35.

rousing E-flag raisings. You will see a great many 'don't blame the dealer' ads, and a surprisingly small number of war bond mentions. You will discover that not very many advertisers really get down to work on conservation, or morale or nutrition or salvage or bonds or the other urgent needs the public needs to be sold on."[51] Considering the advertising industry's commitment to the promotion of government campaigns, these troubling trends were not to be taken lightly.

The public's opinion of war-theme advertising was based on what people saw and heard, and the reactions were mixed. A 1942 study by the Advertising Research Foundation revealed that both men and women were interested in war-related ads and that they responded favorably to copy that described a company's role in the war effort or directly appealed to them for support.[52] Consumers did not object to product advertising, but they had little patience with manufacturers who boasted about their war contributions. People wanted information about how to make goods last longer and about manufacturers' plans for preventing postwar unemployment. Much to the advertising industry's relief, a nationwide study conducted in April 1942 by the Association of National Advertisers (ANA) found negligible public support for Consumers Union's demand that advertising be eliminated in wartime.[53]

How well, then, did the mass media adhere to the government's call for assistance? A study of more than two thousand advertisements from weeklies, women's service magazines, and mass-circulation monthlies between May and September 1942 concluded that 40 percent of the ads contained some sort of war appeal. The ratio was highest for the weeklies (48.9 percent) and lowest for women's service magazines (17.9 percent).[54] A survey titled "Public Sentiment toward Wartime Advertising" conducted by the ANA in the summer of 1943 revealed the following: 63 percent of the respondents believed that advertising had done a good job of explaining how rationing worked; 82 percent praised its job in selling war bonds; 55 percent thought it had done a good job of delineating America's objectives during the war; 56 percent viewed advertising as an instrumental force in the planning of victory gardens; and a whopping 84 percent of those surveyed concluded that it contributed to the general war effort.[55] This, according to the ANA, was a strong indication that the public was expressing "growing confidence in advertising for promoting the war effort."[56] The Advertising Federation of America, on the other hand, was slightly more critical; a resolution issued at its June 1943 convention deplored the "bad taste, vulgarity and willful perversion of legitimate wartime themes" by a few irresponsible advertisers.[57]

The temptation to capitalize on the war situation was not limited to the press. In mid-1942, for example, General Motors (GM) began sponsoring a weekly radio broadcast called *Cheers from the Camp*. Designed to "touch the emotional heartstrings of ordinary American families," the program was broadcast directly from training camps, where soldiers served as unpaid talent. Each week featured a different camp, with a parent, wife, or girlfriend brought in to meet "their" soldier and be interviewed on the air. Establishing itself as a mediator between the average American and new recruits, GM offered a mix of "down-home" music and sing-along hymns, often putting soldiers on the air to speak to the people back home. Other GM programs, such as *Victory Is Our Business*, dramatized the company's wartime production and news from the fighting front. Reaching several hundred thousand GM workers and millions of radio listeners, it often featured GM employees with sons in the military or returning war heroes. In the words of advertising historian Roland Marchand, it came to "represent a kind of Main Street on which local patriotic 'parades' took place." Other corporations, including Westinghouse, Bausch and Lomb, Eastman Kodak, and United States Steel, quickly followed GM's lead and created similar programs.[58]

Boastful advertising aroused resentment and ridicule not only in civilian circles but among enlisted men as well. Overseas military personnel liked advertising for its informational value. They enjoyed reading what people back home were wearing and buying. (In fact, they expressed a strong dislike for special magazine editions that did not carry advertising.) Not all forms of advertising passed muster with them, however. Soldiers objected to ads that described war in glamorous and exciting terms. They often found the depictions of military scenes and personnel to be inaccurate and trite.[59] "When men like these pick up a magazine or paper, read advertisements in which the copy writer has sought to give a military flavor to his copy by dragging in a picture of a male model in uniform, they resent it," stated *Printers' Ink*. "They resent it because it is giving a kind of musical comedy flavor to something that's important. To them the army is men, men they know and trust, working very hard under great risks. It is mud and dirt and a chance of getting killed or wounded."[60] Charles G. Mortimer Jr., vice-president of General Foods and a member of the Advertising Council's Executive Committee, warned the advertising community that the public was not amused when "the agony of death on the battlefield" was used to lure people to "consider the superlative qualities of a cigarette."[61]

Soldiers found manufacturers' tendency to credit their own products for military successes to be particularly annoying. This was well demonstrated when the copy used by a maker of minor aircraft parts included the line "Who's Afraid of the Big Focke-Wulf?" (referring to a deadly German fighter plane, the Focke-Wulf 190). An American bomber pilot ripped out the ad, writing "I am" across it, and had his entire squadron sign it before he mailed it back to the advertiser.[62] "He [the soldier] knows the true value of that equipment," warned *Printers' Ink*. "His life depends on it—but he knows its faults like a mother."[63] "Lay off the gallant airmen, valiant tank drivers, glorious American boys bull," advised an advertising executive turned army officer. "Quit playing upon the glories of war with copy by a bunch of guys who never heard a bomb fall and lay off the 'we are Americans we can't lose optimism.'" He called for advertisements to depict more realistic war images: "No one gives a damn about Mrs. So and So's silk stocking now serving in the parachute corps."[64]

There was an ongoing debate about how to write an effective war-theme ad. Many advertisers were enthusiastic about this task and approached it with gusto; one even went so far as to suggest that the term "aidvertising" be used during the war because it so accurately reflected what advertisers were doing.[65] Others, including Thomas D. Beck, president of the Crowell-Collier Publishing Company, agreed, contending that people were just as interested in home-front information as they were in overseas news about the war: "They want to know just what is being done at home to back up fighting men facing the enemy. And in this connection, business and industry have a factual, truthful and inspiring story to tell, one that will bolster the faith and confidence of the people in the American way of life, and a story, consequently that will bear constant repeating through educational advertising."[66]

While some advertisers believed that ad copy should appeal to consumers' sense of reason, others considered an emotional approach to be more effective.[67] One of the most acclaimed advertisements of World War II, "The Kid in Upper 4," was calculated to make readers misty-eyed rather than stimulate their adrenaline. Created early in the war and without the Advertising Council's assistance, the ad by the New Haven Railroad apologized for crowded passenger cars, explaining its policy of giving soldiers on their way to war first priority for a seat or berth.[68] It described the emotions of a young soldier as the train carried him away from home: "Wide awake . . . listening . . . staring into blackness . . . thinking of . . . the taste of hamburger and pop . . . the feel of driving a roadster over a six-lane highway . . . a dog named Shucks or Spot, or Barnacle Bill. . . . It told of the lump in his throat and the possibility of a tear in his eye." The copy concluded on a poignant note: "It doesn't matter, Kid. Nobody will see . . . it's too dark."[69] The advertisement was widely

Figure 6. "Don't look now—but here comes 444 ladies stockings." Ads such as this one from Shell Research often failed to meet with soldiers' approval. For another example of an unrealistic depiction of the war experience, see fig. 14 on p. 132. *Saturday Evening Post*, November 23, 1944, 3.

Figure 7. "The Kid in Upper 4" was a highly acclaimed advertisement by the New Haven Railroad. *Saturday Evening Post*, January 9, 1943, 43.

quoted and reprinted; it even inspired a song by the same name. *Printers' Ink* pronounced it the "most-talked-of ad of the year."[70]

A series of war bond advertisements in the August 1942 issue of *Family Circle*, on the other hand, took a far more rational approach, promising readers that saving during the war would enable them to purchase refrigerators, automobiles, electric ranges, and other consumer durables once such items became available again. Others promised dream homes with every new appliance imaginable and a private plane, helicopter, or brand new car to boot.[71] A Hoover advertisement cleverly pegged the wartime purchase of savings bonds to the rewarding feeling of buying a new Hoover vacuum cleaner once the fighting had ended.[72] While admitting that such advertising had a self-serving aspect, *Advertising Age* defended the practice as a "legitimate and useful activity" that strengthened an advertiser's position and was helping to pave the way for the important process of postwar adjustment.[73]

The OWI Shakeup and the Birth of the War Advertising Council

In the spring and summer of 1943, the OWI's Domestic Branch came under severe attack from Republican members of Congress and conservative Southern Democrats who accused the government's domestic information organization of a long list of sins, among which was the claim that the office had been turned into an expensive propaganda outlet for the New Deal. They also charged that the staff was inept or too inexperienced to do their jobs and that the OWI's ubiquitous nature had made it a stalking horse for invisible and insidious attacks on representative government—implying *left wing*, *socialist*, or worse. Some went so far as to accuse the agency of serving as a safe haven for men seeking to avoid military service.[74] Elmer Davis denied all such charges, but he could not prevent the heated debate that ensued over the government's information program. When the dust finally cleared a few months later, the OWI's information program had undergone a major organizational shakeup. Many key officers resigned their positions, and the Domestic Branch's budget was drastically cut, causing an even heavier dependence on support from the advertising industry.

The trend had been gradual. In early 1943, Gardner Cowles Jr., himself a liberal Republican, had become concerned that the Republican-dominated Congress would not appropriate sufficient funds to keep the Domestic Branch operating. Anticipating a tough fight, he decided to streamline his agency's operations in a way that would appease its opponents. Part of his strategy was to make sure that the Bureau of Campaigns did not do or say anything that would upset critics. Cowles terminated all controversial and extraneous functions, eliminated the production of pamphlets and posters, and decided to rely more on help from the private sector. He told William Lewis, the former vice-president of CBS, to directly supervise the bureau's writers and appointed motion picture executive James Allen as Lewis's assistant. Price Gilbert, the former vice-president of Coca-Cola, was brought in to head the Bureau of Graphics and Printing.[75] After firing Pulitzer Prize–winning historian Henry Pringle as head of the Bureau of Campaigns' Writers' Division, Cowles appointed New York book publisher Harold Guinzburg in his place. The director of domestic operations also convinced Elmer Davis that Lowell Mellett, head of the office's Motion Picture Bureau, should resign because he was a New Dealer who had used the division's movies to promote the president.

Not surprisingly, the purge met with its share of resistance. Most of the Writers' Division staff signed a statement accusing Cowles of trying to take the guts and spirit out of domestic information. Soon all of them, including the newly appointed Guinzburg, had resigned their positions, complaining that the "high pressure promoters who prefer slick salesmanship to honest information" had made their job impossible.[76] The reaction was just as severe in the Bureau of Graphics and Printing. In a thinly veiled attack on the advertising industry's influence, noted artist Ben Shahn and bureau chief Francis Brennan objected to the idea that men who treated people "as if they were twelve-year-olds" should be entrusted with the government's information campaigns. In a gesture designed to mock the increased federal reliance on help from American business, they created a poster embodying their idea of bureau head Gilbert's requirements. It depicted the Statue of Liberty holding aloft not a torch but four frosty bottles of Coca-Cola, with the caption "The War That Refreshes: The Four Delicious Freedoms!"[77] In a letter to Davis, Brennan outlined his decision to leave the OWI: "The advertising men," he wrote, "utilize every trick of the trade to make necessary civilian action appear palatable, comfortable, and not quite as inconvenient as Guadalcanal. . . . To our shame, while American soldiers rotted in the desert heat, the Graphics Division was designing posters about ordering coal early."[78] He admitted that some industry techniques, such as the fairly simple job of getting messages printed, distributed, and read, greatly benefited the government's campaign strategies, but he refused to let the advertising industry interfere with their psychological approaches, content, and ideas. Such techniques, Brennan stated, had "done more toward dimming perception, suspending critical values, and spreading the sticky syrup of complacency over the people than any other factor."[79]

Historian Sidney Weinberg argues that Cowles's opposition to the writers' pamphlets and their political messages was as much a matter of political necessity to save the Domestic Branch as it was an expression of personal preference. The problem, however, was that Cowles never discussed the situation with those who were directly involved. Davis sympathized with the writers, but he did not want to interfere with Cowles's program, so he declined to come to their support. In spite of all this political maneuvering, however, Cowles did not manage to sway enough votes in Congress to secure the Domestic Branch's allocations. Drastic budget cuts forced him to close twelve regional branches, eliminate the Motion Picture Bureau, and abandon publications altogether.[80]

The advertising community used the upheaval not only to gain more influence over the OWI's Domestic Branch but also to moralize. *Advertising and Selling*, for example, wrote that the OWI itself was to blame for the drastic appropriations cuts because it had never convinced Congress that it knew what it was doing. What the organization needed, the journal argued, was a staff of practical workers capable of disseminating information to the public. The government was trying to do "the biggest job in the world" while being saddled with incompetent civil service people who had been unable to find work in business during the prewar years.[81] Speaking at a Senate Appropriations Committee hearing in June 1943, Chester LaRoche presented the Advertising Council as a practical, nonpolitical, and well-designed organization that was fully up to the task of informing the public about Washington's directives. He claimed to speak "not from any theoretical ivory tower, but out of a year and a half of practical experience" and on behalf of professional people who had devoted their lives to the study of public opinion and public persuasion and to promoting the usefulness of "a young business now coming out of its sloganeering stage to a new sense of its social obligation and its power to help the people play their full part in total war."[82]

In spite of a spirited defense from the Advertising Council and members of the OWI, the allocations for "domestic propaganda" were dramatically reduced, forcing the Domestic Branch to cut its personnel from 1,285 to 491.[83] As a small concession to the council, the OWI folded the Bureau of Campaigns into the Office of Program Coordination, an agency with a much heavier reliance on help from the advertising community. And unlike other divisions, which saw their staff and appropriations cut, the newly created office was allowed to add personnel, effectively boosting the presence of advertising in the OWI. Realizing the potential benefits of the new situation, advertisers now became great defenders of the Domestic Branch.[84] "The most striking difference between the new Domestic OWI and the old is that there is now an understanding of what we might almost call the Science of Information," commented LaRoche. "The new Domestic OWI uses modern opinion polling techniques, modern research methods. It makes use of radio, motion pictures, advertising, and news releases, on a timed and coordinated basis. . . . The Ivory Tower Days are long since over. . . . Experienced, practical men have replaced well-meaning theorists. Newly formed industry committees of newspaper and radio executives contribute practical suggestions."[85] The feeling was mutual. Palmer Hoyt, the editor and publisher of the *Oregonian*, who had replaced Cowles as director of the Domestic Branch, expressed his appreciation for the advertising industry's support in the reorganization.[86]

In response to the changes, the Advertising Council renamed itself the War Advertising Council (WAC), adopting "A War Message in Every Ad" as its goal and slogan. This, according to LaRoche, more accurately described the organization's work and its goals. He urged individual advertisers to double their 1942 contributions to the council, asking for a total of $500 million in donations before the end of 1943. During its first eighteen months of existence, the Ad Council had been active in a long series of home-front campaigns and had donated several hundred million dollars' worth of space, time, and talent.[87] Now it wanted advertising to play an even more significant role in the government's information work.[88] It alerted the advertising community to the pressing need for organized war-theme advertising and asked advertisers to devote a third of their copy to promotions with war themes based on WAC directives.[89] "These official campaigns," said LaRoche, "are all things that virtually anybody would agree need doing. They have nothing to do with politics. They have a lot to do with winning the war." War advertising was not simply advertising that showed pictures of tanks and planes, marines and soldiers, or that told about a company's contribution to the war effort. It was "advertising which induces people, through information, understanding or persuasion, to take certain actions necessary to speedy winning of the war."[90]

Elmer Davis came out in full support. "Whole-hearted cooperation by advertisers will help us enormously on the home front," he said, explaining that war-theme advertising should serve three major functions: it should tell the people how they could help win the war, it should inspire people to take the desired action, and it should make them want to do so immediately.[91] In July 1943, Davis and several other government officials, including Donald Nelson, James F. Byrnes (now a Supreme Court justice), and Marvin Jones, joined

LaRoche in a seventy-five-minute-long closed-circuit broadcast to an estimated thirty thousand business leaders over NBC to discuss "the important part which advertising can play in furthering the cooperation of the whole people."[92] The WAC described the broadcast as "a history-making 'conference of the air.'" "For the first time," reflected the council, "the wartime advertising policy of the government was clearly defined," and business was willing to take on the job of informing the American people about what they must do and not do to speed victory. Speeches from the broadcast were collected in a booklet for distribution to advertisers, agencies, media, and trade groups.[93]

The council followed up with a series of letters to every national advertiser with an annual budget exceeding $100,000, asking for their support in placing "A War Message in Every Ad." The mailings included copy and layout suggestions and a brochure on "How Industry Can Tie-in with the Official Information Program."[94] LaRoche stressed the WAC's uniqueness and its "entirely unselfish purpose." Successful war advertising, he said, followed agreed-upon themes, and the best results were achieved when all advertising on a given subject adopted the same approach, told more or less the same story, and made more or less the same appeals.[95] Hoyt quickly developed a more efficient working relationship with the WAC, instituting changes that greatly improved coordination between Washington and Madison Avenue.[96]

Dealing with Washington

In spite of these developments, the advertising industry was constantly on the alert, never convinced that things were on solid footing. Thus there was great concern when Senator Harry Truman, then chairman of the Senate Committee to Investigate the War Program, pointed out that the "large contribution" that advertisers were making to the war effort was actually being partially underwritten by American taxpayers.[97] Truman did not question the Treasury's decision to give tax deductions to advertisers who donated part of their advertising space to government campaigns. Neither did he object to letting manufacturers whose production had been altered by the war enjoy the same privilege. His concern centered on a third group of advertisers: those who profited from production changes brought on by the war. Much like Colston Warne, the industry's old arch-enemy, Truman questioned the fairness of giving manufacturers with only a limited postwar market to protect the same right to deduct the cost of huge advertising campaigns for the purpose of creating goodwill and future market positions. He was concerned that much of the government-sponsored advertising was used to create false impressions or to counteract criticism that had "legitimately been directed at the corporation." Standard Oil, for example, had spent "a lot of taxpayer money" to distract the public's attention from its role in helping the German Nazi regime develop synthetic rubber in the prewar period. The senator was equally upset with the Curtiss-Wright Corporation, a manufacturer of airplanes and aircraft parts, which after General Motors was the largest recipient of war defense contracts. Not only had the company failed to deliver the highest-quality planes and dive bombers, but it had spent huge amounts of money on tax-deductible advertising to convince the American people that its manufactured products for the government were of superlative quality.[98]

Although nothing ever came of Truman's proposal, the advertising trade press sounded its usual call to arms, with *Business Week* worrying that it had misinterpreted the general attitude in Washington.[99] In a sense this was a predictable reaction, because there were times when government sources believed that advertising interests were getting ahead of themselves. Washington's means of conveying these sentiments were often quite subtle. For example, President Roosevelt had traditionally endorsed a statement prepared by the Advertising Federation of America to be read at its annual convention. In 1943, at the same time that the OWI was being widely attacked from the right, Roosevelt declined to sign the federation's self-congratulatory letter praising "good advertising" as the most important factor in the national recovery effort and urging advertisers to maintain their "constructive efforts to bring the volume of sales of American products up to needed levels" and to "continue those efforts which make advertising a vital force in trade and commerce."[100] In its stead, he (or his aides) provided the AFA with a sober reminder of the task ahead:

> The people of the United States have only one thing to sell; only one product to merchandise. That is victory at the earliest possible date. Splendid support has been given to many campaigns in the war effort, for which your organization is to be congratulated. We can, however, in this day and time always do more than we are already doing. Let me urge your members to renew and increase their contribution—since we, as a nation, will be rewarded in proportion to the unselfish devotion we give to our common causes.[101]

The WAC was not easily discouraged, however, and it continued working tirelessly to increase the advertising industry's significance to the war effort and to win the government's approval. In late 1943, when the OWI had an urgent need for "about six able men" to work on "special and important assignments" as program managers on specific campaigns, the council was adamant that these men be drafted from the advertising community. Industry leaders were not immediately excited about lending financial support, but the general manager of the council, Theodore S. Repplier, kept pressing. "I know there is a disposition on the part of some people in the agency business to feel that these jobs represent a boondoggle of some kind," he wrote to the AAAA's Frederic R. Gamble, also a WAC member. "I am sure you realize that this is not true, and that the work is about the most useful thing an advertising man can do in this war to serve."[102] Exactly who was serving whom was not completely clear, since the WAC increasingly viewed the OWI as supporting the council rather than the other way around. "Regardless of the strength or weaknesses of the OWI," argued the WAC, "it performs a coordinating and planning function that we simply could not get along without unless we doubled or quadrupled our present budgets."[103] The admiration was mutual—so much so, in fact, that the OWI's assistant director, Robert Ferry, suggested that the Domestic Branch be split into two sections, a news division and a war program branch, staffed entirely by admen. The proposal received serious consideration, but for reasons unknown, it never materialized.[104]

The relationship between the WAC and the OWI, and more broadly between the advertising industry and the government, was growing ever closer as the war entered its third year. "I have just finished reading the War Advertising Council's second annual report, and I am struck once again with the tremendously important war job your organization has been doing," wrote Elmer Davis in a letter to the WAC, describing the council as one of the government's "most powerful focal points for directing vital information on home front problems to the American people."[105] The chummier relationship was made clear in March 1944, when a conciliatory President Roosevelt invited a group of executives from the advertising community to what would later become an annual meeting between high-ranking government officials and advertising representatives. During what the White House characterized as "'off-the-record' indoctrination talks," officials from the War Department, the Navy Department, and other executive departments and agencies were on hand to meet and chat with delegates.[106] The conference was sponsored by the army, the navy, the War Production Board (WPB), the OWI, and the WAC. One hundred advertisers, fifty ad agency representatives, and twenty-five members of the mass media were asked to attend, as was the entire WAC board, who were invited to dine at the head table with key people from various government agencies. The chief speakers at the dinner were Donald Nelson, General H. H. "Hap" Arnold of the U.S. Army Air Forces, and council chairman Harold B. Thomas.[107]

"The basic reason for this meeting," claimed the organizers, "is to restate the need for continued support of [the WAC's programs] until the war is not thought to be, but *is* won. We hope to show that now, and until victory, there is even greater need for a united public doing those things which will speed victory right down to the last Jap."[108] The attendees spent their morning sessions at the Pentagon, where the program had been turned over to the army and navy. The afternoon was devoted to a frank question-and-answer session with the chairman and vice-chairman of the WPB. One of the highlights was the opportunity to meet an enthused President Roosevelt, who had sent a glowing letter praising advertisers' war contribution and asking that it be continued.[109] Industry leaders responded with enthusiasm to these developments. "That meeting," concluded the ANA's Paul B. West, "will go a long way toward enabling us to continue to deliver this tremendous voluntary effort by business on the information front for the various government programs until the war job is successfully concluded."[110] West was even more effusive in writing a letter of thanks on behalf of the WAC. "Everyone liked the meeting with the W.P.B. immensely," he wrote to George Healy, the new head of the OWI's Domestic Branch. "The meeting with the president was, of course, the high spot of the day and I was really amazed at the genuinely favorable attitude on the part of everybody with the president and what he had to say."[111]

The meeting also provided industry representatives with an opportunity to talk with members of the Senate Committee to Investigate the War Program. Speaking on behalf of the council, Harold B. Thomas characterized the discussions as "highly satisfactory." For their part, the committee members were pleased that the advertising industry was making a serious effort to improve itself; they also expressed trust in the council's ability to "continue to develop the usefulness of advertising in the war effort."[112]

Conclusion

By mid-1943, the War Advertising Council was well on its way toward attaining the advertising industry's goal of improved public relations. The battle over paid government advertising had been solved to its satisfaction, and thanks to Washington's faith in the WAC's abilities, the industry now enjoyed an even better and closer relationship with the government and was entrusted with a large share of its promotional needs. This amounted to a vote of confidence from the government—and one that the industry knew to cherish. This did not mean, however, that advertisers could rest on their laurels.[113] In order for the council to function smoothly and provide the best possible public relations for itself, public and official reactions to its projects had to be closely monitored. That would prove to be a tough battle, requiring a great deal of perseverance and an organized approach by the War Advertising Council.

6

The Increasing Role of the
War Advertising Council

By the end of 1943, the advertising industry had established itself as an indispensable component of the government's domestic wartime information operations.[1] The quarrel over the Office of War Information had resulted in increased government reliance on the War Advertising Council, putting advertisers in a position to make dramatic public relations gains. In contrast to the atmosphere of mistrust and widespread criticism that had existed only a few years earlier, the industry was enjoying greater credibility and legitimacy in the eyes of the public, the government, and the business community as a whole.

This, however, put increasing pressure on the WAC to successfully complete its mandate. To botch this assignment could undermine all of its hard work to date and leave the advertising industry exposed to a new round of attacks in the postwar period. As it turned out, the council's greatest obstacle in fulfilling its mission during these final months came from major advertisers themselves. Industry leaders, who understood the immediate and long-term importance of the WAC's goal, had to go to great lengths to convince individual advertisers to sacrifice money, resources, and creative independence to make the many campaigns successful. There was considerable short-term incentive for individual advertisers to downplay wartime themes vis-à-vis commercial sales messages, or to use the war in self-serving ways that might generate more public opprobrium than approval. In short, this was a classic conflict between the trade associations' long-term perspective for the well-being of the entire industry and the short-term self-interests of individual firms. The first part of this chapter thus recounts the council's activities during the last part of the war, particularly its ongoing efforts to coax individual advertisers into cooperating.

Most of the government's requests were for help with noncontroversial campaigns, which meant there was little chance that participating advertisers might arouse public anger or resentment. An exception was the highly controversial anti–venereal disease campaign that the WAC signed on to in 1943. The second part of this chapter explores that campaign, which came to pit the council's wartime promises to the government against individual advertisers' commercial concerns.

"A War Message in Every Ad"

The task of getting individual advertisers on board and cooperating had been a struggle throughout the war, and an ongoing coordination problem between the OWI and the War Advertising Council only exacerbated the problem. As late as one year into the war, many campaigns prepared at the government's request were not attracting advertiser support and thus were failing to reach the public. The problem, someone pointed out, was that neither the WAC nor the OWI was responsible for seeing that a particular campaign was actually set in motion. The council considered its part done as soon as it had worked out campaign plans and provided copy suggestions and examples of ads that advertisers could incorporate into their own product promotions. Federal officials did not feel comfortable lobbying advertisers to adopt the various campaigns. As a result, plans equivalent to several million dollars' worth of good ideas were "rotting on shelves in agencies, in government bureaus, and in many other places."[2]

Recognizing the need for procedural changes, the council acknowledged that its job was not complete until the campaigns appeared in the pages of mass-circulation newspapers and magazines. An equally concerned OWI directed the heads of government agencies to more aggressively help the WAC obtain sponsor endorsements.[3] In the early part of 1943, Miller McClintock left the council to become the president of the Mutual Broadcasting System, while Chester LaRoche took a leave of absence from Young and Rubicam to become the council's chairman and full-time operating head.[4] Writing to Gardner Cowles a few weeks before he assumed his new position, LaRoche stressed the importance of a good working relationship: "Our channels of communication to the American people are the most efficient in the world. Not to fully understand them, their capabilities, is dangerous; not to use them to the fullest is to hamper the war effort, the equivalent of a military error. . . . If this plan doesn't work, then we should go to Government-paid advertising, and fast."[5]

Eager to create momentum, the WAC organized the Committee to Co-ordinate War Advertising, a task force made up of media representatives, agency people, and advertisers with a mandate to develop better campaign instructions for potential sponsors and to assist Washington in its dealings with advertisers.[6] The push for improved efficiency on the local level was reflected in a "Community War Plan" that outlined the council's expectations of local advertisers and advertising groups. The AFA and the Pacific Advertising Association were responsible for its implementation.[7] Supportive of these measures, the OWI stressed emphatically that the advertising industry was unique in its ability to "put these government programs before the public in simple, exact terms *often enough* and with *enough power* and with *enough control* to get results," and it pleaded for the donation of an even larger share of advertisers' promotional budgets to the war effort.[8]

The summer of 1943 found the War Advertising Council in charge of more than thirty projects. Its annual budget had increased to $125,000, and its promotional efforts included campaigns on a variety of issues, including war bonds, food and nutrition, wartime housing, and transportation.[9] A survey of 1,250 advertisers found that slightly more than half of them lent promotional support to the war savings bonds campaign and that a quarter supported the second most popular campaign, on nutrition. Two separate rationing campaigns, a campaign to promote tire and car conservation, the manpower-womanpower campaign, and the campaign to promote victory gardens were all supported by approximately 8 percent, while campaigns stressing economic stability, household appliance conservation, farm goals, crop corps, absenteeism, black markets, and scrap and fat salvage were less popular. Only eleven advertisers, or less than one-half of 1 percent, supported the campaign to prevent forest fires.[10] The high level of compliance, however, did not mean that each of the advertisers produced the kind of copy that the government and the WAC believed to be most beneficial to the war effort. Thus the council was left with the not-so-simple task of pressuring advertisers into fulfilling their responsibility in the information campaigns and making sure that there was "A War Message in Every Ad."[11] Another survey of slightly less than three hundred advertisers in the fall of 1943 revealed brand-name preservation as the strongest motivating factor behind their advertising efforts. Goals such as "improving and maintaining dealer relationships," "helping to sell War Bonds," "improving public relations," and "sale of products for the present market" were mentioned, but less prominently so.[12]

One problem, as far as the council was concerned, was that many of the government's campaigns did not easily lend themselves to commercial tie-ins. While food and car manufacturers, for example, could integrate nutrition and scrap metal salvage campaigns into their commercial copy with relative ease, other manufacturers were discouraged to find campaign themes such a poor fit for their products that they gave up and continued their peacetime advertising practices.[13] In fact, one study showed that 50 percent of all advertisers avoided any mention of the war, sticking instead to traditional product selling.[14] Another problem, in spite of the council's constant urging, was that many advertisers continued to prefer their self-designed war-theme advertising to ads developed according to the WAC's directives. This was highlighted during the third war bond drive, in September 1943, when only an estimated one-third of the 89,000 advertisements printed in daily newspapers were prepared in accordance with the council's guidelines.[15] For example, 7-Up's "Get the 'Fresh up' Smile," with its call for Americans to become "fighter backers," demonstrates advertisers' inclination to make up their own slogan independent from the War Advertising Council's directives (see fig. 14 on page 132).

Hoping to drum up more support, the council arranged an exhibit at the Brooklyn Museum in New York to highlight effective advertisements. Almost two hundred ads by some sixty firms were on display, showing how WAC campaigns on "conservation," "economic stabilization," and "absenteeism" could be successfully created for use in newspapers, magazines, outdoor displays, and direct mail.[16] Council member and ANA chairman Charles G. Mortimer reminded advertisers that it was in their self-interest to support the council because "conformity with normal practice of developing campaigns is preferable to having some Washington Executive make demands on the head of the company."[17]

When the ANA released its fourth public opinion poll on wartime advertising in late 1943, it revealed that a whopping 76 percent of the public desired advertising that combined product information with instructions about the civilian war effort.[18] Encouraged by the findings, the WAC continued to stress the importance of advertisers adhering to its official campaigns, calling it "an unparalleled opportunity for sound business public relations."[19] That said, the council made it clear that a contribution of one-third of all advertising to the war effort was an overall industry goal, not a demand that each individual advertiser dedicate that exact percentage to war themes. It was expected that some would do more than a third to compensate for those that did less.[20]

The level of support among advertisers continued to be a problem, however, and now, with the war nearing the second-year mark, sponsors were

Figure 8: "What to do about those war-weary typewriters." This Smith-Corona ad delivered on customers' desire for information that could make their products last longer and thus help the home front effort. *Life*, November 22, 1943, 105.

growing tired of war and impatient with the council's endless pleas for support. "We have made more than a beginning," observed council member Frederic R. Gamble, the managing director of the AAAA. "But there is more to be done in the future. The novelty is beginning to wear off and the early enthusiasm with it. We are settling down to the slogging part of the job."[21] Asserting that overconfidence was America's biggest enemy, a nondefiant council issued a pamphlet asking for advertisers' continuous support. Written by ad agency owner Leo Burnett, *They Are Taking Away the Sandbags* included a ringing appeal to the industry to "get back some of that white heat" from right after Pearl Harbor and to take stock of itself in relation to the war situation: "We advertising people who pride ourselves on being 'molders of public opinion' can measure our postwar prestige, not by anything we have done in the past, but by our efforts from here on out."[22] Sharing the frustration, OWI head Elmer Davis pleaded with advertisers to work harder to encourage the American people to intensify their war efforts. This meant "more war messages and harder hitting messages carried to more people in more advertising, by more media" and a dependence on the WAC to keep advertisers in line and focused on the task.[23]

Sensing the urgency, the Office of Censorship delivered some much-needed help. During the dark early years of the conflict, when the Allied Powers were experiencing defeat on many fronts, it was the agency's policy to censor photographs that portrayed the war effort in a grim light. The fear was that overly realistic depictions would lessen support for the war and discourage potential soldiers from enlisting. (For example, it was forbidden to publish photos of dead GIs, even though everyone understood that war involved fighting and dying.) When the secretary of the American Jewish Congress asked for help in early 1943 in exposing Nazi atrocities, Domestic Branch director Gardner Cowles Jr. and council chairman Chester LaRoche declined the request. The Office of Censorship changed its image-release policy in 1943 as the Allies turned the tide and began to win battles. To fight "war weariness" among the public (including advertisers), it allowed the release of photographs showing blood and carnage, sweat and suffering. In effect, civilians were being asked to compare their own sacrifices on the home front to the sacrifices of the soldiers who were fighting on the front lines.[24]

Whereas early war advertisements had shown little in the way of blood and suffering except in broad, generic terms (such as clouds of smoke and fire or fleets of aircraft overhead), many advertisers now followed the OWI's request for increasingly grim depictions.[25] The council's second war bond drive, in May 1943, initially failed to produce the desired response from the

American public, but when some advertisers began to depict Japanese soldiers executing American fliers in order to stir people to action, the reaction was swift and impressive. "The money was rolling in from banks and institutions," reflected *Advertising and Selling*. "The people—whom the government wants for customers because this is a people's war—were not coming through at all well until the Jap story broke."[26]

Both the OWI and the War Advertising Council revised their campaign instructions in hopes of making it easier to attract individual advertisers. Recognizing that its "Program Books" had lost some of their appeal for advertisers, the OWI launched an "Advanced Bulletin" to alert sponsors to upcoming campaigns, followed by a "Fact Sheet" on each project. A "Program Book" with more detailed campaign information was made available to any advertiser who requested it. The WAC matched the effort by redesigning its "Campaign Folders." Far more appealing to the eye, the new version contained new council procedures, which offered more wiggle room for advertisers. Folders provided a few sample ads, but sponsors were not required to copy them directly. The council's main request was that advertisers compare their final ad copy against a checklist it provided.[27] A brief reference guide called the *War Theme Digest* followed a few months later. It provided quick access to campaign data, suggested copy slants and slogans, and contained information about the various campaign schedules.[28]

Also as part of the renewed effort, the WAC established a Sponsorship Committee under the leadership of John Sterling of *This Week* magazine in hopes of bringing in more local advertisers. Its task was to form several divisional War Advertising Council groups and to work closely with advertisers on the local level, a responsibility of utmost importance to the council. By the end of 1944, WAC sponsorship committees could be found almost everywhere in the United States.[29]

Wartime advertising that adhered to the council's directive was classified into five groups. "All Out" advertisements devoted their entire space to promoting the government's campaigns and were, according to the WAC, "the purest form of selfishness—and the best public relations." These ads did not just "claim virtue"—they demonstrated it.[30] A "Double Barreled Job" was an advertisement that devoted most of its copy to war themes while selling the sponsor's merchandise on the side. Advertisers got in a "Sneak Punch" by skillfully incorporating war themes into their product advertisements. "Plug in a Slug" ads, on the other hand, mentioned war themes only in passing, limiting their campaign messages to a drop-in box in a corner or at the bottom. The last, and largest, category was made up of advertisers who engaged

Figure 9. "Slugs and Boxes." Ca. 1943. Small drop-in ads such as this one were prepared by the War Advertising Council for inclusion in commercial advertisements. For examples of their application, see figs. 7 and 13 on pp. 111 and 131.

Figure 10. "Please help bring my Daddy home." "All Out" ads such as this example from the Electric Auto-Lite Company devoted the majority of their content to promoting a war theme. *Saturday Evening Post*, February 2, 1944, 4.

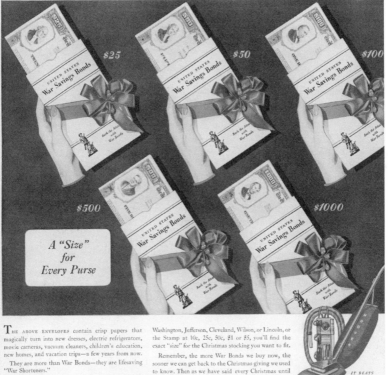

Give her a War Bond

and you give her the best . . .

$25 $50 $100

$500 $1000

A "Size"
for
Every Purse

THE ABOVE ENVELOPES contain crisp papers that magically turn into new dresses, electric refrigerators, movie cameras, vacuum cleaners, children's education, new homes, and vacation trips—a few years from now.

They are more than War Bonds—they are lifesaving "War Shorteners."

The money you pay for these crisp papers goes directly into tanks, planes, submarines and ammunition for fighters to fight with, clothes for them to wear, food for them to eat.

They are marked, respectively, $25, $50, $100, $500, and $1,000. You pay for them, only $18.75, $37.50, $75, $375, and $750 respectively. You earn the difference between each pair of figures.

Whether you choose the Bond with the picture of Washington, Jefferson, Cleveland, Wilson, or Lincoln, or the Stamp at 10c, 25c, 50c, $1 or $5, you'll find the exact "size" for the Christmas stocking you want to fit.

Remember, the more War Bonds we buy now, the sooner we can get back to the Christmas giving we used to know. Then as we have said every Christmas until Pearl Harbor, the makers of The Hoover Cleaner again will say . . .

IT BEATS
AS IT SWEEPS
AS IT CLEANS

"Give her a HOOVER and you give her the best

 ## The HOOVER

THE HOOVER COMPANY, NORTH CANTON, OHIO

Figure 11. "Give her a War Bond and you give her the best." "Double Barreled" ads such as this example from Hoover communicated two different messages, one devoted to a war theme and the other to promoting a product. *Life*, December 6, 1943, 10.

Figure 12. "SALADS help build strong Americans!" This ad for Kraft Miracle Whip exemplifies what the War Advertising Council referred to as a "Sneak Punch," integrating a war theme into regular product advertising. *Saturday Evening Post*, June 13, 1942, 89.

OLDSMOBILE WORKERS HAVE BEEN DOING IT FOR NEARLY TWO YEARS... BACKING UP OUR FIGHTING MEN WITH VOLUME PRODUCTION OF FIRE-POWER

AMERICA is "passing the ammunition" today to almost every corner of the globe. From the skilled hands of her millions of workmen ... to the eager hands of her millions of fighting men ... the planes and ships and tanks and cannon and shell are passing in a never-ending stream.

From Oldsmobile, for example, come automatic cannon for fighter planes—long-range cannon for tanks—shot and shell for tanks and the artillery. Oldsmobile is carrying out these vast assignments in close co-operation with more than 130 sub-contractors, working with them as an All-American "Keep 'Em Firing" team. They're part of the free industry of a free country, and they're working to keep it that way. "Let's pass the ammu-nition," American industry is saying, "and we'll all stay free!"

You Can Help "Pass the Ammunition" —Buy U. S. War Bonds and Stamps

KEEP 'EM FIRING!

OLDSMOBILE DIVISION OF GENERAL MOTORS
★ VOLUME PRODUCER OF "FIRE-POWER" FOR THE U. S. A. ★

Figure 13. "Pass the Ammunition!" This Oldsmobile ad is an example of what the War Advertising Council referred to as a "Plug in a Slug," with no mention of a war theme in the text but including a slug. (For examples of slugs, see fig. 9 on p. 128.) *Saturday Evening Post*, January 16, 1943, 33.

Figure 14. "Get the 'Fresh up' Smile!" This advertisement for 7-Up was an unofficial "Plug in a Slug." "Be a 'Fighter-Backer': Work for Victory" was a self-composed slogan. *Saturday Evening Post*, February 5, 1944, 83.

He carries his life in a tiny package

This tiny package is a vital item in the equipment of every American soldier on the fighting front. It contains the famous sulfa drug. Thanks to the discovery of this powerful new guard against infection, thousands upon thousands of lives are being saved on the battlefield.

Du Pont Cellophane helps protect the precious contents of this package. Where could a few square inches of Cellophane render greater service than in safeguarding the medicine that may save a soldier's life?

Other wartime jobs of Du Pont Cellophane are important, too. It protects food rations and medical supplies for our Army and Navy—and even has uses that are military secrets.

The rigorous demands of war provide a striking demonstration of the remarkable protective qualities of this familiar packaging material—and show how well it serves you in preserving the freshness, goodness and cleanliness of many essential products you buy for your family.

Wartime uses of Cellophane prove its protective value for the things you buy

▶ Below (shown actual size) is the sulfa drug package found in every soldier's first-aid kit. Note the Cellophane wrap used by the Office of the Surgeon General. Use of Du Pont Cellophane on this and many other medical and food supplies of the armed forces is evidence of its outstanding protective value on products at home.

Figure 15. "He carries his life in a tiny package." "Business as Usual" ads such as this one for Du Pont Cellophane made no direct mention of war themes but tried to forge a positive association between a product and the war effort. *Saturday Evening Post*, February 27, 1942, 101.

Have a Coca-Cola = Merry Christmas

...or how Americans spread the holiday spirit overseas

Your American fighting man loves his lighter moments. Quick to smile, quick to enter the fun, he takes his home ways with him where he goes . . . makes friends easily. *Have a "Coke"*, he says to stranger or friend, and he spreads the spirit of good will throughout the year. And throughout the world Coca-Cola stands for *the pause that refreshes,* — has become the high-sign of the friendly-hearted.

* * *

Our fighting men are delighted to meet up with Coca-Cola many places overseas. Coca-Cola has been a globe-trotter "since way back when". Even with war, Coca-Cola today is being bottled right on the spot in over 35 allied and neutral nations.

It's natural for popular names to acquire friendly abbreviations. That's why you hear Coca-Cola called "Coke".

COPYRIGHT 1943, THE COCA-COLA COMPANY

Figure 16. "Have a Coca-Cola = Merry Christmas." This holiday ad is another example of "Business as Usual." *Life*, December 20, 1943, 45.

Figure 17. "The Ammunition is being passed." This Budweiser ad is another example of "Business as Usual." *Life*, December 27, 1943, 119.

in "Business as Usual," meaning that they ignored the council's exhortations altogether.[31] A magazine survey conducted in the spring of 1944 revealed that only 2 percent of advertisers used the "All Out" approach, while 6 percent lent support through "Double Barreled" ads. Four percent took advantage of "Sneak Punches," while 20 percent had used a "Plug in a Slug." This left a full 68 percent of the advertisers to do "Business as Usual."

Advertising and Selling alerted advertisers not to put too much stock in the fact that only one ad out of fifty went "All Out," claiming that "Double Barreled" ads were often just as effective. The trade publication was much less charitable when it came to ads with a "Plug in a Slug," which it characterized as "nearly worthless." Thus, while it appeared that a third of the ads had "gone to war," actually only one out of eight had done so: "the All Outs, Double Barrels, and Sneak Punchers." Despite criticism, the trade journal defended the large number of advertisers who did not appear to be concerned about using war themes in their print ads, claiming that some of them made stronger war-theme contributions in other media.[32]

Believing that its members were sometimes unfairly tainted by accusations of "objectionable" wartime advertising, or what council member James Webb Young referred to as "a stench in many influential quarters," the AAAA asked the National Association of Better Business Bureaus for help in determining the extent of the problem.[33] That organization, in turn, commissioned a group called the War Advertising Survey Committee to closely read ads that had appeared in a select group of magazines and newspapers during the months of October and November 1943 and evaluate their use of war themes. Ads that used WAC suggestions or material were excluded from the review. Two basic questions guided the inquiry: Did the copy express its war-related theme in a way that was constructive and of interest to the public? And what advertisements might be judged "offensive to the reader"? The committee was particularly concerned with advertisements that exaggerated or exploited the war effort and ads that misrepresented the company's role, used scare tactics, or resorted to "over-emotionalism."[34] After examining 4,296 ads with these criteria in mind, committee members concluded that many of the ads had "failed to take advantage of an important opportunity to make a greater contribution to the war effort and to reflect credit on advertising."[35] While this observation was clearly food for thought, the AAAA sought some solace in the fact that only eighty ads, or less than 2 percent, were deemed objectionable.[36] AAAA president Gamble was elated by the finding, claiming that correcting the relatively few flaws would be an easy task.[37]

"I think advertising fared extremely well at the hands of this group," said Thomas D'Arcy Brophy, president of the Kenyon and Eckhardt advertising agency, "and my hat is off to whoever had the idea of having such a committee review our wartime work."[38] His enthusiasm was tempered, however, when an advertisement produced by his own agency fell victim to the committee's criticism.[39] The ad, prepared for Hudnut, a manufacturer of beauty products, took an unauthorized—and in the War Advertising Survey Committee's opinion rather weak—stab at an independent version of the WAC's womanpower campaign.[40] "To help you save time . . . even in a small way," it promised, "Richard Hudnut has prepared a series of beauty shortcuts from the DuBarry Success School so that you can work for victory and stay as lovely as you are now." Brophy became greatly upset when the committee found this ad to be "so far-fetched as to be an offensive use of the war theme."[41] In addition to being a prominent advertising executive, Brophy was a highly regarded member of the WAC's board of directors. Thus it was paramount for his agency to provide shining examples of good war-theme advertising. Hoping to avoid a potentially embarrassing situation, Brophy explained that the Hudnut ad was designed to use advertising to combat women's resistance to war work. Many women, he claimed, hesitated to take on war work out of fear that it would ruin their appearance. This particular advertisement was merely an attempt to address those concerns. He warned the AAAA against being too critical and asked that the recurring problem of obtaining adequate sponsorship for the WAC's campaigns be kept in mind. "It is a nice theory that advertisers will devote their own paid space to the exclusive promotion of a government-sponsored project," said Brophy, "but it doesn't work out this way. Some advertisers have done it, but even the most important ones are inclined to cooperate on a token, rather than a continuing basis."[42] Considering the source, this did not bode well for a strong commitment to the council's efforts.

Public opinion surveys continued to keep advertisers on their toes. A Gallup poll conducted in February 1944, for example, found that a quarter of the nation's households—nearly nine million—were uninformed about the paper salvage campaign, and that only 53 percent of the respondents salvaged paper on a regular basis.[43] Yet another survey, this one sponsored by the AAAA and the ANA in November 1944, revealed that 47 percent of the respondents had serious complaints about specific types of ads and advertising practices.[44] *Advertising and Selling* blamed a few misbehaving companies while urging the entire advertising industry to "reach for that broom" and "give its vastly improved house the cleaning it so obviously needed."[45] The WAC alerted advertisers to the difference between purely commercial campaigns and those that carried war messages. The former could be considered successful even if they affected only a small percentage of people. War campaigns, on the other hand, needed to influence "ALL the people . . . get them to ACT . . . and to keep on ACTING in ways that will help win the war. If a commercial advertising campaign sells only a small segment of the public, a very satisfactory sales result will be obtained. But a war campaign must reach and convince as nearly as 100% of the people as possible." If even a quarter of the people engaged in practices that triggered inflation or passed on military information, then the success of the whole program was threatened.[46]

One year later, the AAAA's Committee for the Board on Wartime Advertising prepared a list of "sins" that advertising agencies should avoid when they prepared copy for their clients.[47] These included advertising that bragged and seemed to suggest that the contributions of an individual industry were winning the war; the use of war themes and battle scenes as a lead-in to advertisements that promoted commercial products of a trivial character; advertisements that exaggerated the contribution of a product to winning the war; appeals that exploited war emotions for commercial purposes; the use of extravagant or wasteful ads to promote products that were unavailable to the general public due to war; and references to postwar products that might seem to suggest that the war was soon to end, thus diverting public attention from the task at hand. "None of us," stated the association, "wants criticism of current advertising, even though some of it may be misdirected, to reach a point where the Treasury may have to revise its present practice of allowing advertising as a deductible expense from taxable income."[48] But as Robinson Murray of the AAAA had put it a year earlier, it was the millions of dollars in volunteer advertising contributions that kept the American people well-informed about the home-front campaigns. And in spite of the occasional lack of good taste, a tendency toward exaggeration, and a bit of "selfishness here and there," the results could not be matched "short of a completely owned and operated government propaganda system along the lines of that of Goebbels in Germany."[49]

Conflicting Impulses: The VD Controversy

Most of the council's many campaigns were noncontroversial and well received. After all, what patriotic American could disagree with the WAC's pleas for conservation, salvage, or the purchase of war bonds? Nor could many object to the council's numerous manpower and recruiting campaigns, or its pleas for victory gardens and good nutrition.[50] But there was always the possibility that what the government regarded as a socially necessary campaign subject could have negative repercussions for the industry. In the summer of 1944, the WAC encountered just such a crisis, requiring the council to be politically and bureaucratically adept.

Venereal disease and its prevention had been a topic of discussion since the late nineteenth century, and the subject had picked up considerable momentum during the Progressive era, when reform-minded individuals pushed for a renewed educational effort. Not surprisingly, this met with considerable resistance from conservative and religious individuals who viewed information about prevention and treatment as an enticement for (young) people to engage in inappropriate sexual behavior. While publications that catered to a sympathetic audience felt at liberty to discuss the reformers' agenda, more mainstream publications did not. Many, no doubt, still freshly recalled that a series of articles on venereal disease in the *Ladies' Home Journal* in 1906 had caused its publisher to lose seventy-five thousand subscribers.[51] Thus, in a tradition that would prevail for decades to come, it seemed safer to keep people ignorant, and therefore infected with venereal disease, than to approach the issue head on and insult the socially conservative segment of the population. The onset of World War I only intensified the need for an informed approach. Almost 13 percent of new World War I recruits were diagnosed with venereal diseases at the time of their admission, a fact that, as Allan M. Brandt points out, reflected a general lack of public information and a huge civilian problem.[52] The War Department used a range of presentations, including lectures, pamphlets, posters, handbills, and even an instructional film called *Fit to Win*, to enlighten enlisted men about venereal infections and their cures.[53]

Despite the best efforts of the War Department, its educational approach failed to reach the population at large. In fact, as sexual mores relaxed in the decades after the war, venereal disease continued to be a big problem. But now, more than ever, withholding information about prevention and cure was viewed as a bulwark against sexual permisssiveness. An estimated one in every ten Americans was suffering from syphilis in the early 1930s, and an additional 700,000 contracted gonorrhea every year. Rates of infection were even higher among African Americans, the poor, and the young. Each year, 60,000 babies were born with congenital syphilis, and 9,000 deaths were tied to the disease in its advanced stage.[54] Clearly, the conservative approach of preaching sexual continence was not enough to stem the spread of disease.

Thus, soon after his appointment as surgeon general in 1936, Thomas Parran set out to bring national attention to the situation. Armed with a scientific, bureaucratic approach, he called for free diagnostic centers, treatment, and public education. Parting from the social hygienists, Parran downplayed the moral argument, emphasizing instead the need for cure and disease containment. Well received among Washington's New Dealers, his initiative helped pass a National Venereal Disease Control Act in 1938.[55]

The new law notwithstanding, there was a sharp increase in venereal infections throughout the country during World War II, posing a threat to the armed forces, civilian workers, and consequently the nation's entire war program. In 1943, an estimated 600,000 new cases of syphilis (a 21 percent increase over 1942) and 300,000 new cases of gonorrhea (a 28.3 percent increase over the previous year) were diagnosed. One year later, the total number of cases was approaching five million and still growing. Hoping to reverse the trend, a greatly concerned U.S. Department of Public Health Service contacted the OWI, which in turn approached the War Advertising Council to request "an unusually competent Task Force."[56] Due to the heavy controversy surrounding the issue, it was understood that the copy theme for the venereal disease program would be particularly challenging and that it would be necessary for all cooperating advertising agencies to work closely with the Public Health Service officials and be guided by their advice and expertise.[57] Many Americans continued to associate venereal infections with risky or promiscuous sexual behavior, and some viewed them as punishment for moral weakness and lack of adherence to religious instructions. It was also commonly believed that VD was primarily a problem of the poor and minorities and that it rarely affected the American middle and upper classes. A study conducted by the OWI in early 1944 revealed that whites in some areas, predominantly in the South, greatly overestimated the infection rate among African Americans, and that eminent officials and physicians shared this view. One high-ranking state official went so far as to predict that there would never be a cure for syphilis "because Negroes would always have it."[58]

Charles Levitt, the leading information specialist at the OWI, was right: the copy theme for the venereal disease program presented "an unusually complicated problem," prompting his office to offer specific recommendations about how the campaign might be handled. One of the those ideas was for copywriters to forge a semantic connection between VD and TB (tuberculosis), attempting to frame them both as "a disease, not a disgrace." "Syphilis and Gonorrhea must be brought out into the open" and should be "discussed frankly as serious diseases, rather than as the consequence of 'sin,'" the OWI instructed. Copy should stress prevention and the fact that only a licensed physician could accurately diagnose and cure venereal diseases. Thus, each advertisement should provide information about "where to go or whom to see for advice and treatment."[59]

In preparing the campaign, the WAC was asked to emphasize the huge social costs of VD, which included death, blindness, insanity, paralysis, and sterility, and to mention the resulting drain on the nation's workforce, including the military. Venereal diseases were highly infectious and affected predominantly young people, and these infections had to be brought under control. The council accepted the assignment in June of 1943 but then hesitated when questions arose about the wisdom of getting involved with the somewhat controversial project. Douglas Murphy, director of the Metropolitan Life Insurance Company, who had been appointed council coordinator for the council's VD campaign, and council member Paul B. West were both concerned. "We all know that this subject is one of the most highly controversial social, religious and political issues and on any one of these counts we cannot afford to put advertising in the middle of it, even granting that advertising could do a job which I seriously doubt," said West, reminding the industry to be careful because advertising was still in a vulnerable situation due to "the great lack of understanding on the part of virtually everybody outside of the advertising business." The council had been given a "golden opportunity" for creating an improved public understanding of advertising's "rightful place as a powerful influence in a Democracy," but much of this could be lost if its leaders failed to select their campaigns with the utmost care.[60] The council was in a tough spot. "I do think that this program is something that should be handled, or it will handle us," reflected council member Allyn B. McIntire. "In any event now that we've got a train started out of a station, let's see where it takes us."[61]

In order to continue its participation, the council made a series of demands, to which the U.S. Public Health Service agreed. A new and informal arrangement allowed the WAC to focus on the curable as opposed to preventive aspects of VD. That freed the council from addressing mores of sexual behavior and dealing with the controversial issue of prophylactics. Hoping to avoid hostility from those with "a professional interest in opposing contraceptives," the council preferred to talk about prevention in terms of abstinence from extramarital sexual relations on moral grounds and avoided "reference to mechanical or chemical prophylaxis," a controversial issue among Catholics in particular.[62] The OWI was relieved. "It is my feeling," wrote Levitt, "that much misunderstanding is now eliminated and that the Office of War Information and the War Advertising Council can now find a thoroughly clear, non-controversial path to assist U.S. Public Health Service conduct an informational and educational program directed at VD as a menace to the war effort."[63]

The council tasked the Warwick and Legert advertising agency with developing promotional material, and representatives from the agency soon found themselves in frequent meetings with the WAC and the OWI to discuss the best strategy for getting individual advertisers to adopt the campaign.[64] Because of the subject's controversial nature, it was recommended that Domestic Branch director Palmer Hoyt, or even Elmer Davis, should give the final clearance, although it is unclear whether these high officials became actively involved.[65] By December, Thomas Parran had given the promotional campaign his stamp of approval, and the OWI was ready to "move right ahead."[66] It mailed out a campaign guide titled *Hidden Enemy: V.D.*, which drew attention to the contagious nature of venereal diseases and the personal suffering associated with them and asked for advertisers' support in fighting them. Accompanying the slogan "Stamp Out VD" was an image of Uncle Sam's foot upraised over the letters "VD." The campaign advised advertisers to use a straightforward and emphatic approach when addressing the public, urging them to stress the preventable and curable nature of the diseases and asking for employers to show compassion when dealing with afflicted employees.

The accompanying campaign folders assisted copywriters in attaining the most effortless tie-ins, suggesting model ads and adaptations to all media and showing examples of VD campaign ads that had been run or were about to be released by advertisers in various fields. Background and contact information, including facts about campaign methods and organization, and a list of WAC and OWI personnel involved with the effort were also included. Additionally, the folders contained progress reports, campaign facts, bulletins with advice and news, and success stories from manufacturers whose war-information advertising had won them "higher readership ratings, improved in-plant morale, favorable comments from dealer organizations and others, letters of recognition and thanks from ranking government officials."[67] The council cautioned advertisers against "preaching" and warned them not to describe the diseases in an overly permissive or horrific manner. The OWI shared the same concern, stressing that although venereal disease did not respect "sex, race, creed or economic status," it carried a certain stigma because "delinquency, prostitution, promiscuity, ignorance, poverty and public indifference" contributed to

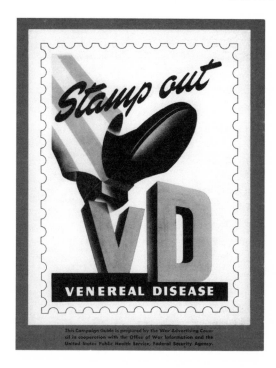

Figure 18. "Stamp Out VD." Ca. 1943. This was the official "slug" for the War Advertising Council's campaign to "Stamp Out Venereal Disease"—a goal that was never realized. Courtesy Ad Council Archives, University of Illinois Archives, RS 13/2/207.

its proliferation.[68] "How does your daughter pronounce syphilis, gonorrhea?" asked one council poster designed for endorsement by advertisers. "That's easy. She doesn't." Other posters let the consuming public know that "Science Says VD Can Be Cured" and that "Hiding VD Is Foolish." The council assumed that national advertisers would support this campaign, just as they had supported the war bond, manpower, and salvage drives. It did not anticipate a backlash from critics upset with what they saw as an unwillingness to discuss the moral aspects of venereal diseases.[69]

Immediately after *Hidden Enemy* had been distributed, it became apparent that many Catholic organizations found the campaign repugnant. The *Catholic News*, a New York–based newspaper, condemned it on the grounds that it condoned "the immorality on which most cases of venereal disease are based." The paper went so far as to call the WAC's effort "A Fraud on Patriotism" and criticized the government's participation. Members of the Catholic clergy and a number of other Catholic newspapers publicly attacked the campaign as well. They claimed (falsely, as the WAC would point out) that the Council's VD information was funded by the public and thus was a waste of public money.[70] The New York chapter of the Knights of Columbus

Figure 19. "How much does THIS bogey-man cost YOU?" The image in this advertising mat prepared by the War Advertising Council for the "Stamp Out Venereal Disease" campaign is startling on several levels—not least because an explicit goal of the campaign was to avoid stigmatization. Ca. 1943. Courtesy Ad Council Archives, University of Illinois Archives, RS 13/2/207.

Figure 20. "Was It a Pickup?" Ca. 1943. The cartoonish appearance of this ad prepared for the War Advertising Council's "Stamp Out Venereal Disease" campaign suggests that it was intended for a pulp magazine along the lines of *True Romance*. Courtesy Ad Council Archives, University of Illinois Archives, RS 13/2/207.

and the New York and New Jersey Catholic War Veterans voiced similar objections. The *Catholic Herald* characterized the VD campaign as "an affront to American decency and morality" and called for a boycott of manufacturers and distributors who promoted it. "There's a time for talk and a time for action—and the time for talk has passed," it warned.[71]

The WAC defended itself by claiming that it was acting only through the OWI's directives and that it had no direct responsibility for the campaign. It stated that it had presented the entire project to the U.S. Public Health Service (whose director, Surgeon General Parran, was himself a Catholic) for review and that representatives from the Catholic community, including a member of the clergy, had been consulted. Indeed, because of the program's controversial nature, the council had taken extra care in clearing it with religious and medical authorities.[72] But the critics were not appeased. "The young and inexperienced," fumed the New York State Council of the Knights of Columbus, "should receive information, but at the proper time and from the proper sources." A general advertising campaign was not the appropriate medium or a satisfactory substitute for private counsel from a parent, teacher, or spiritual adviser. It urged the WAC to "promote morality and clean living rather than the open and shameless discussion of the checking of diseases contracted through sinful practices" and characterized the council's effort as a "perversion of patriotism."[73] The campaign, complained the *Providence (R.I.) Visitor*, "ignores entirely the question of sin in connection with venereal disease" and "is likely . . . to cause an increase in the number of people affected."[74] Others concurred: "An honest campaign must be a moral education, not suggesting ways and means of avoiding infection while enjoying sin."[75] The national commander of the Catholic War Veterans, Edward T. McCaffrey, promised that local chapters of the organization would lodge strong protests and share their misgivings with members of the Senate and the House of Representatives, newspapers, magazines, radio stations, and large business concerns.[76]

This did not mean, however, that the Catholic Church would close the door on the War Advertising Council itself. On the contrary, argued the Reverend John F. O'Hara, the WAC could use its resources to advertise "self-respect, sanctity of the home, justice and health" to the American people. He explained that the council and the VD campaign had both been criticized, but for quite different reasons. The VD campaign was condemned on the grounds that it was immoral, unscientific, and dishonest, whereas the WAC was denounced for showing carelessness and neglect by getting involved. "In line with your code of 'Truth in Advertising,' you have a moral duty to analyze the ethical content of what you are asked to publicize," said O'Hara.[77] "It seems to us unfortunate," commented *Advertising Age*, "that church leaders, who must admit that the restraints of religious training have not done much to solve this problem, are inclined to attack what after all is a practical method of eradicating a blight on civilization. When religion finds it impossible to control human nature, science must come to the rescue." The journal hoped that advertisers would be courageous enough to continue their campaign.[78] "Those who criticize the effort to teach citizens how to understand and cooperate with the scientific control of venereal diseases have a tremendous job of their own in gaining acceptance for the way of life which would prevent them," concurred Dr. Parran.[79]

Not wanting to draw more attention to the issue, the WAC decided not to take part in a public debate with the *Catholic News* and other Catholic newspapers.[80] Hesitant advertisers were assured that they were not on the front lines or carrying the whole load in building public support for the VD program. Advertising was just one part of a much larger OWI campaign that included the whole media gamut, using magazine articles, booklets, posters, and movies to gain support for the cause.[81] The problem, however, was that the overall effort was being tainted by the WAC's involvement.

Prior to the OWI's invitation to the advertising community, the Metropolitan Life Insurance Company and the advertising-free *Reader's Digest* had discussed the VD situation in public service advertisements and articles without incurring much criticism, but now, with the council drawing increased attention to the effort, their contributions, along with other aspects of the VD campaign, became the target of right wing criticism. This was made very clear when the U.S. Public Health Service released an educational documentary on VD in the spring of 1944. Catholic interest groups joined the Legion of Decency in demanding that *To the People of the United States* be withdrawn.[82]

In spite of admitting that the film treated its subject matter in a dignified and restrained manner, the legion was aghast about its failure to adequately stress promiscuity as the principal cause for the spread of VD. The legion claimed that the film violated the Motion Picture Industry's production code and that it would open the floodgates for motion pictures with lurid and pornographic content. The legion maintained that the film inadequately highlighted promiscuity as the principal cause for the spread of VD. After an emergency meeting between the U.S. Public Health Service Advisory Committee and members of the Legion of Decency, the former conceded, admitting that it would not be wise for the Public Health Service to sponsor a national theatrical release of the film. Fearing that a fight about the film might hurt other aspects of the VD effort, which was just beginning to show results, the Surgeon General's Office retracted its original plan, deciding to restrict the film to controlled distribution at local health departments, army posts, and welfare offices.[83] It should come as no surprise that the scolding, threats, and adverse publicity affected the council's ability to attract sponsors, forcing the Public Health Service to call a meeting with the WAC and the OWI in an effort to further modify the campaign.[84] Intent on keeping the effort afloat, Dr. Parran pleaded with the council to continue its cooperation, underlining the importance of its work. Not only was the campaign backed by scientific facts and approved by competent medical authorities, but it dealt with a serious health matter that was affecting an increasing number of Americans.[85]

Worried that the WAC was losing support among advertisers, the OWI suggested a safety valve for those who were not comfortable squaring off with religious and right-wing forces. If necessary, individual advertisers could protect themselves by including some reference in their ads to the importance of avoiding infections by obeying religious and moral laws.[86] The WAC jumped at the opportunity, quickly moving away from its earlier insistence that VD be portrayed as a disease as opposed to a disgrace and asking advertisers to emphasize the role that "character-building institutions" such as churches, schools, and civic organizations played in its prevention. But despite strong support from the U.S. Public Health Service and the surgeon general, the council could not persuade advertisers to adopt even the new and revised directives. The campaign was unraveling.[87] "It is possible that some campaigns can be developed which meet the approval of religious groups," the WAC said. "But because of the highly controversial nature of the campaign as it now exists, the council feels it has an obligation to avoid requesting advertisers to sponsor a program which may generate some ill will toward them."[88] Most of the rejections had come from the New York area, where the Catholic forces had been particularly aggressive. In a last-ditch effort to save the campaign, the council suggested the creation of several local advertising campaigns as opposed to one national one.[89]

Despite having followed the same procedures as for the approximately one hundred other war-related campaigns and having taken particular care to clear the campaign with qualified religious and medical authorities, the WAC was forced to admit that the VD program was buckling under the intense and constant criticism. Thus, in late September of 1944, a defiant council informed the Public Health Service that it was no longer able to assist with obtaining sponsorship for the VD campaign. "It is now apparent that the question of whether or not this particular campaign is a good one, or whether there should be any educational campaign at all, is something that generates a good deal of sincere emotions on both sides," stated the council. Therefore it no longer felt that it could "put itself in the position of judge and jury in this matter."[90]

The council had learned a lesson. Prior to the VD campaign, it had tended to adopt noncontroversial causes such as paper drives and victory gardens, which were intrinsically patriotic contributions to the war effort.[91] But just as association with those campaigns could serve as a good PR vehicle, an ill-chosen one might backfire on the industry's overall effort. Although criticism of the VD campaign had come from a relatively small group, its leaders were highly influential and could potentially sway participating advertisers in a damaging way. Thus the debate over the VD campaign exposed the ongoing struggle between advertisers' need for immediate customer approval and their desire to take a principled stand for the war effort in a strategy to build more general support for the institution of advertising on a long-term basis. Thereafter, the council steered clear of anything that might be viewed as controversial.

Maintaining Discipline with an Eye on the Prize

With the D-Day invasion and the subsequent liberation of France in the summer of 1944, victory in Europe seemed assured, perhaps before the end of the year. Many Americans assumed that peace was close at hand. This optimism (or rather over-optimism, as it proved) presented a problem, because it diverted public attention from the war effort. This was especially true for the WAC, which was having a difficult time keeping advertisers committed. As one advertising official put it cynically, "good war news" from abroad translated into "bad news on the home front."[92] Instead of focusing on the war effort, many advertisers had become overly confident that peace was right around the corner, and their ads reflected this view.[93] "The prestige of the advertising profession," stated a concerned advertising executive, "can be affected by its behavior during the next few months more than at any time since the early stages of the war."[94] Industry observers went so far as to declare complacency the new national enemy. "This attitude," argued one, "is causing a definite shift away from war industries by workers; it is leading to announcement of post-war plans which take our minds off the war that is still to be fought, and in fact, is leading to a general letting down of war spirits. In the meantime, the Japs are talking about a 100-year war."[95]

The WAC renewed its efforts to devise activities that would spark involvement. It considered special get-togethers for small groups of select advertisers as well as the possibility of an industry-wide meeting to inspire the continuous effort. "A renewed push by us over the period of the next few months," observed WAC board member Theodore S. Repplier, "might tip the scales with many advertisers and agencies who are now on the fence about continuation of war themes."[96] The council was helped in this effort when Time, Inc., agreed to underwrite production of an inspirational publication titled *Are We Getting a Little Tired of the War?* The booklet, by Charles L. (Roy) Whittier of Young and Rubicam, was aimed at reenergizing and inspiring the public. Whittier was full of ideas, having just returned from a three-month special mission for the Treasury and War departments that had taken him to the battlefields of France, Germany, and Italy. There, he said, he had learned firsthand from American GIs the real meaning of "war weariness." His booklet reflected "the point of view of those to whom winning the war is still the most important mission in life; those who believe that no war effort should be relaxed until both the Krauts and the Nips give us the green light of unconditional surrender; those who feel that as long as our men are suffering mutilation and death in battle, our advertising has a responsibility to discharge."[97] The pamphlet played heavily on sacrifice, even showing photos of dead and wounded soldiers as a means of comparing home front "sacrifices" with those made on the fighting front. Its final page depicted three war casualties under the captions "This man gave half an arm. . . . This man gave half his eyes. . . . Will you give half your ads?" The bottom of each page reminded advertisers that "There will be no post-war until the last gun is fired!"[98]

The council was delighted to receive scores of letters requesting *Are We Getting a Little Tired of the War?*, making it the WAC's most widely distributed publication.[99] "Sometimes the whole war theme idea gets to looking like a dying horse," reflected Young. "We must keep industry alive to what we are doing."[100] At the same time, however, that it insisted advertisers intensify their support for the government's war effort, the council itself was busy with postwar planning. This was a shrewd move, given its role as the advertising industry's primary public relations agency. Although promoting the war effort was advertisers' most pressing task, the council could not take the risk that peace might arrive before it had designed a postwar strategy. An underlying fear was that the WAC would be unable to make a smooth transition from war to peace, and that this would end up affecting it negatively.[101]

Uncertain how to handle the dual job of coaching the industry toward intensified wartime efforts while simultaneously keeping a close eye on the postwar situation, the council decided to "leak" its postwar plans to *Advertising Age*, leaving the industry shielded from criticism should the trial balloon burst.[102] "The successful conversion of the country to a peacetime basis," the trade publication dutifully reported, "will be primarily a selling job in which advertising must inevitably play a leading role." It asked advertisers to prepare their campaigns in such a way that they could be put into use as soon as Germany surrendered. The timing had to be right, however. *Advertising Age* warned that advertising could not "afford" to resign from its wartime tasks while millions of men were bracing themselves for the hardest jobs of their lives: "By all means let us have advertising pointed toward peace and free enterprise and private initiative; let us have plans for advertising that will sell peacetime goods, and sell them effectively. But at the same time, let us keep a realization of the fact that advertising still has a multitude of wartime jobs to do—jobs of explaining, exhorting, morale building—which it cannot resign until victory is not only in sight but in hand. Let's keep our timing right."[103]

By late 1944, the WAC's board of directors had pledged to continue the council's work beyond the conclusion of the war, promising that "its methods of operation should be revised to meet the new conditions."[104] A permanent postwar Advertising Council not only might be the solution to many postwar problems, but might make for a smart business move to boot.[105] In no way, however, did the council want these postwar plans to imply, or invite the suggestion, that it was shirking its wartime duties.[106] "In peace as in war," the WAC stated, "the Council's purpose shall be to utilize some of the power of advertising in the interest of all the people; to give by its use an example of advertising as a social force; to give a continuing demonstration of the willingness of business to cooperate with national leaders . . . and by these means, to conduct on the highest plane, the finest type of public relations possible for advertising and for business."[107] The idea of a postwar continuation earned a strong endorsement from President Roosevelt, who nevertheless reminded the council of the need to continue its efforts till the bitter end. "I cannot emphasize this point too strongly," he said. "Those who are assisting in bringing information to the people have a responsibility to help prevent any letdown on the home front."[108]

Conclusion

By 1944, the WAC could look back on close to three years of intense activity. Whereas its involvement in 1942 had been limited to fourteen campaigns, its accomplishments by the end of 1944 encompassed sixty-two projects. During the same period, the number of government agencies the council served had grown from eight to twenty-seven.[109] By late 1944, the advertising community had contributed close to $800 million worth of time, space, and talent to government campaigns through the WAC.[110] By any criterion, the council had grown dramatically and had played a significant part in the domestic war effort. But while there is no doubt that many of those connected with the WAC displayed a strong patriotic sentiment, its overriding raison d'être was always to provide public relations benefits to the advertising industry. This was the context for understanding the council's motives and actions when dealing with recalcitrant advertisers and government officials. And as measured by public relations, the WAC's last two years were a marked success. "I feel that we should recognize at the outset what already has been accomplished in the way of public relations," said one industry observer near the war's end. "We have accomplished a good deal in a short time." Indeed, the War Advertising Council had fired the imaginations of the entire industry, enabling many of its practitioners to see the benefits of maintaining such an organization in the postwar world.[111] As the war entered its final year, it was increasingly acknowledged across the advertising community that the council should remain in existence at war's end. Its mission would be to continue providing public relations services to advertising and to American business generally.

7

Peace and the Reconversion
of the Advertising Council

The War Advertising Council had been created with the understanding that it would be a temporary organization, to be terminated at the end of the war. Its success at improving the advertising industry's standing had far exceeded expectations. In just a few years, the formerly hostile relationship between the industry and Washington had changed to one of mutual respect and cooperation, leading the organization's officers to agree that continuing its activities would be a wise strategy.[1]

In contrast to the war years, when the WAC's main role was to communicate the government's home-front instructions, the postwar council selected campaigns from proposals submitted by both government agencies and private interest groups, using them strategically for its own political ends while staying safely within the parameters set by the federal government. This chapter traces the history of the War Advertising Council as it evolved back into the Advertising Council. The chapter explores the trend toward politically explicit postwar campaigns and shows how the council's projects helped the advertising and business communities take on an important role in the fight against communism and in building a postwar economic system based on business dominance.

The War Advertising Council Looks Ahead

The Allies' invasion of Normandy on D-Day, June 6, 1944, signaled the end of the war. By September the WAC had established a Post-War Planning Committee, with Chester LaRoche in charge. Warning that reconversion would be a tumultuous period, and that "the white light of information and persuasion" would be needed "as perhaps never before," the council began to seriously consider its postwar options.[2] Soon the discussion about the possibilities for a formal postwar advertising organization spread to the business community at large, prompting *Tide* to sponsor a debate on advertising's social responsibilities. A powerhouse panel was convened in early 1945, headed by public relations and management counsel to the American Home Product Corporation Leo Nejelski. It also included clergyman and professor of applied Christianity at Union Theological Seminary Reinhold Niebuhr, former chairman of the Federal Communications Commission James L. Fly, Yale University professor Harold D. Lasswell, Columbia University sociologist Bernhard J. Stern, and the president of the WAC, James Webb Young.[3]

Niebuhr, who would later become a member of the postwar council's Public Policy Committee, joined Lasswell and Stern in expressing concern that public service advertising would now be more attuned to the needs of business propaganda than to the public's need for useful information. As one of the country's experts on propaganda, Lasswell was particularly worried that advertising's special relationship with the commercial mass media would give it an unfair advantage over its political opponents in getting its views before the public. In response, Young said simply that it was up to the opponents of any issue to take care of themselves.[4] Concerns such as these reinforced the importance of crafting a postwar council that would studiously avoid controversy and emphasize public service above all else. Although the purpose of the postwar organization—to facilitate a business-friendly environment—was implicitly political, its legitimacy would collapse if the new group came to be viewed as a partisan entity producing self-interested propaganda.[5]

Pointing to the "many critical national problems" that would require the understanding and cooperation of each and every citizen, President Roosevelt considered it "vitally important that the working partnership between business and government, which so successfully brought information to the people in wartime, continue into the post-war period."[6] And in a move that calmed an always jittery advertising community, Harry S. Truman, who during his tenure as head of the Senate Committee to Investigate the War Program had caused advertisers a great many worries, emerged as a full-fledged supporter of the council after his presidential inauguration in 1945.[7]

Creating the Postwar Council

As the postwar plans came together, there was an important new twist: a Public Policy Committee (initially called the Public Advisory Committee) and an Industrial Advisory Committee were added to the council to assist with selecting campaigns. The former was chaired by Evans Clark, the executive director of the Twentieth Century Fund, and consisted of "leaders of public opinion" drawn from diverse fields of American society, who would serve the council in a capacity similar to that of the trustees of a large foundation.[8] This did not mean that the council's board of directors would defer independent judgment with regard to campaigns. The committee's role, after all, was to advise them, not to dictate their actions. Thus the council rejected any suggestion that the Industrial Advisory Committee, which was filled with people from corporate America, had a "private axe to grind," and it stressed its right to accept or reject any project, regardless of origin.[9]

For the council to continue, however, there would have to be broad-based support from advertising leaders and the business community, a situation that was complicated by the broad range of opinions about what its future goals and objectives ought to be.[10] Some in the advertising industry hoped that the postwar council would serve in an educational capacity, explaining advertising and its role in society to the American public. Others wanted it to be "the voice of progressive elements in American business," demonstrating the business community's willingness to assume "progressive leadership." Still others envisioned a role for the Council in teaching the public about national problems, functioning as a "mediator and force for unity." By demonstrating an unwavering commitment to the public welfare, the advertising industry would ultimately be successful in increasing its prestige.[11]

There were also those who wanted to limit the council's postwar involvement to campaigns along the lines of its wartime projects. Fearing, perhaps, that campaigns to explain tax rules, charitable fund drives, and conservation of natural resources approximated its earlier tasks too closely, the WAC was adamant that it not come across as "a war-time organization attempting to perpetuate itself."[12] The postwar council, stressed LaRoche in what would soon become the majority opinion on the issue, should capitalize on its newly earned reputation and continue to serve as a liaison between business and government, providing guidance and leadership in making advertising a more effective tool both for business and for society as a whole, and thereby proving itself as a "unifying force of great value."[13]

Talking candidly among themselves, however, WAC executives revealed that there were more self-serving reasons behind their desire for the council to continue beyond the war. They hoped that their work would leave the public with a positive impression of advertising. "There is a popular misconception among some people that we are proposing a great humanitarian project," said Young.[14] "But just as when a man wants to do a public relations or character-building for himself, he can do it better by *acting* as a good citizen instead of just talking about himself as one, so can an advertiser or industry do a better public relations job for himself by demonstrating good citizenship instead of talking about it."[15] Warning that the stability of private enterprise was being threatened by a host of social and economic disturbances, Don Belding, a council member and partner at Foote, Cone and Belding in Los Angeles who also served as president of the Pacific Advertising Club, advocated for a postwar council that would work to develop "educational techniques" to help keep the activities of "anti-advertising groups" in check, so that advertising would be "properly respected by consumers." He envisioned an effort "to win labor to advertising's side" and to promote "the free enterprise system," but he warned against becoming entrapped "in any political quicksands which might reflect discredit to the industry in general."[16]

The Advertising Council, Inc.

The heated debates notwithstanding, in July 1945 the council's board of directors voted overwhelmingly to continue operations. *Advertising Age* welcomed the decision as perhaps "the finest contribution of this generation of advertising people," both "to the future of America" and "to the long range interests of the whole field."[17] Wasting little time, the reenergized council held meetings with top executives and created a speakers' pool staffed with professional men and women who were available to speak with interested groups about the council's postwar plans. The transformation involved a full publicity program, with the general press—including Washington correspondents, columnists, chief editorial writers, radio commentators, magazine editors, and trade press representatives—encouraged to report and comment.[18]

By October, the War Advertising Council had officially gone back to its original name, the Advertising Council, Inc. It proudly announced that it would have a budget of at least $30 million a year to deal with "future campaigns growing out of an act of Congress, requiring public understanding or action; or problems certified in the public interest" as determined by a three-quarters vote by its Public Policy Committee.[19] While promoting the effort as one that could "help business as a whole, protect it from vicious attacks by biased critics, keep government officials sold on advertising as a powerful weapon for good, and augment further the public goodwill business now enjoys from its unstinted, voluntary effort during the war," the council's president, Paul B. West, and chairman, Charles G. Mortimer Jr., also believed that it would benefit the general public because, as West put it, "Democracy is healthy in proportion as the people are well informed."[20]

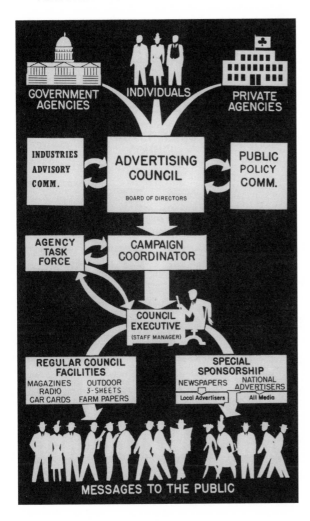

Figure 21. "Messages to the Public." Advertising Council flowchart, ca. 1951. Courtesy Ad Council Archives, University of Illinois Archives, RS 13/2/207.

The postwar council involved a plan to increase the number of sponsors and the addition of a new "contributing members" category for those who were willing to make an annual donation of at least $10,000 toward the council's operating expenses.[21] Washington, D.C., was quickly selected as the best location for a permanent headquarters because a presence in the nation's capital would make it possible to closely monitor issues before Congress. With the bulk of American advertising agencies located on Madison Avenue, however, there was considerable support for maintaining a second, smaller office in New York City.[22]

A great deal of thought went into the Ad Council's postwar relationship with the government. Although the Council had never been part of the Office of War Information, the mutually close relationship that had developed between Washington and advertising during the war had blurred some of the prewar boundaries between the two institutions. The OWI was officially dissolved in September 1945 and replaced by a temporary agency, the Office of War Mobilization and Reconversion (OWMR), with John Snyder, a bank executive and longtime close friend of President Truman, in charge.[23] A Media Programming Division headed by Andrew Dudley, who had served as Ken Dyke's deputy chief in the Bureau of Campaigns early in the war and was now a retired commander in the Office of the Secretary of the Navy, was made part of the OWMR's operations from the start and given responsibility for mapping the various government agencies' promotional needs.[24]

The Media Programming Division invited the Advertising Council not only to coordinate actual advertising efforts but also to handle all dealings with the outdoor advertising industry and oversee "car cards," the advertising posters that were displayed in trains, subways, and buses. It also asked that the council assume responsibility for the government's radio allocation plan, which secured airtime for Washington's messages.[25] One year later, at the Ad Council's request, the division officially became a unit of the Executive Office of the President, a move that provided the council with ready access to the White House.[26] The Office of Government Reports (OGR), which had been the government's information agency before the war, was reactivated in December 1946. The Media Programming Division was then transferred to the OGR as its Advertising Liaison Office, in which capacity it continued to serve as a point of contact between the government and the advertising community. Heralding the industry's increased entrenchment in Washington's corridors of power as "striking evidence of advertising's new status," the council willingly appeared before Congress to request funding for the newly created office, presenting estimates that it would attract more than $100 million in donations of time and space to the government. It easily won bipartisan approval.[27]

Advertising's increased stature was also reflected in the council's amicable dealings with key government officials and a continuation of the confidential off-the-record "summit meetings" between Washington officials and industry leaders that had been held since 1944.[28] In September 1946, for example, council leaders were invited to a series of informal meetings at the White House so that they could be directly apprised of major national problems requiring "public understanding."[29] There were no formal speeches at these gatherings, which meant that council representatives had ample time to interact and ask government officials any questions they wished.[30] "Sometimes," director and president of the Mutual Broadcasting System Edgar Kobak later commented, "men in industry forget that the men in government are just ordinary folks—and vice versa. Rubbing elbows, exchanging ideas help to clear the air."[31] Unable to attend the 1946 meetings, President Truman sent his regrets. He was pleased, however, that the two sides were working so well together. "In peace as in war," he declared, "there is no substitute for teamwork between business and government in the solution of problems which both agree are in the public interest."[32]

The Advertising Council still needed to proceed with extreme caution. Although Washington was vastly different now than it had been during the years when it was filled with aggressive New Dealers, the relationship between government and the business community was not always a smooth one, and the council's primary mission was to serve the advertising industry in a public relations capacity. Thus, as key players in business, labor, and government disagreed about political goals and how to achieve them, the council was forced to become extremely adept at strategizing its campaigns.[33]

Labor and the New Deal as Threats to Business

The end of World War II brought "an array of unresolved controversies about authority, status, and power" in America.[34] The Depression, the New Deal, and the war had ushered in a prolonged period of stress, causing large segments of the public to yearn for more stable conditions. Although business and labor had different visions for the future and different strategies for realizing those visions, both groups promised Americans that an age of prosperity, stability, and economic growth was at hand. Perhaps most importantly, influential business leaders worried that the United States might follow the British in electing a government that would support labor and attempt to nationalize the country's major industries.[35] (Britain's wartime leader, Winston Churchill, was turned out of office by the Labour Party almost as soon as the war ended.) Britain's course was the direct opposite of what the U.S. business community envisioned as postwar normalcy; it seemed like a nightmarish extension of the worst of the New Deal from the years leading up to the war. Business and labor each knew that "the good life" was predicated, at least to some degree, upon its own role in society being elevated at the expense of the other. In short, this was a contest in which there could be only one winner—or at least a contest in which one side would have to do the lion's share of compromising. Considering the stakes, it is not surprising that the conflict between capital and labor was an emerging theme even before the war came to an end.[36]

During the war, organized labor had gained strength and popularity, building upon its rapid growth in the late 1930s. In spite of the long-standing feud between the Congress of Industrial Organizations (CIO) and the American Federation of Labor (AFL) and other internal problems, almost 70 percent of all U.S. manufacturing workers were union members as the war came to an end. This is not to suggest, however, that labor was more powerful than business, only that it was far more powerful than it had been in decades, if not in all of American history since the Industrial Revolution. Thus, the most conservative segment of America's business community proceeded into the postwar era as if it were engaged with labor—or at least with its most militant elements, such as the CIO—in a battle of life or death. Concerns over labor's increasing powers were also reflected in the collective efforts of moderate business groups to replace the Wagner Act of 1935 with the far less labor-friendly Taft-Hartley Act in 1947. The latter prohibited certain kinds of strikes, made it illegal for unions and corporations to donate to candidates running for federal office, and required all union officers to sign noncommunist affidavits.[37]

The National Association of Manufacturers (NAM) and the even larger U.S. Chamber of Commerce (USCC) were the nation's leading, and most inclusive, employers' organizations. Actively opposed to the labor movement, the two groups hoped that by lobbying policymakers they could gain more power for business in regulating labor matters. Their fear was that organized labor, with its vastly enlarged membership and newly acquired strength, was poised to take a much bigger role in the private enterprise system, and that labor's active involvement in management might seriously undermine the prerogatives and privileges of business.[38]

The Business Advisory Council (BAC), formed in the 1930s, and the Committee on Economic Development (CED), established in 1942–43, took their inspiration from the National Resources Planning Board (NRPB), a small, moderate research arm of the White House that advocated a nonconfrontational approach to resolving the ideological tension.[39] Unlike the NAM and the USCC, which counted a large number of businesspeople and small manufacturers among their members, the CED and the BAC reserved membership for the presidents and board chairmen of America's largest corporations. The CED, for example, consisted of eighteen leading industrialists and economists. (It liked to characterize itself as a "nonpolitical" group.)[40] And unlike the NAM and the USCC, which used rhetoric that evoked industrial conflict, the BAC and the CED employed more conciliatory tactics, seeking to modify and work with the New Deal rather than destroy it.[41] They wanted central planning—to be influenced primarily by business—to ensure post-war prosperity.[42] In exchange for a promise that the Democratic mainstream would not seek to expand New Deal reform, the BAC and the CED agreed not to join with right-wing forces (represented by groups such as the NAM and the USCC) to attack major elements of the New Deal as it was presently being implemented. Further, they promised to support an effort to create a bipartisan foreign policy to contain communism.[43] On this point their mission would eventually overlap with that of the Advertising Council. Much like the council, the CED believed in "socially responsible risk-taking for the common good, with the hope of private profit as an incentive."[44]

A series of wartime polls had shown strong support for the social-democratic aspects of Roosevelt's New Deal. A *Fortune* poll conducted in 1942, for example, found that a majority of the respondents were in favor of universal medical insurance and social security benefits for retired workers. They also wanted full employment, unemployment insurance, and government regulation of banks. Although 40 percent of the respondents were opposed to socialism, fully 25 percent declared themselves in favor of it, while 34 percent were undecided. In other words, remarked an exasperated *Advertising Age*, "The American people do not want new 'systems' or new ideologies, but they want jobs, public works, medical care, and social security. . . . They want the deed, not the word."[45]

The trade publication was equally concerned when a later Gallup poll found that only 30 percent of Americans knew the definition of *free enterprise*. The remaining 70 percent were either ignorant of the concept or had a "definite antagonism" toward it. It was time, warned *Advertising Age*, for the advertising industry "to start working hard on the vital problem of presenting the story of the free enterprise system in such a way as to sell the 70 per cent who either don't understand it or are opposed now to what they think it means."[46]

Just as disturbing from the point of view of business were the results of a 1944 survey by the Association of National Advertisers (ANA). While a majority of those respondents preferred a private takeover of government-owned war plants after the war, they also had "serious misconceptions" about the amount of manufacturers' war profits, and they believed that private business had an obligation to keep people employed and to ensure good working wages. A later survey, conducted in 1945, found a slight increase in the number of respondents who believed that Washington was better equipped than business for "straightening things out after the war."[47] As with any poll, the results were subject to a variety of interpretations; there were no absolute answers. But it is safe to say that the country's top business leaders did not feel confident about their postwar prospects. It was here that the (War) Advertising Council saw itself as playing an important role. Capitalizing on its skills and an impressive network of connections, the council was in a unique situation to "sell" the American public on free enterprise and the advantages of a capitalist economy.

Both the NAM and the CED believed that *free enterprise* and a *capitalist economy* were the only route to postwar prosperity, viewing the terms as interchangeable with notions of a *free society* and a *democratic way of life*; and each sought an alliance with what was then still the War Advertising Council.[48] But whereas the WAC lent a sympathetic ear to the well-funded NAM, it declined to enter into formal cooperation with a group that so publicly attacked labor and "New Deal–Fair Deal liberalism," preferring instead to work with the CED, whose philosophy was more in line with its own.[49]

While industry groups were encouraged by their members to vigorously promote a conservative agenda, the council's task was more complex. Most, if not all, of its members and sponsors had a public affiliation with well-known trade names that enjoyed cross-political support among consumers. To push a heavy partisan agenda and potentially alienate a sizable section of a sponsor's consumer base could prove risky and unwise. Thus, and perhaps with the failed VD campaign still fresh in memory, the council aimed for a political middle ground. This strategy was facilitated by the fact that the council was taking its cues from an increasingly conservative, albeit Democratic, government, and its willingness to work with postwar civic groups gave the appearance that it was not trying to advance any particular agenda. In contrast to the NAM campaigns, which hammered on a set of political demands, the council claimed to represent all sides and not give preferential treatment to anyone. That, of course, was not really the case. All campaign proposals were carefully chosen and vetted to make sure that they reflected well on the council and its overarching goals. The strategy was to combine "a little statesmanship with its salesmanship," allowing "the best and most liberal elements of business" to "work hand-in-hand with labor and government."[50] Or, as the council itself put it, the best public relations program for advertising—and, indirectly, for the nation's businesses as a whole—was the rendering of "unselfish public service" through the postwar Advertising Council.[51]

Postwar Campaigns and the Freedom Train

The postwar Advertising Council was inundated with pleas for help as soon as it got off the ground. During 1948 alone, it received 123 proposals from private organizations and government departments. Of those, 57, or slightly less than half, were given some level of assistance.[52] "Requests," write Robert Jackall and Janice Hirota, "came from organizations of every stripe addressing the panoply of human ills and social issues endemic to an industrial social order, from tuberculosis control to accident prevention, from blood drives to advocacy for atomic energy, from group prejudice control to raising the prestige of the army."[53] The council continued its U.S. Saving Bonds promotions and launched campaigns for "the Girl Scouts, the Marine Corps, the National Safety Council, the Famine Emergency Committee, the Salvation Army, the Infantile Paralysis Association, the Cooperative for American Remittances to Europe (CARE), the National Society for Crippled Children, and the National Conference of Christians and Jews," as well as a largely unsuccessful and somewhat controversial "Peace" campaign promoting U.S. membership in the United Nations.[54] In 1949 it joined forces with the newly formed National Citizens' Commission, which had been awarded a grant by the Carnegie Corporation to encourage the improvement of public schools.[55] Many of the campaigns, argues Robert Griffith, were designed to appease groups that had been critical toward advertising in the past, such as educators, clergy, and physicians. Others were designed to produce "collateral benefits" for individual industries. The campaign to prevent forest fires, popularized through the invention of "Smokey the Bear," was a boon to the lumber-related industries, while campaigns to prevent highway accidents reflected well on their sponsors in the automobile and insurance industries.[56] Still, as Griffith points out, many of the council's campaigns carried subtle political messages, sometimes only by omission. For example, while the "Better School Campaign" encouraged the establishment of independent community groups to work toward improving public education, it never discussed federal aid as a tool for this purpose; and while the campaign on highway safety was heavy on individual responsibility, it never mentioned poor highway or automobile design as a cause of traffic deaths.[57]

In late 1946, council executives Thomas Brophy and Theodore Repplier attended a large meeting of business and professional leaders arranged by Attorney General Tom C. Clark. Clark issued a warning about subversive forces and foreign elements that might "undermine and discredit" the American system of government and suggested that an "indoctrination in democracy" was needed to blend the nation's diverse groups into "one American Family."

Moved by the attorney general's concerns, which so closely reflected his own, Brophy helped organize a new group called the American Heritage Foundation (AHF) and appointed prominent banker Winthrop W. Aldrich as its chairman.

Before long, the foundation had launched the "Freedom Train," a one-year traveling exhibit that used the railroad to take original documents of national significance directly to the American people, with a goal to "strengthen the nation against the poisonous flood of Communist propaganda from within and without." The campaign was quickly accepted by the Advertising Council, and W. B. Potter of Eastman Kodak was put charge of coordinating the massive project, which required the volunteer help of ten advertising agencies.[58] Between September 1947 and October 1948, the train stopped in 322 cities, and each day some 8,500 people came aboard to view original drafts of the Constitution, the Declaration of Independence, the United Nations Charter, the Emancipation Proclamation, and other documents that had been lent to the AHF by the National Archives, the Library of Congress, and several individual collectors and institutions.[59] More than twenty-six thousand newspaper advertisements and three thousand billboards across the nation helped announce the thirteen-month journey, often adding a local touch. Additionally, and as part of the campaign, the council distributed more than 1.5 million copies of a booklet on "the duties and privileges of citizenship" prepared by the Leo Burnett Agency and took pride in the more than two thousand articles and editorials and more than six billion radio "listener impressions" that the campaign had generated.[60]

President Truman praised the Freedom Train and its documents as "landmarks of the advance of freedom and democracy."[61] The selection of those documents, however, as Stuart J. Little argues, reflected an idealized vision of American history, one that tried to merge and reconcile positive abstractions such as "individual freedoms and the democratic process" and "the abundance and opportunity of capitalism" with broader social tensions and concerns as the essence of Americanism.[62] And among those concerns was the growth of racial tensions in the United States. The nation's treatment of African Americans, especially returning black service members who had done their part to help win the war, was eliciting a significant amount of anger and concern overseas. Worried that a failure to properly address the issue might provide ammunition for Soviet propaganda, the National Conference on Christians and Jews, the Anti-Defamation League, the American Jewish Committee, and the Institute for American Democracy had turned jointly to the council. The result was the "United America" campaign, which stressed "the professed American tradition of tolerance." Citing the economic, social, and "international consequences of domestic racism," the Ad Council was now actively involved in the effort to fight prejudice.[63]

Thus the organizers of the Freedom Train were unprepared when civil rights leaders accused the project of racism and characterized some of the documents as reflecting "the traditional white supremacy way of life."[64] The famous performer Paul Robeson, an outspoken communist, pointed out that there were "no Negroes on the American Heritage Foundation's Board, nor any Negroes on the train's personnel." In addition, visitors to the exhibits in southern states were often segregated by race. Considering Attorney General Clark's failure to end lynching and the use of terror against African Americans, Robeson pointed to the hypocritical nature of the "freedom" campaign and was highly frustrated when Clark would not address the issue of discriminatory access to the train's exhibits. It was perversely ironic that the Freedom Train concept had originated from an old Negro spiritual and that the trains used to smuggle escaped slaves from the South before the Civil War were commonly referred to as "freedom trains." Many people were also struck by the hypocrisy of an exhibit that included an original copy of the Emancipation Proclamation being viewed by visitors who had been separated into groups by race.[65]

The AHF did not know how to handle the situation at first, and President Truman's praise of the campaign offered little guidance.[66] But when viewers were once again segregated at stops in Virginia, South Carolina, and Georgia, the foundation realized that it had to take a stand against the practice in order to save the project's integrity. Exhibits that had been planned for segregated crowds in Birmingham, Alabama, and Memphis, Tennessee, were quickly canceled.[67] "In rejecting this one manifestation of the Jim Crow system," argues Little, "the Foundation had responded to black leaders and the threat of adverse publicity," and it received high levels of praise from the civil rights movement as a result. Despite the AHF's racially inclusive ideology, however, many of its ideals were still reflective of white America.[68]

The council's collaboration with the American Heritage Foundation, albeit a major project, was only part of its activities. As the Freedom Train traveled from town to town attempting to define the essence of America, the council became involved with a new campaign, an ambitious plan to define the "American Economic System" that clearly pushed the political envelope but was designed to reach out to the American mainstream.[69]

Promoting the "American Economic System"

Warnings about an imminent communist takeover had been around since World War I and frequently came in response to a real or perceived threat to business. By the latter part of the 1930s, anticommunist crusaders had stepped up their efforts. Groups and individuals who had expressed varying degrees of criticism against U.S. capitalism were lumped together as subversive elements about to undermine the social fabric of American society. That an increasingly popular consumer movement and many of its leaders were accused of such activities and forced to testify before the Dies Committee, the forerunner to the House Un-American Activities Committee, says a lot about the political jitters in the ultraconservative camp. Although the war had put a damper on most of these activities, the criticisms had never really gone away, and they regained momentum as the nation entered reconversion. Conservative groups, including the NAM, the Hearst newspaper chain, and the American Legion, took up their old cause. Notable among the groups and individuals who picked up the mantle was J. Edgar Hoover, director of the Federal Bureau of Investigation, who launched a campaign in 1946 to educate the public about the "Communist Party menace." Hoover sent information pulled from FBI files to reporters, congressmen, publishers, religious leaders, columnists, and anticommunists in the labor movement and the entertainment industries in hopes of building his case.[70] The result was a growing sense of fear and paranoia and a warning to citizens from the business community that "the decline of America's values, morals, and freedoms" now threatened the stability of their existence.[71]

In the spring of 1947, after more than a year of preparations, a newly created Joint ANA and AAAA Committee on Understanding Our Economic System presented plans for a comprehensive campaign to foster understanding of "the American system of free enterprise." Eager to participate in the educational effort, the Advertising Council appointed a special subcommittee of the Public Policy Committee to work closely with the ANA and AAAA in developing a plan that would secure the support of labor. It delegated the execution of the campaign to Foote, Cone and Belding. Having observed the numerous "free enterprise" campaigns conducted by other organizations and individual advertisers over the years, the chairman of the general planning committee, Howard Chase, was determined to top them all. Not only had his people worked diligently to keep the campaign completely unbiased, but it was "absolutely free" of material that favored business interests over other groups. The material had been prepared in "cooperation with labor, religious, consumer, and women's groups," with care taken to ensure that a range of viewpoints were reflected. Also, because the program would be administered by the Advertising Council, "which by government charter may operate only in the public interest," its nonpartisanship was guaranteed.[72]

The campaign to promote the "American Economic System" had two separate but closely related tracks. One was directed at industrial plants, aiming to correct workers' misconceptions about industrial profits and restore their pride in and sense of being part of the capitalist economy. The Joint Committee was convinced that this could be accomplished if workers were equipped with an improved understanding of capitalism's fundamental principles and the benefits it offered them. The enemy of free enterprise, they claimed, was not labor; in fact, it was not even an internal entity. The forces that needed to be harnessed were the proponents of "controlled enterprise" and their increasing communist propaganda. Theodore Repplier, now the Ad Council's president, called for "radical measures" to fight an "ideological war," the seriousness of which few people had yet come to understand.[73]

The second phase of the campaign, which was not to be activated until the first stage was well under way, was to be directed at the public and would follow the same themes, emphasizing that the "superiority of the American standard of living and wages of the American worker compared to those in other countries."[74] Although Americans professed to be in favor of the free market, complained Jack Smock, the Foote, Cone and Belding advertising executive who was in charge of the campaign, their knowledge about its basic principles was lacking. Unless this ignorance could be properly addressed, the country would be facing a grim economic future.[75]

Thus it was essential to demonstrate that management, labor, and other major interest groups were in agreement about "the basic objectives of better living, adequate housing, clothing and nutrition and good health for all, with ever greater opportunities for individual development," and to drive home the idea that these objectives could be realized only by embracing the "American system." Not surprisingly, given the somewhat vague ultimate goal and the limitations of an advertising campaign for conveying complex ideas, the program did not aim to explain "the complicated mechanisms of production, finance, and distribution patterns under the economic system," but, similar to what had been done with the "Freedom Train" campaign, the "American Economic System" campaign sought to reconcile positive abstractions in an effort to instill a feeling of pride and superiority among Americans.[76]

Unlike previous council campaigns, the "American Economic System" project added an outreach component modeled loosely on the broader public relations campaigns that the NAM and other business-interest organizations had developed back in the 1930s. Its ten points covered freedom of employment, of private affairs, of private management, and of speech; individual security; limited government action in economic affairs; free competition; collective bargaining; expanding productivity; and increased recognition of human values. The campaign included an impressive arsenal of booklets, motion pictures, and radio shows. Campaign kits were made available to any group or company with an interest in disseminating the program among its members or employees. The goal was to continue the campaign until every American had been "re-educated."[77]

Obtaining advertiser support for ideologically charged campaigns proved difficult. In light of past experiences, that must not have come as a complete surprise. The task of devising an effective campaign slogan proved to be a major challenge, subjecting the four major advertising agencies that were serving as a volunteer "task force" to endless rounds of writing, rewriting, revising, scrapping, and replacing of copy ideas.[78] Newly elected council chairman Charles Mortimer was not blind to the challenges involved. "The boys who write glowingly of soap and how it will make you a success can't do the same with this idea—it's not so simple," he acknowledged. "We're going to sell the system, not defend it, in easily understood, action-provoking terms."[79] But, as he said, "There will be no enterprise and no right to advertise unless the swing to the left is checked."[80]

Advertisers reacted positively to the part of the plan that focused on outreach to industrial plants, but they were far more skeptical about the public outreach portion. Their concern was that their ads would appeal only to the already converted and thus have little general impact.[81] Some feared that worries about a potential consumer backlash might prevent commercial sponsors from lending support, while numerous advertising directors complained that the campaign was too similar to efforts by the NAM and the USCC.[82] That was not enough, however, to deter the Advertising Council. After more than two years of preparation and a great deal of determination, it finally got the campaign off the ground in November of 1948. "Sure, America's going ahead if we all pull together," read ads in the November issues of national magazines, with a subsequent $1-million-dollar campaign along similar lines in newspapers, on radio, and on outdoor billboards.[83] During its first year, the campaign generated well over two billion radio listener impressions, as many as were generated by one hundred episodes of the highly rated *Bob Hope Show*.[84]

Between January and June of 1949, the number of sponsors nearly doubled, offsetting a drop in support from magazine publishers. In addition to advertisers who followed the Joint Committee's "blueprint," there were no

Figure 22. "How to tune a piano!" 1949. This ad was part of a series prepared by the Advertising Council for its "American Economic System" campaign. The message, of course, is that the American economic system did not have to be destroyed (by labor); it simply needed some fine-tuning (by business). Notice the relatively small space for the sponsor's brand name. Courtesy Ad Council Archives, University of Illinois Archives, RS 13/2/207.

fewer than 1,500 additional supporters who implemented some element of the committee's suggestions. Advertisers had clearly overcome their hesitations. By summer, the council estimated that 70 percent of all Americans had been reached by some aspect of the campaign. Helping to spread the message was *The Miracle of America*, a booklet explaining the "American Economic System." By early 1950, *Scholastic* magazine had issued 535,000 reprints of the publication, boosting its combined circulation to schools, civic groups, the military, and the population at large to more than 1.5 million. Some copies were ordered by business for general distribution, while others were mailed to individuals upon request. Magazines, newspapers, and radio made frequent references to the booklet, and after an endorsement by the popular radio host Arthur Godfrey, more than 27,000 people asked for a copy.[85]

The Crusade for Freedom

As time went on, the council's campaigns became increasingly reflective of the anticommunist sentiments that were permeating American politics. Whereas the campaign to explain the "American Economic System" had maintained a national focus and warned Americans about subversive forces within their own borders, the scope of campaigns in the early 1950s was broadened to include fighting communism overseas. But unlike the earlier campaigns to promote the "American Economic System" and to publicize the Freedom Train, campaign initiatives with a political bent now came not from private business organizations but from the federal government. Washington had reacted to the threat of communism with direct military action against Chinese interests in Korea, but it took a different tack in its attempt to prevent the communist ideology from spreading in Eastern Europe. At the same time, the Advertising Council experienced a substantial increase in requests for campaign material promoting the "American Economic System" from other countries, including Japan, Australia, and New Zealand. One Canadian newspaper was asked by the local Board of Trade to order all the available advertising mats for Canadian adaption and use.[86] This came on the heels of Canada's interest in creating its own Advertising Council, modeled after the American original, and by the early 1950s, American business interests, led by the Ad Council, were entertaining the idea of an "International Advertising Council," with backing from the American Advertising Council and U.S. advertising groups.[87]

In 1948, at the request of the U.S. State Department's Office of International Information, the Advertising Council designed a major overseas information campaign to educate the people of Western Europe about the Marshall Plan and correct their "misconceptions about the United States." American-made products were highly regarded in Europe, and the State Department thought that international ads for those products might be the perfect medium for "selling" the American system itself. Detailed campaign guides were sent to key officials at all American companies involved in overseas advertising and to agencies that handled export accounts. Designed to complement the Voice of America, a broadcasting system created by the State Department to combat communism in Europe and, later, Asia, the ad campaign followed the practice of the "American Economic System" campaign in not directly discussing economic issues. The hope was that the ads themselves would convey "Americans' love of individual liberty," and how this liberty helped create "individual opportunities and competitive ingenuity leading to high production and living standards."[88] Whereas other council projects came with specific directives, sponsors of this particular campaign were merely given a detailed outline of information to be incorporated into advertising messages and asked to adapt it to local conditions. They were warned, however, that boastful or poorly worded copy might give communist sympathizers a chance to twist things in a way that would reflect poorly on the United States. As part of the effort, a campaign guide called *Advertising: A New Weapon in the World-Wide Fight for Freedom*, prepared by Foote, Cone and Belding, International, was mailed to all businesses that advertised in foreign countries and to all agencies that handled foreign advertising accounts.[89]

Such efforts, however, could do only so much to fight what seemed like a growing communist menace, and in early 1950, when the members of the Advertising Council met with top government officials at their annual confidential White House conference, Secretary of State Dean Acheson announced an all-out effort to win the ideological battle over communism. "Unless we as a people recognize the realities of Total Diplomacy just as we realized those of Total War, our future is indeed grim," he said. It did not mean that the U.S. would be taken over in the next year or even the next decade, but some parts of the world would not be so fortunate.[90]

Within weeks, Senator William Benton (D-CT) took to the floor of Congress, calling for "the establishment of a non-governmental agency to help, inspire, and guide the efforts of millions of private American citizens who might use their talents, resources, and contacts overseas in furtherance of the program." After outlining a detailed plan to bring "facts about the U.S." directly to Europeans, Secretary Acheson wasted little time in asking the Advertising Council to take on the task. While acknowledging that advertising had shortcomings when it came to communicating complex ideas, and that some foreign governments might object to the rather unorthodox approach to goodwill building, Acheson was eager to get the plan moving, especially because he suspected that the strategy might be upsetting the Kremlin.[91] Unlike most requests for council assistance, this campaign dealt with national policy as set by acts of Congress and required a three-quarters majority from its Public Policy board, a vote that was quickly secured.[92]

Aimed at "winning the 'cold war' against the Kremlin," the council's "Crusade for Freedom" was launched in August 1951 with the slogan "Help Truth Fight Communism—Join the Crusade for Freedom" as its slogan (see fig. 23). Its planning phase coincided with the release of *Red Channels*, a pamphlet by the right-wing journal *Counterattack* that listed 151 broadcasting entertainers, writers, and producers who were suspected of being communists or communist sympathizers. Similar accusations had been launched against the film industry since 1946, but this was a crusade aimed directly at the television industry during a time when American anticommunist hysteria was reaching fever pitch. Thus it was probably no coincidence that in addition to the more than 100 national advertisers who incorporated the Crusade for Freedom into their display copy and in-house magazines, some 107 television stations and all 4 radio networks welcomed the Ad Council's campaign kits and enthusiastically promoted the project.[93] This was followed by *Here's How You Can Help Truth Fight Communism*, a booklet prepared by Hewitt, Ogilvy, Benson, and Maher, which explained the campaign, its strategies and goals, to individual advertisers and provided them with sample scripts for radio and television in addition to the more traditional examples of print ads.[94] "Give us this day . . . Our daily *truth*," read one campaign ad addressed to the general public. "This is the whispered prayer of millions behind the iron curtain—'give us our daily truth . . . our daily hope.'" "With your help, a beachhead for freedom has been established in the hearts and minds of captive people. With your continued help, the *cold* war against Communism can be won—and a horrible global *hot* war prevented. . . . Help Truth Fight Communism—Give to the Crusade for Freedom."[95]

Whereas the Ad Council during its first decade of existence had limited its involvement to behavior modification, telling Americans how to think and behave in a patriotic manner, the Crusade for Freedom introduced a more direct approach, actively soliciting funds ($4 million in 1952 alone) for the continuation and expansion of Radio Free Europe, a private counterpart to the State Department's Voice of America. (A Radio Free Asia had been established in 1951.) The council also collected funds and signatures for "Freedom Grams," leaflets touting the superiority of the free enterprise system that were air-dropped behind the Iron Curtain.

Figure 23. "Help Truth Fight Communism." Ca. 1951. This advertisement was prepared by the Advertising Council as part of the "Crusade for Freedom" campaign. It is another example of an "All Out" advertisement, in which the sponsor takes a backseat to the message. Courtesy Ad Council Archives, University of Illinois Archives, RS 13/2/207.

Even a Boy can fight Communism with Truth

Kids on Radio Free Europe Send Hope To Pals Behind Iron Curtain

Twelve-year-old Karel Paces, a young Czech found in a German refugee camp, is broadcasting over Radio Free Europe to his Czech friends behind the Iron Curtain.

He is telling them familiar children's stories in their native tongue—stories now denied them by their Communist masters. These stories have a very real meaning to Karel's friends, a meaning ingrained in the folklore of their country.

Karel Paces is giving his friends, the boys and girls of his beloved Czechoslovakia, the truth of their own country and the free world. It is this truth which every American must support now so

that it can be used to fight the deceit, darkness and despair which Communist tyranny is spreading through the satellite countries of Europe.

Day and night, Radio Free Europe is exposing Communist lies and propaganda, and sustaining the hope of oppressed millions that some day they will live in a better world.

At least $4,000,000 is needed this year to support and expand the operations of Radio Free Europe and Radio Free Asia. In addition, the Crusade for Freedom is seeking the signatures of Americans, on Freedom-Grams. These will be your personal pledges of hope for a free world.

This Crusade cannot succeed without your help. Your contribution is needed *now* to help support Radio Free Europe and Radio Free Asia . . . to help fight red lies with truth and to win the cold war.

Support this truth campaign now and help bring to millions the promise of future freedom.

Send your contribution to
Crusade for Freedom,
c/o your local Postmaster

Help Truth Fight Communism
Give To Crusade For Freedom

 Contributed in the public interest by

SPONSOR'S NAME

Figure 24. "Even a Boy can fight Communism with Truth." 1952. This ad was part of the Advertising Council's "Crusade for Freedom" campaign. Courtesy Ad Council Archives, University of Illinois Archives, RS 13/2/207.

The White House continued to blur the traditional distinction between government politics and commercial policy. Just as Washington officials confided in the Advertising Council and used its communication channels to further the government's political aims, so the council began to dabble in politics, arranging "Round Table Discussions" on issues such as "Basic Elements of a Free, Dynamic Society," "Our Concepts of Political and Civil Liberties," and "The Moral and Religious Basis of the American Society."[96]

The cooperation between the Advertising Council and the federal government continued into Dwight Eisenhower's presidency and beyond, maintaining a fine balance between promoting advertising as a public servant and preserving a bipartisan (albeit never nonpolitical) agenda. Much to the business community's delight, Eisenhower had great faith that advertising could solve the nation's problems. In addition to "washing machines, soap, and services," he reflected in 1948, advertising was also needed to "promote an understanding of what made these products possible, what is necessary for a free market, and what our free market means to the individual liberty."[97] Council campaigns throughout the Eisenhower presidency continued to reflect these ideals.[98]

Conclusion

Thanks to the Advertising Council's relentless work and political maneuverings, Madison Avenue had arrived in Washington, and it enjoyed a good working relationship with the government. The advertising industry had made an impressive move out of the line of fire in which it had found itself a decade or so earlier. In 1941, right before the Japanese attack on Pearl Harbor, one optimistic industry observer had envisioned a day when government reliance on the promotional industries' time and talent would overcome advertisers' fear of federal interference and allow "Mr. Advertising himself" to walk "jauntily down the Main Street, publicly recognized as a tried and true defender of the American Way."[99] That had proved to be an accurate prediction.

The difference between the stature of the advertising industry in the late 1930s and in the early 1950s was almost night and day. Thanks to the Advertising Council's relentless work and political maneuverings, the days of the TNEC hearings and prewar regulatory worries were all in the rearview mirror. Having positioned itself as a patriotic institution able to sell war and peace, advertising was now comfortably established as an essential and noncontroversial component of American society. This would become even more evident as the nation transitioned into the postwar "Consumers' Republic."[100]

Although scholars have acknowledged the importance of advertising and its broad acceptance among policymakers and the general public in the post–World War II era, only limited attention has been paid to the events that facilitated this development.[1] The goal of this book has been to explore the political processes and maneuvers that, in the span of only a few years, helped change advertising's image, transforming it from a scorned industry with a tendency toward monopoly building—and thus a damper on the free enterprise system—into a necessary institution for the protection and promotion of political and economic freedom.

The key factor in this transformation was the (War) Advertising Council's tireless work on behalf of the advertising community. Displaying an excellent sense of timing and direction, the WAC coached, chastised, and cajoled individual advertisers, pleading for their compliance in what it believed to be a fantastic public relations opportunity. During 1,307 days of war, advertisers, under the Ad Council's direction, encouraged Americans to spend more than $800 million on war bonds and to plant some 50 million victory gardens. In addition to raising several million dollars for the Red Cross and National War Fund drives, they helped fight inflation, recruit military personnel, spread information about a wide variety of salvage campaigns, and enlist workers for industrial war plants. At the war's end, the council had been involved in more than 150 different home-front campaigns and had by its own estimate contributed more than $1 billion in time, space, and talent to the war effort.[2] The war experience had shown that just as advertisers were capable of dispensing advice on cigarettes, body odor, and the keys to social success, they were equally adept at guiding the public through issues of political magnitude.

Directly and indirectly, as a result of the council's efforts, the advertising industry had fought back against regulation and taxation and raised its stature among policymakers and the public at large.[3] By the end of the war, advertising was firmly entrenched as an integral component of U.S. democracy and the American way of life. Advertising itself had not changed: its methods were the same, and the weaknesses critics dwelled upon had not disappeared; indeed, it could be argued that they were magnified as advertising blossomed in the postwar era. The change was in how advertising was perceived—by the public, by policymakers, and even by consumer activists.

When the Cold War heated up in the late 1940s, the Ad Council again wrapped its activities and motives in the rhetoric of citizenship, democracy, and patriotism. It moved seamlessly from one war to another, this time to the seemingly permanent war for national survival, while emphasizing the positive aspects of consumer capitalism along with vague and uncontroversial liberal values and a disdain for communism. The council had used its wartime campaigns to ask people to plant vegetables and purchase war bonds to show their patriotism, and its postwar campaigns redefined the meaning of that noble sentiment. Patriotism was now pegged to the unconditional acceptance of free enterprise, which some termed *People's Capitalism*.[4]

Unlike the 1930s, when business and Congress often had conflicting agendas, the postwar era brought the two institutions into closer alignment. The Advertising Council added a Public Policy Committee after the war to lessen any perception that it was motivated by ideology, but there is no denying that the increasingly conservative policies of the Truman administration closely matched those of the council and the campaign partners it selected from the business community. As sociologist C. Wright Mills observed at the time, the newly achieved consensus between government and business interests reflected a troubling trend. The war had blurred the boundaries between the military and the economic and political worlds, and a new *Power Elite* had come to view the government as an umbrella under which they could operate with impunity.[5]

Whether the council's wartime campaigns originated from government or from business, their overarching goal was to portray the American economy as "a uniquely productive system of free enterprise" and the nation itself as "a dynamic, classless, and benignly consensual society."[6] In the 1930s, such campaigns had been the prerogative of conservative business enterprises, most notably the National Association of Manufacturers, but now, in the postwar era, these sentiments were being adapted by the government and conveyed to the American public through product advertising in the commercial mass media. The overall promise, as Charles F. McGovern argues, was that "the postwar world would be brought to Americans by corporate largesse, typified by American values of freedom and enterprise, and ratified by the American equation of market and democracy."[7]

"For the first time in a generation," concluded a writer for *Advertising Age* in 1948, "Washington seems to be getting back to Business as Usual."[8] There was concrete evidence to support this assertion. In 1951, the Twentieth Century Fund released a monumental survey showing that *imperfect competition*—a term used by economists to describe markets with monopolistic tendencies—still plagued the American economy and that brand-name advertising was still part of the problem. This should not come as a real surprise, because advertisers' ability to preserve their brand names for the war's duration had enabled oligopolies to weather the war and emerge from it in remarkably good shape. In contrast to the 1930s, however, when the Twentieth Century Fund's work on these issues had aided the Temporary National Economic Committee's investigations, the postwar report warranted no calls for heavier enforcement of antitrust laws in government circles.[9] And whereas there had been numerous attempts to limit the economic advantages of advertising during the period of national defense in the early 1940s, the postwar economic climate was far less conducive to such proposals. Responding to growing concerns over inflation in 1951, the Congressional Joint Committee on the Economic Report tested the waters by suggesting that advertising be taxed as a means of bringing the situation under control. The proposal was met with weak support at best from the committee's bipartisan members, who quickly backed away from the idea. Consequently, the plan never even made it to Congress.[10]

The improved postwar relationship between Washington and the advertising industry is relatively easy to document, but assessing the extent to which the war experience had changed the average American's perception of advertising is more of a challenge. The historian Robert Griffith cautions us not to assume that there was a simple cause-and-effect relationship between the Ad Council's efforts and the seemingly high level of cultural consensus in the 1950s. But he also advises that we not underestimate the "repetitious, pervasive and unchallenged" messages that surrounded Americans "with an omnipresent if distorted reflection of their society and thus help[ed] shape, to a degree no less real for being difficult to measure, the political culture of postwar America."[11] What is certain is that the push for federal regulation of advertising, which had gained considerable traction before the war and had ignited a large consumer movement in the 1930s, had lost its appeal for the American public.

In a survey conducted in 1951, nearly 70 percent of three thousand respondents drawn from a cross-section of socioeconomic backgrounds expressed a high level of confidence in advertising and believed that advertised products were more likely to be of good quality than unadvertised products; a full 80 percent thought that advertising played an important part in lowering prices and improving the quality of goods.[12] Nearly four out of five believed that the continued use of advertising during the war, when products were in short supply, had helped to create postwar jobs. A little over 76 percent viewed advertising as helping to "make our lives happier, more comfortable," while nearly 90 percent regarded it as educational.[13]

Between 1946 and 1950, advertising played an instrumental role in convincing American consumers that they needed to buy 21.4 million automobiles, more than 20 million refrigerators, 5.5 million electric stoves, and 11.6 million television sets.[14] Billions of dollars were spent on household appliances and furnishings. Between 1940 and 1950, the proportion of families who owned a mechanical refrigerator rose from 44 to 80 percent, a dramatic increase that would soon be replicated with the sale of television sets.[15] Advertising volume rose in tandem. In spite of a reduction in consumer products for the domestic market, advertising expenditures had increased by 17 percent between 1942 and 1943. By 1945, $2.875 billion, or 1.4 percent of the gross national product, was spent on advertising; ten years later, that number had more than tripled to $9.194 billion, or 2.3 percent of GNP.[16] Postwar planning and telling consumers what they could buy for their war bonds savings once the war had ended had been an early preoccupation with advertisers, starting as early as in the summer of 1942 and continuing throughout the war.[17] Still, and as consumer advocates were quick to point out once the war was over, manufacturers did not come close to delivering on their wartime pledge to use their war-related technologies to bring "new and improved" products to market. Although consumers were probably not overly disappointed that private helicopters had not replaced the family car, as some manufacturers had promised, they had reason to be upset when postwar durables turned out to be "postwar" in production date only. During the first years of reconversion, the "world of tomorrow" that had been promised in many wartime ads, with its abundance of consumer products derived from war-related scientific discoveries, was not reflected in the marketplace. In fact, argues art historian Cynthia Lee Henthorn, the only product introduced in 1946 whose technology had been developed as a result of the war and that was thus properly a "postwar product" was the ballpoint pen. The designs and materials used in most advertised postwar products were still of prewar quality and style, a point that Consumers Union, the advertising industry's old arch-enemy, was quick to publicize.[18]

In 1945, with the goal of continuing its prewar activities, CU established an office in Washington to monitor the many important reconversion battles, especially the continuing fight over price control legislation.[19] Much like the Advertising Council, which also established a formal presence in Washington around this time, CU believed that having this office would make it easier to work with labor and liberal groups and would simplify the task of keeping an eye on federal agencies that had jurisdiction over consumer issues. A Washington office was also important for furnishing material to *Bread and Butter* (which subsequently folded in 1947) and provided ample opportunity for information from CU's two publications to be read into the *Congressional Record*.[20]

The organization had high hopes for the future. For the 1946–47 fiscal year, it budgeted $15,000 to study consumer-related issues, including grade labeling and standardization, housing, postwar living costs, taxes, and health insurance. It also planned to bring the TNEC antimonopoly material up-to-date and to publish those findings both in special pamphlets and as articles in *Consumer Reports* and *Bread and Butter*. Further, it envisioned itself making a political comeback, using said findings in testimony before congressional committees and in helping to help draft congressional bills. CU's ambition was clearly to become "the intellectual leader and spokesman for the consumer movement and large sections of the public."[21]

As the 1940s drew to a close, however, key individuals in the organization were becoming less comfortable with its activist role. They wanted it to become an independent, non-membership-based, nonpolitical enterprise whose sole purpose would be to test products and make the results available to the consuming public. Only after a vote by the board of directors did President Warne's vision of CU as a "democratically-controlled, pro-labor" membership organization prevail.[22]

However, the biggest challenge to postwar consumer activism did not come from within. The 1930s had ended with a right-wing crusade to destroy the consumer movement. That effort, which labeled consumer leaders as communists and their messages as subversive, was backed by only a small minority of Americans, but it received a great deal of attention because of

Figure 25. "Serving the Armed Forces." Unlike manufacturers with unrealistic postwar promises, Emerson Electric was far more modest in claiming how wartime technology would benefit the postwar consumer market. *Saturday Evening Post*, February 27, 1943, 57.

its well-connected supporters. The National Association of Manufacturers and the Advertising Federation of America, which arguably was the most conservative of the advertising organizations, encouraged the accusations, and the idea of a communist-inspired consumer movement found a ready audience in sympathetic journalists, certain political leaders, and newspaper chain owner William Randolph Hearst Jr. The Dies Committee (which became the House Un-American Activities Committee in 1946) eventually cleared consumer leaders of their alleged transgressions, but there is no denying that the event had scarred the movement.[23]

The witch hunt against the consumer movement slowed during the war, but some, including the Pacific Advertising Club, did their best to keep it alive.[24] CU downplayed this effort, considering it far less of a threat than the 1930s attacks, but the organization became increasingly worried when a congressional fact-finding committee in California claimed to have proof that several of the major consumer groups had been infiltrated by communists and were serving as "Stalin's agents" and "transmission belts" for the cause.[25] The elimination of advertising, according to the report, was part of a larger communist plot "to undermine and destroy the capitalist system of free-enterprise." A subsequent investigation by the Advertising Club of Los Angeles in collaboration with the Pacific Advertising Club supported the claim, warning, much as red-baiters had done a few years earlier, that there had been "an amazing spread of Communist propaganda" in certain "consumer books." It called the attention of libraries and teachers' organizations to consumer classics such as *100,000,000 Guinea Pigs*; *Skin Deep*; *Counterfeit*; *Eat, Drink and Be Wary*; and *Guinea Pigs No More*, which it said "wittingly or unwittingly" contained subversive information.[26]

The allegations did not stick at first, but as the anticommunist zeal peaked in the early 1950s, Consumers Union was again tagged as suspect. At the same time that the Advertising Council was working closely with the Truman administration on the Crusade for Freedom campaign, which had advertisers across the nation asking consumers to "Help Truth Fight Communism," CU was in Washington fighting for its political survival. This was a stark contrast to the power balance that had existed during the TNEC hearings at the height of the New Deal. Back in the late 1930s, the advertising industry had been on the hot seat, with members of the consumer movement testifying about the less desirable aspects of advertising. A little more than a decade and a war later, it was CU that was now forced to defend itself before Congress.

The anticommunist crusade was at its high-water mark in March 1951 when the House Un-American Activities Committee released its *Guide to*

Subversive Organizations and Publications, listing Consumers Union among the suspected communist organizations. CU was subsequently flooded with urgent letters from individuals, many wanting to cancel their subscriptions to *Consumer Reports*.[27] Several school districts, including the public school system in Cincinnati, Ohio, wrote to say that they had decided to stop using the publication in the classroom. The risk of being investigated by the House Un-American Activities Committee, said the Cincinnati school superintendent, far exceeded the value of keeping *Consumer Reports* as library reference material.[28] Not all of the magazine's subscribers crumbled under the pressure, however. The Detroit public school system formed a special committee to assess the publication's subversive nature, but it found little about which to be concerned and decided to maintain its subscription.[29] Additional support came from a wide range of organizations and individuals, including college professors and even leaders of the National Better Business Bureau. The latter angered some of their local chapters by vouching for CU as an organization with "a deep basic loyalty to what may roughly be called 'the American system.'"[30]

Still, the task of defending itself against a number of highly unfavorable political allegations was a drain on the organization's time, money, and human resources.[31] Convinced that the same forces that had tried to destroy the organization in the 1930s were at work again, CU was profoundly concerned about its future and worried that the right-wing accusations would gain more public traction in the postwar political climate. Fearing that the organization's work was in jeopardy, the board of directors responded with a public statement that rejected communism "and all other forms of totalitarianism" and declared a strong commitment to "the free enterprise system." The consumer organization was at a loss to understand why there might be confusion about its political loyalties. "So deeply is the philosophy of Consumers Union based on the free market, the competition of products, and the free choice of the consumer who wants to buy the best for his money—all mechanisms which are essential to the free enterprise system—that it is utterly obvious to us (and, we feel sure, to our readers who have been with us for any length of time) where we fit into the scheme," it stated. "Freedom of enterprise includes freedom of scientific research, freedom for citizens to form voluntary groups for the pursuit of common purposes, and freedom of communication." In fact, argued CU, its existence was conceivable only in a free enterprise society where the production of goods and services was "guided by the free choice of consumers." The success of its efforts would depend "fundamentally upon high-level national income, upon the existence of a broad variety of national brands, and upon the maintenance of a competitive marketplace in which the consumer can exercise complete freedom of choice."[32]

So desperate was CU to rid itself of the communist allegations that its research director, Arthur Kallet, trumpeted the fact that the Distributive, Processing and Office Workers Union of America (a group that had been expelled from the CIO because of communist activities) had accused the organization of discrimination. Additional proof of CU's patriotic credentials, according to Kallet, was that it had been attacked by the communist newspaper the *Daily Worker* for labor discrimination against African Americans and Jews.[33] The organization also tried to dissociate itself from the notion that its only purpose was to solve the "buying problems" of the poor and the working class. To the contrary, said CU, it was middle- and high-income families, those who were interested in purchasing consumer durable goods such as automobiles and freezers, who constituted the main readership of *Consumer Reports*.

In order to maintain its expanding rating service, CU employed a full-time staff of about 130. The organization occupied eight floors in two buildings in New York City, with total floor space of about fifty thousand square feet. Its annual payroll was more than $500,000, and its gross annual income from subscriptions and the sale of its publications exceeded $2.5 million. It was soundly and conservatively financed and was becoming widely respected, both in industry and in technical circles, for the integrity and the quality of its work.[34]

The charges against CU tapered off after the Army-McCarthy Hearings in 1954 and the fall from grace that same year of Senator Joseph McCarthy (R-WI). The anticommunist fervor continued for years, but CU was no longer in the spotlight. In 1954, after thirteen years of red-baiting, the organization was finally cleared of the suspicion of communism, but the experience had taken its toll. While CU eventually strengthened its educational program and became involved with other consumer education associations, most consumers in the 1950s and 1960s equated it with *Consumer Reports* and the helpful navigation it offered through the profusion of products that characterized American postwar affluence.[35]

As a result of the postwar increase in consumption, CU experienced an extraordinary spike in interest in its rating services. In July 1949, *Consumer Reports* had 250,000 subscribers; three years later, that number had risen to 550,000, and by May 1953, some 700,000 people were receiving the magazine every month.[36] As impressive as those numbers were, however, they were more reflective of people's interest in making good choices among the many brands that were gradually being released for purchase than they were of a renewed interest in the kind of consumer activism that had been so important to CU supporters in the past, and that had been the core reason for the group's formation in the 1930s. During the early postwar era, CU had every intention of resuming the political work that had been interrupted by the war. After a few years of struggle and a series of unanticipated events, however, the organization came to accept its new role in helping to develop a consumer society built on capitalist values.

Despite CU's ability to land on its feet, there is no doubt that the winner in all of this was the advertising industry. As postwar consumerism peaked, the industry was riding high. Its prewar problems were now well behind it, and the two institutions responsible for keeping the business community's feet to the fire were now firmly in its camp. Thanks to the Ad Council's ongoing public relations work, the advertising industry was now a political ally and confidant to the government, conferring with high federal officials and helping Washington in the shared fight for "free enterprise" and a global capitalist economy. At the same time that right-wing forces had effectively squelched most forms of radical consumer activism, consumers' postwar preoccupation with consumption had aided the transformation of CU into a highly effective testing outfit and an integral component of the postwar consumer-spending ethos.

This is not to claim that nobody took advertising to task after World War II. The postwar decades were rife with satire on the asininity of advertising, but the nature of the criticism had changed. The sociologist David Riesman received plenty of attention for his views on the corrupting influences of material abundance, and Vance Packard caused a stir with *The Hidden Persuaders* and other exposés of advertising methods, but no demand for advertising laws and regulations emerged as a result. Nor did works by C. Wright Mills, David Potter, or John Kenneth Galbraith, or more subtle forms of criticism expressed through popular culture, trigger a public debate about how to impose structural restrictions on commercial forces.[37] While postwar advertising could be lampooned—through films such as *The Hucksters* and publications like *Mad Magazine*—and advertising practices could be criticized, the institution itself was now fundamentally off-limits for debate.

The same reluctance to deal with advertising on a structural level was reflected in other contexts. As Victor Pickard discusses in his work on postwar radio, the complaints, ridicule, and anger that were directed against radio commercials served primarily as an outlet for people to vent their unhappiness over excessive commercialization and helped, along with the merciless red-baiting of radio reformers, to divert attention from the real structural changes that could have made the medium more democratic. It is also worth noting that the new medium of television faced no challenges to its purely commercial format, a development that clearly worked against efforts to make radio less commercial, especially when the two media were controlled by the same corporate interests.[38]

The key point is that the kind of criticism to which commercial messages had been so routinely subjected in the 1930s and early 1940s had been pushed to the far margins of acceptable commentary. It seemed implausible that there could be a good society without advertising as people had come to know it. Nevertheless, the absence of organized public opposition to the advertising industry's conduct in the war and postwar years should not be interpreted as absolute support. Scholars warn that most histories of postwar America fail to account for the psychological complexity of the period, including the vitality and variety of subordinate cultures. "If consensus did indeed characterize America's national culture in the 1950s," Robert Griffith remarks, "it was perhaps to a degree we have not fully appreciated, a consensus manufactured by America's corporate leaders, packaged by the advertising industry, and merchandised through the channels of mass communication.[39] The future would bring new challenges, but as a pillar in the shiny new "Consumers' Republic," the advertising industry could bravely face them with unprecedented security and self-assurance.

The evidence in this book, and its predecessor, *Advertising on Trial*, demonstrates that advertising's role in our culture is not the result of careful public debates, and informed consent does not provide the basis for the industry's existence or prominence. Our commercial landscape is the result of a series of well-designed public relations strategies, and advertising's position has been maintained through a constant massaging of public opinion. The fact that advertising could indeed be re-regulated or even significantly reformed is rarely presented to the American public as an option—not because it would be an unpopular or inappropriate subject for consideration, but because the industry and the advertising-supported media, institutions, and politicians who benefit from the status quo are loath to raise the subject.

Also working in the industry's favor has been an ongoing effort to shift responsibility for advertising-related policies from Congress to regulatory agencies and the court system. Whereas in 1942 the U.S. Supreme Court was adamant in its ruling in *Valentine v. Chrestensen* that commercial speech was not protected under the First Amendment, lower courts in the 1970s opened the door for a reversal.[40] By 2010, the Court had changed its position, ruling in *Citizens United v. Federal Election Commission* that limiting corporate "speech" would indeed be a First Amendment violation.[41] This decision, which will have immense political, economic, and social ramifications, was reached without any of the congressional debate or public "interference" that the advertising industry had found so troubling in the 1930s and 1940s.

The point of this research is not to dwell on battles long lost, but to use past events to understand our present situation. It is through an appreciation of the social, economic, and political forces that have established advertising as a seemingly inviolable American institution that we can gain the necessary guidance for a new public debate on what has become, for better or for worse, a defining aspect of America. Our objective should be to arrive at a democratic solution, triumphing over Madison Avenue and its advertising slogans.

Notes

Abbreviations

ACA	Advertising Council Archives, University of Illinois Archives, Urbana
BBP	Bruce Barton Papers, 1881–1967, Mass Communications History Collections, Wisconsin Historical Society Archives, Madison
CBC	National Archives, Textual Archives Services Division—Archives II, College Park, Md., Record Group 208, Records of the Office of War Information, Entry 39, Records of the Office of War Programs, Records of the Chief, Bureau of Campaigns, August 1942–January 1943
CEWP	Colston E. Warne Papers, Consumers Union Archives, Yonkers, N.Y.
CUA	Consumers Union Archives, Yonkers, N.Y.
CWJF	Files of Charles W. Jackson, Harry S. Truman Papers, Harry S. Truman Library, Independence, Mo.
DCBC	National Archives, Textual Archives Services Division—Archives II, College Park, Md., Record Group 208, Records of the Office of War Information, Entry 40, Records of the Deputy Chief, Bureau of Campaigns, September 1941–February 1943
DMR	UAW Washington Office Legislative Department: Donald Montgomery Records, Walter Reuther Library, Wayne State University, Detroit, Mich.
FDR OF	The President's Official Files, Franklin D. Roosevelt Library, Hyde Park, N.Y.
FDR PPF	The President's Personal Files, Franklin D. Roosevelt Library, Hyde Park, N.Y.
GLR	National Archives, Textual Archives Services Division—Archives II, College Park, Md., Record Group 208, Records of the Office of War

Information, Entry 94, Records of the Radio Bureau, Records of the Chief, George Ludlam

HLR National Archives, Textual Archives Services Division—Archives II, College Park, Md., Record Group 208, Records of the Office of War Information, Entry 82, Records of the Deputy Director for Labor and Civilian Welfare, General Records of Deputy Director Herbert Little, October 1943–December 1944

HSTP Harry S. Truman Papers, Harry S. Truman Library, Independence, Mo.

JKGP John Kenneth Galbraith Papers, 1930–1989, John F. Kennedy Presidential Library and Museum, Harvard University, Cambridge, Mass.

JLFP James Lawrence Fly Papers, Rare Books and Manuscripts Room, Butler Library, Columbia University, New York, Box 49

JLVC Jerry Livingston Voorhis Collection, Special Collections, Honnold Mudd Library, Claremont University Consortium, Claremont, Calif.

JRWL National Archives, Textual Archives Services Division—Archives II, College Park, Md., Record Group 208, Records of the Office of War Information, Entry 28, Records of the Domestic Operations Branch, 1926–46, Records of the Office of the Director, General Records of Assistant Director James Rogers and William Lewis

JWGP John W. Gibson Papers, Harry S. Truman Library, Independence, Mo.

NA2 National Archives, Textual Archives Services Division—Archives II, College Park, Md.

NBCP National Broadcasting Corporation Papers, Wisconsin Center for Historical Research, State Historical Society of Wisconsin, Madison

NDR National Archives, Textual Archives Services Division—Archives II, College Park, Md., Record Group 208, Records of the Office of War Information, Entry 84, Records of the Deputy Director for Labor and Civilian Welfare, Records of Natalie Davisen, Program Manager for Homefront Campaigns, July 1943–August 1945

ODR National Archives, Textual Archives Services Division—Archives II, College Park, Md., Record Group 208, Records of the Office of War Information, Entry 28, Records of the Domestic Operations Branch, 1926–46, Records of the Office of the Director

OPC National Archives, Textual Archives Services Division—Archives II, Suitland, Md., Record Group 208, Records of the Office of War Information, Entry 42, General Records of the Office of Program Coordination, July 1943–May 1944

OWI AD National Archives, Textual Archives Services Division—Archives II, Suitland, Md., Record Group 208, Records of the Office of War Information, Records of the Office of Facts and Figures, Records of the Advertising Division, 1942–43

POP   Peter Odegard Papers, Franklin D. Roosevelt Library, Hyde Park, N.Y.

RG   Record Group

RG 208   Record Group 208, Records of the Office of War Information

TCCP   Papers of Tom C. Clark, Harry S. Truman Papers, Harry S. Truman
             Library, Independence, Mo.

TDBP   Thomas D'Arcy Brophy Papers, Wisconsin Center for Historical Re-
             search, State Historical Society of Wisconsin, Madison

TNEC   National Archives, Textual Archives Services Division—Archives II,
             College Park, Md., Record Group 144, Records of the Temporary Na-
             tional Economic Committee, Department of the Treasury

TWAC   Thurman W. Arnold Collection, American Heritage Center, University
             of Wyoming Library, Laramie

UD5, Box 2   National Archives, Textual Archives Services Division—Archives II,
             College Park, Md., Record Group 122, Records of the Federal Trade
             Commission, Entry UD5, Division of Legal and Public Records: Press
             Clippings, Notices & Releases, 1918–1959, Box 2, bound volume labeled
             "Federal Trade Commission Library, Advertising: 1939–42"

UD5, Box 3   National Archives, Textual Archives Services Division—Archives II,
             College Park, Md., Record Group 122, Records of the Federal Trade
             Commission, Entry UD5, Division of Legal and Public Records: Press
             Clippings, Notices & Releases, 1918–1959, Box 3, ring-bound volume
             labeled "Federal Trade Commission Library, Advertising: 1943–"

Introduction

1. Charles F. McGovern, *Sold American: Consumption and Citizenship, 1890–1945*
(Chapel Hill: University of North Carolina Press, 2006); Inger L. Stole, *Advertising on
Trial: Consumer Activism and Corporate Public Relations in the 1930s* (Urbana: Uni-
versity of Illinois Press, 2006); Lizabeth Cohen, *A Consumers' Republic: The Politics
of Mass Consumption in Postwar America* (New York: Vintage Press, 2003); Lawrence
B. Glickman, "The Strike in the Temple of Consumption: Consumer Activism and
Twentieth-Century American Political Culture," *Journal of American History* 88, no.
1 (June 2001): 99–128; Glickman, *Buying Power: A History of Consumer Activism in
America* (Berkeley: University of California Press, 2009); Kathy M. Newman, *Radio
Active: Advertising and Consumer Activism, 1935–1947* (Berkeley: University of Cali-
fornia Press, 2004).

2. Notable exceptions are Blake Clark's account of the Advertising Council in *The
Advertising Smokescreen* (New York: Harper and Brothers, 1943); Frank W. Fox, *Madi-
son Avenue Goes to War: The Strange Military Career of American Advertising, 1941–45*
(Provo, Utah: Brigham Young University Press, 1975); and Mark Leff's seminal article
"The Politics of Sacrifice on the American Home Front in World War II," *Journal of
American History* 77, no. 4 (March 1991): 1296–1318. Adding to the small body of re-

search is art historian Cynthia Lee Henthorn's *From Submarines to Suburbs: Selling a Better America, 1939–1959* (Athens: Ohio University Press, 2006).

3. Fox, *Madison Avenue Goes to War*, chap. 5. For an excellent analysis of actual wartime ads, see Henthorn, *From Submarines to Suburbs*. For a discussion of women's images in war advertising, see Tawnya J. Adkins Covert, *Manipulating Images: World War II Mobilization of Women through Magazine Advertising* (Lanham, Md.: Lexington Books, 2011); Mei-Ling Yang, "Selling Patriotism: The Representation of Women in Magazine Advertising in World War II," *American Journalism* 17, no. 3 (Summer 1995): 304–20; Maureen Honey, *Creating Rosie the Riveter: Class, Gender, and Propaganda during World War II* (Amherst: University of Massachusetts Press, 1984).

4. For a discussion of war-theme advertising in magazines and radio, respectively, see Honey, *Creating Rosie the Riveter*, and Gerd Horten, *Radio Goes to War: The Culture of Propaganda during World War II* (Berkeley: University of California Press, 2002). The use of war-theme advertising in newspapers is discussed in George H. Roeder Jr., *The Censored War: American Visual Experience during World War Two* (New Haven, Conn.: Yale University Press, 1993). Unlike magazines, radio, and newspapers, the World War II movie industry had no direct link to the advertising industry; but as a regulated industry, Hollywood cooperated closely with the Office of War Information and its Motion Picture Bureau in the Domestic Branch. See, for example, Clayton R. Koppes and Gregory D. Black, *Hollywood Goes to War: How Politics, Profits and Propaganda Shaped World War II Movies* (Berkeley: University of California Press, 1987).

5. Richard S. Tedlow, "From Competitor to Consumer: The Changing Focus of Federal Regulation of Advertising," *Business History Review* 55, no. 1 (Spring 1981): 35–58; Daniel Pope, *The Making of Modern Advertising* (New York: Basic Books, 1983), 23. For a discussion of business expenditures on advertising between 1880 and 1942, see Martha L. Olney, *Buy Now, Pay Later: Advertising, Credit, and Consumer Durables in the 1920s* (Chapel Hill: University of North Carolina Press, 1991), chap. 5.

6. John Bellamy Foster, Robert W. McChesney, and R. Jamil Jonna, "Monopoly and Competition in 21st Century Capitalism," *Monthly Review* 62, no. 11 (April 2011): 1–39, quotation from 13.

7. For a discussion of advertising's role in creating national markets, see Susan Strasser, *Satisfaction Guaranteed: The Making of the American Mass Market* (New York: Pantheon Books, 1989); Richard S. Tedlow, *New and Improved: The Story of Mass Marketing in America* (New York: Basic Books, 1990); and Pope, *Making of Modern Advertising*, chap. 2.

8. "A New Deal for Business and Government," National Archives, Textual Archives Services Division—Archives II, College Park, Md. (hereafter NA2), Record Group (hereafter RG) 144, Records of the Temporary National Economic Committee, Department of the Treasury (hereafter TNEC), Box 444, Folder: Digest of Clippings, Speeches, etc. on Monopoly.

9. "Summary Volume of the Study of the Concentration of Economic Power," TNEC, Records of the Executive Secretary, Working Papers, Box 1, Folder: Ch 2.

Popular Assumption—The American Way, 32–33. See also Stuart Ewen, *PR! The Social History of Spin* (New York: Basic Books, 1996), chap. 3.

10. "A New Deal for Business and Government." See also William G. Roy, *Socializing Capital: The Rise of the Large Industrial Corporation in America* (Princeton, N.J.: Princeton University Press, 1997); Naomi Lamoreaux, *The Great Merger Movement in American Business, 1895–1904* (Cambridge: Cambridge University Press, 1985); Richard L. McCormick, "The Discovery That Business Corrupts Politics: A Reappraisal of the Origins of Progressivism," *American Historical Review* 86, no. 2 (April 1981): 247–74.

11. Lamoreaux, *Great Merger Movement*, 3.

12. The classic statements remain Thorstein Veblen, *The Engineers and the Price System* (1921; reprint, New York: Viking Press, 1938); and Veblen, *Absentee Ownership and Business Enterprise in Recent Times: The Case of America* (1923; reprint, New York: Viking Press, 1954). See also Paul A. Baran and Paul M. Sweezy, *Monopoly Capital: An Essay on the American Economic and Social Order* (New York: Monthly Review Press, 1966); and Merle Curti, "The Changing Concept of Human Nature in the Literature of American Advertising," *Business History Review* 41, no. 4 (Winter 1967): 334–57.

13. Stole, *Advertising on Trial*, 2.

14. Consumers' Research started out as a fairly radical enterprise but became increasingly conservative (even reactionary) in its politics after the split with Consumers Union in 1936. Thus the 1941 version of Consumers Research did not have a liberal bias but took its product testing quite seriously. For more information, see Stole, *Advertising on Trial*.

15. "Memorandum for Mr. Arnold, re: Identification Tests on Branded Cigarettes," July 7, 1941, Thurman W. Arnold Collection, American Heritage Center, University of Wyoming Library, Laramie (hereafter TWAC), Box 60, Folder: Legal Case File, 1941, American Tobacco Company et al. (2 of 2 folders).

16. John Kenneth Galbraith, *American Capitalism* (Boston: Houghton Mifflin, 1952), 14–15. Qtd. in Foster, McChesney, and Jonna, "Monopoly and Competition," 19.

17. Milton Friedman, *Capitalism and Freedom* (1962; reprint, Chicago: University of Chicago Press, 2002), 119–20. Qtd. in ibid., 13.

18. Ibid., 16.

19. Stuart Chase and F. J. Schlink, *Your Money's Worth: A Study in the Waste of the Consumer's Dollars* (New York: Macmillan, 1931).

20. Robert N. Mayer, *The Consumer Movement: Guardians of the Marketplace* (Boston: Twayne, 1989), 21; Norman Isaac Silber, *Test and Protest: The Influence of Consumers Union* (New York: Holmes and Meier, 1983), 18. See also Edith Ayres, "Private Organizations Working for the Consumer," *Annals of the American Academy of Political and Social Science* 173 (May 1934): 158–65.

21. Otis Pease, *The Responsibilities of American Advertising: Private Control and Public Influence, 1920–1940* (New Haven, Conn.: Yale University Press, 1958); James Harvey Young, *The Medical Messiahs: A Social History of Health Quackery in Twen-*

tieth-Century America (1967; reprint, Princeton, N.J.: Princeton University Press, 1992).

22. Stole, *Advertising on Trial*, chap. 5.

23. Ibid., chap. 6.

24. Ibid.

25. Harold B. Thomas, "The Background and Beginning of the Advertising Council" (n.d.), Advertising Council Archives, University of Illinois Archives, Urbana (hereafter ACA), RG 13/2/203: Special Publications, 1952–2006, Box 13, Folder: Background and Beginning of the Advertising Council (1952), n.p.

26. "By-Laws of the Advertising Council, Inc.," March 4, 1942, ACA, RG 13/2/201: Meeting Minutes, 1942–98, Box 1, Folder: Advertising Council and Council Executive Minutes, March–April 1942. See also "Advertising Roster," *Business Week,* February 21, 1942, 48–49; "Advertising Coordinates for War Effort; Council Representing Industry Set Up," *Commercial and Financial Chronicle,* February 26, 1942, 869; "Advertising Unity," *Newsweek,* February 23, 1942, 44–45. For a treatment of the circumstances that led to the establishment of the Advertising Council and the council's activities during its first year of existence, see "Advertising Council Serves to Coordinate War Activities," *Advertising Age,* December 21, 1942, 24; Thomas, "Background and Beginning."

27. "Advertising Roster"; "Advertising Coordinates for War Effort"; "Advertising Unity"; "Advertising Council Serves to Coordinate War Activities"; Thomas, "Background and Beginning."

28. Morse, *Consumer Movement,* 106.

29. George Gallup, "An Analysis of the Study of Consumer Agitation," February 9, 1940, National Broadcasting Corporation Papers, Wisconsin Center for Historical Research, State Historical Society of Wisconsin, Madison (hereafter NBCP), Box 76, Folder 11.

30. Fox, *Madison Avenue,* chap. 5.

31. C. Wright Mills, *The Power Elite* (New York: Oxford University Press, 1956), chap. 12; Robert Griffith, "The Selling of America: The Advertising Council and American Politics, 1942–1960," *Business History Review* 57, no. 3 (Autumn 1983): 388–412.

32. Cohen, *Consumers' Republic.* I do not claim to be the first scholar to explore the World War II advertising industry. Frank W. Fox and Mark H. Leff have treated the issue in some detail: Fox, *Madison Avenue;* Leff, "Politics of Sacrifice."

33. Griffith, "Selling of America," 388.

34. Stole, *Advertising on Trial,* 195–96.

Chapter 1. Prelude to War

1. See, for example, "Government Anti-Ad Front Widening," *Broadcasting,* August 18, 1941, 9.

2. "A New Deal for Business and Government," TNEC, Box 444, Folder: Digest of Clippings, Speeches, etc. on Monopoly.

3. Foster, McChesney, and Jonna, "Monopoly and Competition," 1–39.

4. "Business Week Reports to Executives on the Background of the 'Anti-Monopoly' Investigation," *Business Week*, December 24, 1938, 23.

5. Robert Goldston, *The Great Depression: The United States in the Thirties* (Greenwich, Conn.: Fawcett, 1968); Maurice W. Lee, *Economic Fluctuations: An Analysis of Business Cycles and Other Economic Fluctuations* (Homewood, Ill.: R. D. Irwin, 1955), 236; James Arthur Estey, *Business Cycles: Their Nature, Cause, and Control* (New York: Prentice-Hall, 1950), 22–23, chart.

6. For an excellent account of Thurman Arnold's involvement with the antimonopoly probe, see Alan Brinkley, *The End of Reform: New Deal Liberalism in Recession and War* (New York: Vintage Books, 1996), 106–22.

7. Thurman Arnold, "What Is Monopoly?" (address delivered at Advertising Federation of America's Luncheon Session, June 15, 1938), TNEC, Box 276, Folder: Postbound Notebook with News Releases, January 16, 1939–February 5, 1941; Thurman W. Arnold, *The Bottlenecks of Business* (1940; reprint, Washington, D.C.: Beard Books, 2000), 11.

8. Arnold, "What Is Monopoly?"

9. "Business Week Reports," 23.

10. National Association of Manufacturers, "Special Newsletter on Temporary National Economic Committee," August 1, 1938, TNEC, Office of the Executive Secretary, Correspondence of the Executive Secretary, Box 57, Folder: National Association of Manufacturers; Temporary National Economic Committee; Legislative History, 1, 2.

11. Ibid., 3.

12. Brinkley, *End of Reform*, 123. Other members included Garland S. Ferguson from the FTC, Donald E. Montgomery from the Agricultural Adjustment Administration, William O. Douglas (later to become Supreme Court justice) and Jerome Frank from the Securities and Exchange Commission, Herman Oliphant (later replaced by Rear Admiral C. J. Peoples) from the Treasury Department, Assistant Secretary Richard Patterson from the Department of Commerce, and Isador Lubin, director of the Bureau of Labor Statistics in the Commerce Department.

13. "A Memorandum on the Problem of Big Business Submitted to the Temporary National Economic Committee by the Corporation Survey Committee of the Twentieth Century Fox," TNEC, Statements and Reports Submitted to the Committee, Box 35, Folder: Twentieth Century Fund.

14. "Outline of Committee Surveys and Inquiries," TNEC, Office of the Executive Secretary, Correspondence of the Executive Secretary, Box 57, Folder: Legislative History.

15. "Statement of Senator Joseph C. O'Mahoney, Wyoming, on Progress of Work of Temporary National Economic Committee," August 19, 1938, TNEC, Box 441, Folder: Progress Reports Monopoly Studies. Even the *Journal of Commerce* characterized the TNEC as a "Moderate Course"; "The Washington Situation," *Journal of Commerce*,

December 14, 1938, TNEC, Box 443, Folder: Monopoly, December 1 to December 31, 1938; Joseph O'Mahoney "to Ted," October 21, 1939, TNEC, Box 429, Folder: Correspondence: Treasury Study on Laws and Restraint of Trade, Monopoly, etc.

16. Richard C. Patterson Jr., Assistant Secretary of Commerce, "An Inventory of Business," address, September 27, 1938, TNEC, Box 444, Folder: Digest of Clippings, Speeches, etc. on Monopoly.

17. "Ugwug, Agwag, and Wiffwaff," *Business Week*, March 18, 1939, 52.

18. "Our TNEC Faculty," TNEC, Box 429, Folder: Correspondence re: Treasury Study on Laws of Restraint of Trade, Monopoly, etc.

19. Memo starting with "Caution: This outline of the testimony of Leon Henderson," n.d., TNEC, Statements and Reports Submitted to the Committee, Box 28, Folder: Leon Henderson, 5.

20. News Release, Department of Justice, July 14, 1938, TWAC, Box 103, Folder: Professional File, 1938–1940, General Antitrust Policies (1 of 2 folders).

21. Ibid.; "Report of Assistant Attorney General Thurman Arnold in Charge of the Antitrust Division," TWAC, , Box 103, Folder: Professional File, 1938–1940, General Antitrust Policies (1 of 2 folders).

22. *Congressional Record: Proceedings and Debates of the 77th Congress, First Session*, Monday, May 19, 1941, vol. 87, no. 93, Senate, 4273–99, AP, Box 104, Folder: Professional File, 1941–1942, General Antitrust Policies, 4287.

23. "Twilight of TNEC," *Time*, April 14, 1941.

24. "Arnold Warns against False Charges," *Advertising and Selling*, January 1942, 28; "Not Anti-Advertising, Montgomery Tells Meeting," *Advertising Age*, March 4, 1940, 26; George Gallup, "An Analysis of the Study of Consumer Agitation," February 9, 1940, NBCP, Box 76, Folder 11.

25. "Concentration of Economic Power That Ought to Be Investigated by the Antitrust Division," May 6, 1941, AP, Box 103, Folder: Professional File, 1941, General Antitrust Policies (2 of 2 folders); Boston Public Library, Temporary National Economic Committee, Online Collections, http://www.bpl.org/online/govdocs/temporary_national_economic_committee.htm (accessed February 1, 2012).

26. Harold Fleming, "Advertising under Pressure; Publishers Denounce Attacks," *Christian Science Monitor*, August 21, n.d., n.p., NA2, RG 122, Records of the Federal Trade Commission, Entry UD5, Division of Legal and Public Records: Press Clippings, Notices, and Releases, 1918–1959, Box 2, Bound Volume labeled "Federal Trade Commission Library, Advertising: 1939–42" (hereafter UD5, Box 2).

27. United States, Temporary National Economic Committee, *Investigation of Concentration of Economic Power: Hearings before the Temporary National Economic Committee, Congress of the United States, Seventy-Sixth Congress, First Session, Pursuant to Public Resolution No. 113 (Seventy-Fifth Congress)*, pt. 8: *Problems of the Consumer, May 10, 11, and 12, 1939* (Washington, D.C.: USGPO, 1939), 3399, 3400, 3401.

28. Ibid., 3402.

29. Ibid., 3403.

30. Ibid., 3406, 3410, 3329–40, 3345–75.

31. "What Consumers Told TNEC," *Business Week*, May 20, 44; "TNEC Digs into Consumer Questions as Mahoney Defends Advertising," *Printers' Ink*, May 18, 1939, 30+.

32. "No Intention to Smear Advertising, FTC Member Says," *Advertising Age*, March 18, 1940, 5. The FTC's final report on advertising as a factor in distribution costs was completed more than four years later. It gave little support to the industry's claims that advertising provided broad social and economic benefits. It concluded that manufacturers of common consumer products such as cooking oils, soaps, cigarettes, cereals, and drugs and medicines spent more on advertising relative to distribution cost than did producers of other items. "Ad Cost Studied," *Business Week*, November 4, 1944, 76.

33. "No Intention to Smear Advertising," 5.

34. "Barton Sees FTC Study as Serious Business Attack," *Advertising Age*, February 19, 1940, 35. Others, including the research director for the Dies Committee, J. B. Matthews, argued along the same lines. See "Not Anti-Advertising." For a discussion of the Dies Committee and its relationship to advertising, see chap. 7.

35. "Advertising's Curb Is Noted by Taft," *Broadcasting*, May 15, 1940, 34. See also "Mr. Taft on Advertising," *Printers' Ink*, May 10, 1940, 81–82.

36. "Arnold Explains Anti-Trust Action," *Baltimore Sun*, October 28, 1940, UD5, Box 2; "Arnold Denies Opposition to Use of Advertising," *Advertising Age*, September 23, 1940, 1. Arnold brought a lot of rigor to his position as assistant attorney general in the Justice Department's Antitrust Division. He was appointed to serve on the TNEC but applied less energy to the latter. See Brinkley, *End of Reform*, chap. 6.

37. "Arnold Explains Anti-Trust Action."

38. "Arnold Denies Suits Are Aimed at Advertising," *Editor and Publisher*, November 2, 1940, 6; "Arnold Warns Priorities May Cut Advertising," *Herald Tribune*, October 8, 1941, UD5, Box 2.

39. "Arnold Denies Opposition," 2.

40. "Advertising Club Hears Arnold Outline Campaign," *Times Herald*, November 6, 1941, UD5, Box 2.

41. "The Sherman Anti-Trust Act and the Newer Problems of Trade Restraint and Competition" (remarks of William L. Ransom, trustee of the Academy of Political Science, former president of the American Bar Association, before the Academy of Political Science, at the Hotel Astor, New York City, November 9, 1938), AP, Box 1057, Folder: Professional File: 1938–1942, General-Federal Trade Commission, 16.

42. "War on Advertising as Monopoly Breeder Is More Than Talk," *Printers' Ink*, August 30, 1940, 9–10; "The Right to Advertise," *Advertising Age*, August 19, 1940, 12; Eugene S. Duffield, "New Dealers May Renew Attack on Advertising during Emergency," *Wall Street Journal*, August 6, 1941, UD5, Box 2; "Mr. Arnold Not Seeking Advertising's Scalp," *Post* (D), October 14, 1941, UD5, Box 2.

43. Thurman Arnold, "Mr. Arnold's Side of the Argument," *Printers' Ink*, October 17,

1941, 13; Thurman Arnold to R. I. Elliot, November 14, 1938, TWAC, Box 59, Folder: Legal Case File: 1938–1941—Advertising, 1.

44. "Right to Advertise."

45. "Is Mr. Arnold Kidding Us?," *Advertising Age*, September 22, 1941, 12.

46. "War on Advertising," 9.

47. "Mr. Arnold's Opinion," *Editor and Publisher*, November 2, 1940, 22.

48. "Advertising under Fire," *Broadcasting*, July 28, 1941, 34; "Arnold Disclaims Any Intention to Hurt Advertising," *Broadcasting*, July 28, 1941, 62.

49. "Arnold Denies Intention of Curtailing Oil Advertising," *Advertising Age*, July 28, 1941, 1; "Arnold Disclaims Any Intention to Hurt Advertising"; "Advertising under Fire."

50. "A Tug of War Is Fun, but . . . ," *Advertising Age*, July 28, 1941, 12.

51. "Edward H. Gardner, "What Did You Want Mr. Arnold to Say?," *Printers' Ink*, October 17, 1941, 82.

52. Ibid.

53. "Chicago Tribune Answers Arnold's Cigarette Charges," *Editor and Publisher*, August 17, 1940, 26; "Questionnaire on Advertising," *Lexington (Ky.) Herald*, August 11, 1941, UD5, Box 2; *Chicago Tribune*, May 4, 1940, UD5, Box 2. Others argued along the same lines. See, for example, "To Cripple the Press," *World Herald*, October 9, 1941, UD5, Box 2; "Cites U.S. Foes of Advertising," *Sun*, August 21, 1941, UD5, Box 2.

54. "Twilight of TNEC."

55. "Will Heavy Defense Taxes Cut Down Consumer Sales?," *Advertising and Selling*, June 1941, 17–18. For a treatment of the advertising industry's fight against taxation during World War II, see Mark H. Leff, "The Politics of Sacrifice on the American Home Front in World War II," *Journal of American History* 77, no. 4 (March 1991): 1296–1318; "Sales Tax Gains Favor as Aid in Meeting Expenses," *Advertising Age*, April 21, 1941, 6; U.S. Congress, House of Representatives, 76th Cong., 3rd sess., HR 9513, "A Bill to Provide Revenue, Equalize Taxation, and for Other Purposes by Mr. Voorhis of California," April 23, 1940, Referred to the Committee on Ways and Means, Jerry Livingston Voorhis Collection, Special Collections, Honnold Mudd Library, Claremont University Consortium, Claremont, Calif. (hereafter JLVC), Box 120, Folder 6.

56. Jerry Voorhis, "The Tax Bill: Extension of Remarks of Jerry Voorhis of California," JLVC, Box 120, Folder 6; also Roland Marchand, *Creating the Corporate Soul: The Rise of Public Relations and Corporate Imagery in American Big Business* (Berkeley: University of California Press, 1998), 320.

57. Sidney Margolius, "Boo! Ad Man Unnerved by Unexpected Publicity Backfire," *P.M.*, December 30, 1940, JLVC, Box 34, Folder T1-1.

58. Ibid.

59. "Is It Patriotic to Save Taxes by Advertising?," *Advertising and Selling*, November 1940, 34; Raymond Rubicam, "Advertising in Last War—and This," *Broadcasting*, June 9, 1941, 12; "Ad Field Pledges Aid in Emergency," *New York Times*, May 29, 1941, 33; "Advertising News and Notes," *New York Times*, March 6, 1941, 6.

60. Margolius, "Boo!"

61. Bruce Barton to S. R. Bernstein, November 20, 1940, Bruce Barton Papers, 1881–1967, Mass Communications History Collections, Wisconsin Historical Society Archives, Madison (hereafter BBP), Box 82, Folder: *Advertising Age*, 1940–44.

62. U.S. Congress, House of Representatives, 77th Cong., 3rd sess., HR 10720, "A Bill to Prevent Avoidance of Taxes by Unlimited Investment in Advertising; to Control Uneconomic Advertising Expenditure Engaged In by the Liquor, Tobacco, and Luxury Trades; to Discourage Advertising on the Public Highways in Order to Derive Revenues Therefrom; and for Other Purposes," by Mr. Voorhis of California, December 9, 1940, Referred to the Committee on Ways and Means, JLVC, Box 34, Folder T1-1.

63. For a full text of the bill, see "Voorhis and His Bill," *Printers' Ink*, December 20, 1940, 17–18. See also "Drastic Advertising Tax Bill Introduced by Rep. Voorhis," *Advertising Age*, December 16, 1940, 1; "Voorhis Bill Called Symptom of Advertising Control Trend," *Broadcasting*, January 1, 1941, 20.

64. "Seven Reasons Why the 'Advertising Tax' Should Become Law," n.d., JLVC, Box 34, Folder T1-1.

65. J. K. Lasser, "Advertising and the New Tax Law," *Advertising and Selling*, November 1940, 28.

66. "Voorhis and Bill," *Tide*, January 1, 1941, JLVC, Box 34, Folder T1-1. This article has good bibliographic data on Voorhis.

67. Margolius, "Boo!"

68. "Tax Deceit," *L.A. Examiner*, December 17, 1940, n.p., JLVC, Box 34, Folder T1-1.

69. "Voorhis and His Bill"; "Drastic Advertising Tax Bill"; "Voorhis Bill Called Symptom."

70. "Voorhis' Proposed Tax on Advertising," *Advertising and Selling*, January 1941, 34.

71. John Benson to Jerry Voorhis, January 29, 1941, JLVC, Box 34, Folder T1-1.

72. "500 Advertisers Would Be Curbed under the Voorhis Bill," *Advertising Age*, December 16, 1940, 48. The argument that advertising was an expression of true "Americanism," not to be found in totalitarian countries, was heard in other connections as well. See, for example, Paul Garrett, "Advertising and Defense," *Printers' Ink*, May 9, 1941, 17–19. However, it must be pointed out that Congressman Voorhis was a left-liberal Democrat and far from a fascist totalitarian!

73. Margolius, "Boo!"

74. "Excess Profits and Advertising," *Advertising Age*, November 25, 1940, 12. Industry observers also argued that advertising had not kept up with business progress since the bottom of the Great Depression and that American companies were underspending on advertising. See, for example, L. D. H. Weld, "Why Advertising Has Failed to Keep Pace with Economic Advancement," *Printers' Ink*, May 2, 1941, 33+; Weld, "Why Advertising Lags as Economic Picture Improves," *Printers' Ink*, June 6,

1941, 21–24; "Advertising Groups Assail Tax Measure," *Broadcasting*, August 18, 1941, 1; "Advertising News and Notes," *New York Times*, August 28, 1941, 35.

75. "More Advertising Will Take Sting out of New Taxes," *Advertising Age*, July 1, 1940, 23; "A Statement by the Editors on Advertising and the New Tax Law," *Advertising and Selling*, December 1940, 29; "Is It Patriotic?"; "500 Advertisers."

76. "AFA Finds Voorhis Is 'Firm Believer' in Advertising," *Advertising Age*, January 20, 1941, 1.

77. "Statement Presented by G. S. McMillan, Secretary Association of National Advertisers, Inc., New York, before the Senate Finance Committee in Opposition of Sections 557 and 601 of H.R. 5417, August 14, 1941," Box 23, Folder 1, Thomas D'Arcy Brophy Papers, State Historical Society of Wisconsin, Madison (hereafter TDBP), 4.

78. From G. S. McMillan to "Dear A.N.A. Member," August, 18, 1941, Box 23, Folder 1, TDBP; "House Group Drops Proposals to Tax Radio and Advertising," *Broadcasting*, July 21, 1941, 9; "Advertising Should Not Be Taxed"; "Radio, Outdoor Interests Rally to Defeat Taxes," *Advertising Age*. August 4, 1941, 1; "AFA and AAAA Assail Proposed Tax on Radio and Billboard Advertising," *Broadcasting*, August 11, 1941, 20; "Advertising in for Fight, Federal Views Indicate," *Advertising Age*, August 11, 1941, 1; "Advertising Groups Assail Tax Measure"; "See Possibility of Scrapping Tax on Outdoor Panels," *Advertising Age*, August 18, 1941, 1; "Advertising Tax Opposed at Senate Hearing," *Printers' Ink*, August 22, 1941, 37; "Senate Committee Knocks Out Taxes on Advertising," *Advertising Age*, September 1, 1941, 1; "Senate Approves Knocking Out Ad Taxes in New Bill," *Advertising Age*, September 8, 1941, 1; Charles E. Murphy to Paul Garrett, January 11, 1941, JLVC, Box 34, Folder T1-1.

79. "Advertising—A Tax Deduction in Defense Contracts?," *Advertising and Selling*, November 1941, 22; "Vinson Bill Would Ban Deductions for Advertising," *Advertising Age*, October 20, 1941, 17.

80. "Advertising—A Tax Deduction?"; "Vinson Bill Would Ban Deductions."

81. "Proposed Advertising Limits Merely in Discussion Stage," *Broadcasting*, May 25, 1942, 54.

82. Raymond Moley, "Advertising in Wartime," *Newsweek*, July 13, 1942, 68.

83. "Government Anti-Ad Front Widening."

84. The ongoing debate over grading and standardization of goods is further explored in chapter 4.

85. "Tearing Up the Road," *Washington Post*, October 10, 1941, UD5, Box 2.

86. "Sell Advertising to Public to End Attacks: Murphy," *Advertising Age*, October 20, 1941, 15; Frank W. Fox, *Madison Avenue Goes to War: The Strange Military Career of American Advertising, 1941–45* (Provo, Utah: Brigham Young University Press, 1975), 39.

87. "Advertising under Fire," *Broadcasting*, July 28, 1941, 34.

88. "Advertising under Fire," *Broadcasting*, August, 25, 1941, 34.

89. "You May Be out of a Job," *Industrial Marketing*, September 1941, 77; "DMAA

Speakers Fly to Defense of Advertising," *Advertising Age*, October 13, 1941, 1; "Government Anti-Ad Front Widening."

90. Fleming, "Advertising under Pressure."

Chapter 2. Advertising Navigates the Defense Economy

1. "You May Be Out of a Job," 77.

2. Meg Jacobs, *Pocketbook Politics: Economic Citizenship in Twentieth-Century America* (Princeton, N.J.: Princeton University Press, 2005); Cohen, *Consumers' Republic*, chap. 2.

3. "You May Be Out of a Job"; Erik Barnouw, *The Golden Web: A History of Broadcasting in the United States, 1933–1953* (New York: Oxford University Press, 1968), 166. Herman E. Krooss states that inflation had been a worry throughout the 1930s but that the outbreak of war in 1939 made the concern more prevalent; Krooss, *Executive Opinion: What Business Leaders Said and Thought on Economic Issues, 1920s-1960s* (Garden City, N.Y.: Doubleday, 1970), 204–9.

4. Henry M. Stevens, "New Horizons Now," *Printers' Ink*, December 19, 1941, 51–52. See also G. A. Nichols, "AAAA Sharpens Tools for Huge Defense Task," *Printers' Ink*, May 9, 1941, 25–26; "Looking Ahead to Peace," *Advertising Age*, April 28, 1941, 12; "You May Be Out of a Job."

5. Nichols, "AAAA Sharpens Tools"; "Looking Ahead to Peace." See also Roland Marchand, *Creating the Corporate Soul: The Rise of Public Relations and Corporate Imagery in American Big Business* (Berkeley: University of California Press, 1998), chap. 8; Henthorn, *From Submarines to Suburbs*, chap. 7.

6. Raymond Moley, "This Habit of Economic Freedom," *Printers' Ink*, December 5, 1941, 11–14; "These Advertisers, Now Great, Began in 1915–18," *Printers' Ink*, August 22, 1941, 97; "Faith in Advertising Pays Rich Dividends," *Printers' Ink*, August 22, 1941, 82. See also Eldridge Peterson, "Why Keep On Advertising When Oversold? Case Histories from World War Times," *Printers' Ink*, October 20, 1939, 25–26; "What's Ahead for Industrial Advertising?," *Advertising Age*, September 16, 1940, 12.

7. Cy Norton, "Advertising in 1942 Will Be Different," *Printers' Ink*, December 5, 1941, 23.

8. Roy F. Irvin, "An Open Letter to the Advertising Agencies of America," *Printers' Ink*, September 12, 1941, 29. Irvin refers to advertising campaigns that the government partially paid for as part of its effort to sell government bonds and increase enlistment in the armed forces. See, for example, Lawrence M. Hughes, "Many Firms Launch Advertising Now to Build Tomorrow's Sales," *Sales Management*, November 1, 1941, 36+; "Advertising Enlisted—for Duration," *Business Week*, August 24, 1940, 38. The USO campaign, on the other hand, was donated by copywriters, commercial artists, and media in order to help the United Service Organizations (USO) raise close to $11 million. The money was used for recreational activities in army camps. See "Advertising Mobilizes in United Service Drive," *Printers' Ink*, June 27, 1941, 19–21. Irvin

was not alone in his opinion. See, for example, Nelms Black, "After Hours," *Printers' Ink*, June 6, 1941, 6; Irvin, "An Open Letter," 26.

9. Paul Garrett, "Advertising and the Economics of U.S. Defense," *Advertising and Selling*, June 1941, supplement inserted between 32 and 33.

10. Hughes, "Many Firms Launch Advertising," 37.

11. Peterson, "Why Keep On Advertising"; "These Advertisers Now Great"; "What's Ahead for Industrial Advertising?"

12. Hughes, "Many Firms Launch Advertising," 37; Paul Garrett, "Advertisers and Defense," *Printers' Ink*, May 9, 1941, 17–19.

13. C. B. Larrabee, "War and War Rumors Not Reducing Volume of U.S. Advertising," *Printers' Ink*, July 12, 1940, 9–11. A 1940 survey of ANA members revealed that 6 percent intended to lower their 1941 advertising budgets, while 38 percent planned to maintain their current budgets. However, 56 percent of the members planned to substantially increase their advertising budgets for 1941. Paul B. West, "A.N.A. Poll Reveals Notable Increases in 1941 Sales and Advertising Budgets," *Printers' Ink*, November 22, 1940, 15–17. See also "Advertisers Plan to Drive Ahead Despite Fog," *Advertising Age*, January 20, 1941, 6.

14. "Ads Mirror the War," *Business Week*, June 29, 1940, 32; "Industrial Copy Ties into Defense," *Advertising and Selling*, September 1940, 28–29.

15. "Defense in the Ads," *Business Week*, April 5, 1941, 34–36.

16. "Advertising Tunes Up for Defense," *Printers' Ink Monthly*, November 1940, 10–11.

17. "Defense in the Ads," 35.

18. P. H. Erbes Jr., "Star Spangled Selling," *Printers' Ink*, August 16, 1940, 15.

19. Norton, "Advertising in 1942."

20. "Government Warns against Illegal Use of American Flag," *Advertising Age*, March 10, 1941, 33; "Advertising Referring to Army and Navy," *Printers' Ink*, June 13, 1941, 67–69; "Use of the Flag," *Advertising and Selling*, July 1941, 66; "The Flag Instead of Products," *Business Week*, June 29, 1940, 32. See also Eleanor Austin, "Our Flag in Advertising," *Printers' Ink*, February 5, 1943, 17; Kenneth W. Akers, "Practical Advertising under Defense Conditions," *Industrial Marketing*, August 1941, 20.

21. "Defense in the Ads," 36.

22. "Advertisers Are Urged to Continue Campaigns during Current Crisis," *Broadcasting*, October 6, 1941, 22.

23. "Patriotism and Public Relations," *Advertising and Selling*, June 1941, 36.

24. "War Advertising Minus Sob Sister Flavor," *Printers' Ink*, October 17, 1941, 20–21.

25. The survey based its findings on the following magazines: *American Weekly, Collier's, Liberty, Life, Puck, Saturday Evening Post, Time, Look, American Magazine, Cosmopolitan, National Geographic, True Story, Good Housekeeping, Ladies' Home Journal, McCall's, Women's Home Companion, American Home*, and *Better Homes and Gardens*. "Defense as an Advertising Theme," *Advertising and Selling*, November 1941, 16–17.

26. "Users of Advertising Must Join in United Fight to Protect It," *Printers' Ink*, November 7, 1941, 11–13.

27. Stole, *Advertising on Trial*.

28. "New Council of Education, AAAA Project," *Advertising Age*, May 9, 1938, 1; "New Consumer Council Ready to Start Work," *Advertising Age*, June 20, 1938, 19; "Four A's Revives Plan for Consumer Relations Council," *Advertising Age*, December 25, 1939, 1; "Dameron Named Head of Consumer Relations Group," *Advertising Age*, January 15, 1940, 4; "Push Progressive Ad Policies," *New York Times*, April 16, 1941, 42; Frederic R. Gamble, "Economic Effects of Advertising—Con and Pro," Annual Meeting, 10th District, Advertising Federation of America, Hotel Tulsa, Tulsa, Oklahoma, October 18, 1941, TDBP, Box 7, Folder 8.

29. Gamble, "Economic Effects," 2; Neil H. Borden, *The Economic Effects of Advertising* (Chicago: Richard D. Irwin, 1942); "Harvard Study Urges New Program to Guide Consumers," *Advertising Age*, December 5, 1938, 8.

30. Paul B. West, "An Opportunity to Do a Vitally Necessary Job for Advertising and for the National Welfare" (typewritten memo, September 2, 1941), TDBP, Box 9, Folder 6, 6.

31. Harold B. Thomas, "The Background and Beginning of the Advertising Council" (n.d.), ACA, RG 13/2/203, n.p.

32. Paul West to Tomas D'Arcy Brophy, October 3, 1941, Box 9, Folder 6, TDBP, 2.

33. Representing the AAAA on the joint committee were Thomas D'Arcy Brophy, president of Kenyon and Eckhardt; E. DeWitt Hill, vice-president of McCann-Erickson; Chester LaRoche, president of Young and Rubicam; William Reydel, a partner in Newell-Emmett; Thomas L. Ryan, president of Pedlar and Ryan; and Frederic R. Gamble, managing director of the AAAA. The ANA was represented by Lee Bristol, vice-president of Bristol Myers Company; A. O. Buckingham, vice-president of Cluett Peabody; Charles Mortimer, vice-president of General Foods; H. W. Roden, president of Harold Clapp, Inc.; Harold B. Thomas, president of the Centaur Company; and Paul West, president of the ANA. Ibid.

34. "Memorandum Regarding Program Jointly Sponsored by the A.N.A, and A.A.A.A.," October 31, 1941, TDBP, Box 9, Folder 6; "Prospectus of Special Joint Meeting," The Homestead, Hot Springs, Va., November 13, 14, and 15, 1941, ibid.

35. "Meeting of the A.N.A. and the A.A.A.A. Steering Committee on Parts I and II Joint Meeting of the Two Associations," October 8, 1941, TDBP, Box 90, Folder 6.

36. Ralph K. Strassman, "Time to Fight," *Printers' Ink*, January 31, 1941, 129.

37. "Users of Advertising Must Join," 77.

38. Everett R. Smith, "What of 1946?" *Printers' Ink*, September 5, 1941, 17.

39. "Prospectus of Special Joint Meeting"; "Advertising Industry Plans War Council," *Broadcasting*, November 3, 1941, 16.

40. "Advertising News and Notes," *New York Times*, October 1, 1941, 30. See also "ANA, Four A's to Scan Attacks on Advertising," *Advertising Age*, October 6, 1941, 2;

"'Most Challenging Problem' Subject of 4A's-ANA Meet," *Advertising Age*, November 3, 1941, 1; "Advertising Industry Plans War Council."

41. "'Most Challenging Problem,'" 32; "Advertising Industry Plans War Council"; "Advertising News and Notes," *New York Times*, October 29, 1941, 39; "Advertising Pledges Aid to War Economy," *Broadcasting*, November 17, 1941, 7–8.

42. C. R. Palmer, "Complete Text of Talks at Hot Springs Meetings," *Advertising Age*, November 17, 1941, 25, emphasis in the original.

43. Thomas, "Background and Beginning," n.p.

44. "Young Presents Forward-Looking Plan for Field," *Advertising Age*, November 17, 1941, 26; "Advertising Pledges Aid to War Economy." For an excellent discussion of John D. Rockefeller's public relations strategies, see Stuart Ewen, *PR! A Social History of Spin* (New York: Basic Books, 1996).

45. See "Advertising Clinic," *Newsweek*, November 24, 1941, 47, for a discussion of Blatt's Hot Springs talk.

46. "Henderson Disclaims Fight on Advertising," *Broadcasting*, November 17, 1941, 9, emphasis in the original; "'You Got Me Wrong,' Henderson Tells Four A's, ANA," *Advertising Age*, November 17, 1941, 1. Henderson's speech received extensive attention in advertising circles. For the full text of this speech, see Leon Henderson, "Advertising Must Survive as Thriving Economic Force," *Printers' Ink*, November 21, 1941, 9–12; Henderson, "Advertising's Crisis Is Everybody's Crisis," *Advertising and Selling*, December 1941, 16; Leon Henderson, "No Monopoly on Trouble," *Vital Speeches of the Day*, November 13, 1941, 109–12.

47. "Advertising Clinic," *Newsweek*, November 24, 1941, 47.

48. C. B. Larrabee, "If You Looked for a Miracle," *Printers' Ink*, November 21, 1941, 13.

49. Thomas, "Background and Beginning," n.p.

50. "Advertising Mobilizes Forces to Preserve Free Enterprise," *Advertising Age*, November 17, 1941, 1.

51. Larrabee, "If You Looked," 13; "Where Do We Go from Here," *Advertising Age*, November 24, 1941, 12.

52. "Should Advertising Defend Itself—or the U.S.?," *Advertising and Selling*, December 1941, 36. In contrast to other trade journals, *Advertising Age* concluded that the meeting was a successful step in the right direction. See "Where Do We Go."

53. "Should Advertising Defend Itself?," 36, emphasis in the original.

54. Thomas, "Background and Beginning," n.p.

55. Ibid.

56. Jack Malcolm Bethune, "A History of the Advertising Council, 1942–1967" (M.A. thesis, University of Texas at Austin, 1968), 34.

57. "War Comes to America," *Advertising Age*, December 15, 1941, 12.

58. "Advertising for Uncle Sam," *Advertising Age*, December 22, 1941, 12.

59. Ibid.

60. This observation was made in late October 1941 at the Pacific Coast Conven-

tion of the American Association of Advertising Agencies. "Sees End to Government Advertising Opposition," *Editor and Publisher*, November 1, 1941, 8.

61. "Advertising Council Serves to Coordinate War Activities," *Advertising Age*, December 15, 1942, 24; Bethune, "History of the Advertising Council," 36.

62. Marchand, *Creating the Corporate Soul*, 89; Robert Jackall and Janice M. Hirota, *Advertising, Public Relations, and the Ethos of Advocacy* (Chicago: University of Chicago Press, 2000), 23. See also Ewen, *PR!*, chap. 6; Stephen L. Vaughn, *Holding Fast the Inner Lanes: Democracy, Nationalism, and the Committee on Public Information* (Chapel Hill: University of North Carolina Press, 1980), chap. 8; Daniel Pope, "The Advertising Industry and World War I," *Public Historian* 2, no. 3 (Spring 1980): 4–25.

63. Roy Dickinson, "Advertising Brains Available for Defense," *Printers' Ink*, June 6, 1941, 37–38; Gilbert T. Hodges, "A.F.A. Defense Committee Explains Operating Plans," *Printers' Ink*, July 4, 1941, 51–52. President Roosevelt heaped praise on the project, causing AFA chairman Paul Garrett to promise continuous use of advertising to maintain national morale and war awareness. Franklin D. Roosevelt to Paul Garrett, May 20, 1941, The President's Personal Files, Franklin D. Roosevelt Library, Hyde Park, N.Y. (hereafter FDR PPF), Box 602 (2), Folder: Advertising Federation of America, 1939–43; Paul Garrett to the President, June 3, 1941, ibid.

64. "Minutes of Meeting of Advertising Council, Inc., January 14, 1942," ACA, RG 13/2/201, Box 1, Folder: Advertising Council Minutes, January–February 1942, 1.

65. "By-Laws of the Advertising Council, Inc.," March 4, 1942, ACA, RG 13/2/201, Box 1, Folder: Advertising Council and Council Executive Minutes, March–April 1942. See also "Advertising Roster," *Business Week*, February 21, 1942, 48–49; "Advertising Coordinates for War Effort; Council Representing Industry Set Up," *Commercial and Financial Chronicle*, February 26, 1942, 869; "Advertising Unity," *Newsweek*, February 23, 1942, 44–45. For a treatment of circumstances leading to the establishment of the Advertising Council and the council's activities during its first year of existence, see "Advertising Council Serves to Coordinate War Activities," *Advertising Age*, December 21, 1942, 24; Thomas, "Background and Beginning," n.p.

66. "McClintock, Ad Council Chief, a Skillful Organizer, Diplomat," *Editor and Publisher*, June 27, 1942, Peter Odegard Papers, Franklin D. Roosevelt Library, Hyde Park, N.Y. (hereafter POP), Box 8, Folder: Advertising, 1942, n.p.; "Minutes of the Annual Meeting of the Advertising Council, Inc., March 4, 1942," ACA, RG 13/2/201: Meeting Minutes, 1942–98, Box 1, Folder: Advertising Council and Executive Minutes, March–April 1942; "LaRoche Announces Makeup of New Ad Council," *Advertising Age*, February 16, 1942, 4. For a complete list of the Advertising Council's original members, see "Advertising Field Mobilizes for War," *New York Times*, February 16, 1942, 10. McClintock resigned from his executive position in November 1942 but continued as an unpaid member of the board and an officer of the council. "Advertising News," *New York Times*, November 12, 1942, 36. See also "Special Meeting of Executive Committee, The Advertising Council, Inc., November 10, 1942," and "Minutes of Meeting of Advertising Council. Inc., November 16, 1942," both ACA,

RG 13/2/201, Box 1, Folder: Advertising Council and Executive Committee Minutes, November–December 1942.

67. "Advertising Council Serves to Coordinate War Activities." Contributions to the council were as follows: the American Association of Advertising Agencies and the Association of National Advertisers each contributed $20,000; advertising media, represented by magazine, newspaper, radio, and outdoor interests, contributed $15,000 each. This left the Advertising Council with an annual budget of $100,000. See "Minutes of Meeting of the Advertising Council, Inc., February 18, 1942," ACA, RG 13/2/201, Box 1, Folder: Advertising Council Minutes, January–February 1942.

68. Advertising Council, "The Advertising Council: A Six Months' Record," TDBP, Box 4, Folder 7.

69. "Advertising Council Reports on Progress," *Printers' Ink*, April 17, 1942, 53–54.

70. "Proposed Advertising Limits Merely in Discussion Stage," *Broadcasting*, May 25, 1942, 54.

71. See list dated January 23, 1942, and letter to Richard Compton from James S. Milroy, January 22, 1942, TDBP, Box 1, Folder 3.

72. "Statement Presented by G. S. McMillan before the State Finance Committee in Opposition to Sections 557 and 601 of H.R. 5417, August 1941," January 20, 1942, TDBP, Box 1, Folder 3.

73. James J. Kimble, *Mobilizing the Home Front: War Bonds and Domestic Propaganda* (College Station: Texas A and M University Press, 2006), 35–36.

74. Ibid., 35–37.

75. "Tax Rule Explains Advertising Status," *Broadcasting*, August 31, 1942, 52–53; "Excerpts from Renegotiation Manual," ACA, RG 13/2/305: Washington Office Subject File, 1942–81, Box 4, Folder: Government Contracts, 1943, 1944. Rather than taxing advertising, the Treasury Department sought revenues from other sources. Part of the final solution was to increase the tax paid by private citizens. This option, which many found grossly unfair, is well discussed in Mark H. Leff, "The Politics of Sacrifice on the American Home Front in World War II," *Journal of American History 77*, no. 4 (March 1991): 1296–318.

76. "Tax Rule Explains Advertising Status"; "Wartime Advertising," *Bread and Butter*, April 1, 1944, 1. See also "Advertising Expense and Corporate Income Tax Returns," *Printers' Ink*, September 4, 1942, 19; William L. O'Neill, *A Democracy at War: America's Fight at Home and Abroad in World War II* (Cambridge, Mass.: Harvard University Press, 1993), 254.

77. "Advertising Tax Status Draws Morgenthau, Henderson Views," *Broadcasting*, June 1, 1942, 51. For a celebratory trade-press account of Morgenthau's decision, see "Morgenthau Clears the Air," *Advertising Age*, June 8, 1942, 12.

78. A. P. Mills, "Anti-Advertising Fears Allayed by Government Steps," *Advertising Age*, July 13, 1942, 1.

79. "Advertising Costs Ruled Deductible," *New York Times*, August 28, 1942, 29. The Bureau of Internal Revenue approved advertising campaigns to change wartime buying

habits. For example, it accepted the use of advertising to educate the public about the need to buy large instead of small bottles in order to save plate for metal caps. It also recognized the use of advertising to speed war production campaigns in offices and plants. See "Wartime Uses of Advertising Acknowledged by Treasury," *Advertising Age*, August 31, 1942, 1–2; "Tax Rule Explains"; "Advertising in Wartime," *New York Times*, August 31, 1942, 16; "Tax Deductions Made for Advertising," *Commercial and Financial Chronicle*, September 3, 1942, 810; "Advertising Expense and Corporate Income Tax"; "Explanation of Treasury Department Attitude on Advertising Expense," *Advertising and Selling*, September 1942, supplement inserted between 16 and 17.

80. "Wartime Uses of Advertising."

81. "Advertising as Government Sees It: An Interpretation," *Printers' Ink*, October 9, 1942, 13, 30.

82. "Advertising and Taxation," *Advertising Age*, October 12, 1942, 12; "ANA Warns against Abuse of U.S. Ad Expense Policy," *Advertising Age*, October 5, 1942, 1–2.

83. "1943 Advertising Okayed," *Advertising Age*, January 18, 1943, 12. The Commerce Department, celebrating the Treasury's decision, published a booklet clarifying advertising's tax-deductible status. See "Vital Need of Advertising during War Shown in Summary by Commerce Department," *Broadcasting*, September 27, 1943, 59.

84. "Political Ads Held Not Tax Deductible," *Advertising Age*, April 10, 1944, 16; "Politics or Ads," *Business Week*, April 22, 1944, 92.

85. David Lloyd Jones, "The U.S. Office of War Information and American Public Opinion during World War II" (Ph.D. diss., State University of New York at Binghamton, 1976), 240.

86. "Getting Your Money's Worth" (discussion outline, n.d.), Consumers Union Archives, Yonkers, N.Y. (hereafter CUA), Education Service Division, Group 3E, Box 1, Folder 4: Discussion Outlines, 1938–1942.

87. "The Battle for Fairer Taxes," *Consumers Union Reports*, April 1942, 107–8; "The Consumer Testifies," *Consumers Union Reports*, May 1942, 136–37.

88. W. P. Tuttle, "Total Advertising," *Printers' Ink*, November 13, 1942, 15.

89. "Stewart-Warner Sees Tax 'Small Price for Freedom,'" *Printers' Ink*, March 5, 1943, 71.

90. Leff, "Politics of Sacrifice," 1306.

Chapter 3. The Initial Year of the Advertising Council

1. Thomas, "Background and Beginning," n.p.; Advertising Council, "The Advertising Council: A Six Months' Record," TDBP, Box 4, Folder 7; "Minutes of Meeting of Advertising Council, February 5, 1942," ACA, RG 13/2/201, Box 1, Folder: Advertising Council Minutes, January–February 1942, 4; "Advertising's Wartime Job," *Industrial Marketing*, February 1942, 74.

2. "The Council Marches On," in the column "The Impact of War on Advertising: Report to Advertising and Sales Management," no. 13, *Advertising and Selling*, July 1942, 18–19.

3. [Author not indicated; probably Bruce Barton], "No Time for Weaklings" (memo for *Time and Space,* June 22, 1942), BBP, Box 1, Folder: Advertising Federation of America.

4. Ralph Allum to Ken R. Dyke, June 12, 1942, and Miller McClintock to Allen Grover, May 1, 1942, both NA2, RG 208, Records of the Office of Facts and Figures, Records of the Advertising Division, 1942–43 (hereafter OWI AD), Box 2, Entry 3B, Folder: Advertising Division Correspondence, 1942; Advertising Council, "Advertising Council," 5.

5. Getting local advertisers to join the Advertising Council's efforts continued to be a problem even a year into the war. "Adclubs to Promise Greater Aid to War Campaigns," *Advertising Age,* December 14, 1942, 16. The task of encouraging additional war activities on the part of local advertising clubs throughout the country was left to the AFA in cooperation with the Advertising Council. The AFA proposed a War Advertising Committee in order to organize all the publicity and promotional activities necessary to the community's war effort. See, for example, "AFA's War Work Concentrated on Local Activities," *Advertising Age,* December 21, 1942, 40; "AFA Local Setup for War Work" (organizational chart), *Advertising Age,* December 21, 1942, 34.

6. "Advertising Council Reports on Progress," *Printers' Ink,* April 17, 1942, 53–54.

7. Confidential memo to William B. Lewis from Ken R. Dyke, May 14, 1942, OWI AD, Box 2, Entry 3B, Folder: Advertising Division Correspondence, 1942; and Gwen Cheney to Ken Dyke, May 15, 1942, ibid.

8. "World's Greatest System of Mass Communication Is at Call of U.S. Government," *Printers' Ink,* April 10, 1942, 38.

9. Sidney Weinberg, "What to Tell America: The Writers' Quarrel in the Office of War Information," *Journal of American History* 55, no. 1 (June 1968): 73–75.

10. "Coordinating U.S. Advertising," *Advertising Age,* March 16, 1942, 12.

11. "The U.S. Needs an Advertising Manager," *Advertising and Selling,* March 1942, 30.

12. Confidential memo to Lewis from Dyke, May 14, 1942, 3.

13. Memo to Vaughn Flannery and William Lewis from Advertising Council, March 14, 1942, OWI AD, Box 2, Entry 3B, Folder: Advertising Division Correspondence, 1942–43.

14. Memo to John B. Baker from Ken R. Dyke, May 29, 1942, ibid.; *Frank W. Fox, Madison Avenue Goes to War: The Strange Military Career of American Advertising, 1941–45* (Provo, Utah: Brigham Young University Press, 1975), 11–12; John Morton Blum, *V Was for Victory* (San Diego: Harcourt Brace Jovanovich, 1976), 22.

15. "'Quote Sheets' for Wartime Copy Offered to Admen," *Advertising Age,* April 20, 1942, 36; R. M. Dobie, "OFF Picks Best War Ads, Sends Them to Advertisers," *Editor and Publisher,* April 18, 1942, 78. See also memo to Miller McClintock from Ken R. Dyke, May 14, 1942, OWI AD, Box 2, Entry 3B, Folder: Advertising Division Correspondence, 1942.

16. "Wartime Advertising Exhibit," Colston E. Warne Papers, Consumers Union Archives, Yonkers, N.Y. (hereafter CEWP), Box 62, Folder 1.

17. Memo to Ken R. Dyke from Porter Bibb Jr., June 11, 1942, OWI AD, Box 2, Entry 3B, Folder: Advertising Division Correspondence, 1942.

18. "The Advertising Council," *Advertising and Selling,* June 1942, 9. See also "Give Advertising Bigger War Tasks, Rubicam Urges," *Advertising Age,* June 1, 1942, 6.

19. "President Roosevelt's Message," *Advertising Age,* June 29, 1942, 12; C. B. Larrabee, "A Thing of Peace, Advertising Is Now Geared to Winning War," *Printers' Ink,* July 10, 1942, 28; see also "Anti-Advertising Fears Allayed by Government Steps," *Advertising Age,* July 13, 1942, 1; "Minutes of Meeting of Advertising Council, Inc., January 14, 1942," ACA, RG 13/2/201, Box 1, Folder: Advertising Council Minutes, January–February 1942, 1–2; and "Minutes of Meeting of Advertising Council, Inc., January 22, 1942," ibid., 2–3.

20. "Advertising Faces Its Biggest Job in Selling War Use of Ads to the U.S. (by an Agency Man with 20 Years Experience)," *Editor and Publisher,* May 30, 1942.

21. Ibid.; "Planning and Production of Government Information Plans," n.d., TDBP, Box 4, Folder 1.

22. Office of War Information, "Report to the President," NA2, RG 208, Records of the Historian, Subject File 1941–46, Box 13, Entry 6E, Folder: President, Final Report by Elmer Davis to the President Concerning OWI 9/15/45. For a detailed description of the OWI, its organizational functions and agencies, see David Lloyd Jones, "U.S. Office of War Information." George H. Roeder Jr., *The Censored War: American Visual Experience during World War Two* (New Haven, Conn.: Yale University Press, 1993), 9; "Davis Given Free Hand as Boss of War Information," *Advertising Age,* June 22, 1942, 16.

23. See, for example, Allan M. Winkler, *The Politics of Propaganda: The Office of War Information, 1942–1945* (New Haven, Conn.: Yale University Press, 1978), chap. 2.

24. "Minutes of the Executive Committee for the Advertising Council, Inc., June 19, 1942," ACA, RG 13/2/201, Box 1, Folder: Advertising Council Executive Committee and Board of Directors Minutes, May–June 1942, 2.

25. Cowles's appointment was influenced by the OWI's desire to appear bipartisan. He initially turned down the job but accepted it after President Roosevelt directly requested his help in heading the agency. See Office of War Information, "Report to the President," 7.

26. For a description of bureaus under the OWI's Domestic Branch offering media facilities and services, see OWI Domestic Branch, "List of Media Facilities and Services Available for War Information of All Branches of the Government," May 22, 1942, NA2, RG 208, Entry 28, Records of the Domestic Operations Branch, 1926–46, Records of the Office of the Director (hereafter ROD), Box 3, Entry 1, Folder: Organization I, Domestic, June–November 1942. In addition to News, Magazine, Book, Graphics and Printing, Motion Picture, and Radio bureaus, the publication also lists the Bureau of Special Services and the Bureau of Program Coordination. In August

1942, the latter two were combined into one agency and renamed the Bureau of Campaigns.

27. "Advertising Gains Stature in War Information Plans," *Advertising Age,* August 10, 1942, 1.

28. Office of War Information, August 7, 1942, NA2, RG 208, Entry 93, Records of the Radio Bureau, Records of the Office of the Chief, General Records of the Chief, William B. Lewis, July 1941–April 1943, Box 606, Folder: Domestic Branch Asst. Director Gardner Cowles; "Admen to Plan War Information Policy, Program," *Advertising Age,* August 17, 1942, 19.

29. "Planning and Production of Government Information Campaigns," TDBP, Box 4, Folder 1; David Lloyd Jones, "U.S. Office of War Information," 221–26.

30. Ken R. Dyke to Stephen E. Fitzgerald, November 20, 1942, NA2, RG 208, Entry 39, Records of the Office of War Programs, Records of the Chief, Bureau of Campaigns, August 1942–January 1943 (hereafter CBC), Box 140, Folder: Advertising Council.

31. "OWI Coordinates U.S. Advertising in New Bureau," *Editor and Publisher,* August 15, 1942, 10.

32. "Admen to Plan War Information." See also "The Salesmanship of Sacrifice," *Time,* September 21, 1942, 77; David Lloyd Jones, "U.S. Office of War Information," 217. When Dyke left the Bureau of Campaigns for an army post in early 1943, Dudley was appointed head of the bureau. "Dyke Takes Army Post; Dudley Is Successor in OWI," *Advertising Age,* January 18, 1943, 4.

33. "Salesmanship of Sacrifice."

34. See, for example, Ken R. Dyke to Ralph S. Butler, May 29, 1942, OWI AD, Box 2, Entry 3, Folder: Advertising Division Campaign Material, 1942.

35. "O.W.I. Bureau to Coordinate Government Advertising," Association of National Advertisers, Inc., *News Bulletin* 26, no. 38 (August 17, 1942), NA2, RG 208, Entry 40, Records of the Deputy Chief, Bureau of Campaigns, September 1941–February 1943 (hereafter DCBC), Box 142, Folder: A.N.A. Confidential Bulletins, 252–53.

36. Paul West to Ken Dyke, June 8, 1942, DCBC, Entry 3B, Folder: Advertising Division Correspondence, 1942, emphasis in the original. See, for example, Ken R. Dyke to Ralph S. Butler, May 29, 1942, OWI AD, Box 2, Entry 3, Folder: Advertising Division Campaign Material, 1942.

37. Ken R. Dyke to G. E. Eckert, June 8, 1942, OWI AD, Box 2, Entry 3, Folder: Advertising Division: Citizen's Manual for War, Prepared by the Office of Civilian Defense (Washington, D.C., 1942).

38. "Editorial," *Editor and Publisher,* n.d., but likely from late May or early June 1942, OWI AD, Box 2, Entry 3, Folder: Advertising Division: Citizen's Manual for War.

39. T. S. Irvin, "What We Need Today Is Fighting Words," *Editor and Publisher,* April 4, 1942, 14. A few months later, the Advertising Council made the same obser-

vations. See "McClintock Says Straight Selling Ads Are Out," *Editor and Publisher*, January 23, 1943, 18.

40. "How Advertising Can Help Win War; Two Workable Plans," *Printers' Ink*, July 31, 1942, 16. See also Advertising Council, Inc., "A Plan for Business to Use One of Its Principal Tools to Help Win the War," OWI AD, Box 3, Entry 3B, Folder: Professional Advertising Organizations—Guides for War-Time Advertising.

41. "Ad Council Seeks 13 Million Fund to Sell Total War," *Advertising Age*, June 29, 1942, 30.

42. "Coordinating U.S. Advertising," *Advertising Age*, March 16, 1942, 12; "Advertising Council Serves to Coordinate War Activities," *Advertising Age*, December 21, 1942, 28.

43. "Salesmanship of Sacrifice."

44. "Minutes of the Meeting of the Board of Directors of the Advertising Council, Inc., August 25, 1942," ACA, RG 13/2/201: Meeting Minutes, 1942–98, Box 1, Folder: Advertising Council Executive Committee and Board of Directors Minutes, July–August 1942.

45. "Minutes of Meeting of Advertising Council, Inc., November 19, 1942," ACA, RG 13/2/201: Meeting Minutes, 1942–98, Box 1, Folder: Advertising Council and Executive Committee Minutes, November–December 1942, 1.

46. Some of the larger projects were assigned more than one project coordinator. The war bond drive, for example, had six coordinators.

47. "Advertising Council Serves," 28; David Lloyd Jones, "U.S. Office of War Information," 219–20.

48. "260 Ad Agencies Volunteer Services for War Effort," *Advertising Age*, June 15, 1942, 8.

49. James Playsted Wood, *The Story of Advertising* (New York: Ronald Press, 1958), 450.

50. The only exception was the payment (a maximum of $10 a day) for travel-related expenses specifically requested of agency employees by the OWI. Gardner Cowles to Chester LaRoche, April 10, 1943, NA2, RG 208, Entry 20, Records of the Domestic Operations Branch, Correspondence of Director Gardner Cowles Jr., 1942–43, Box 12, Folder: The War Advertising Council, Inc.

51. R. M. Dobie, "New Fat Salvage Drive Shows Ad Council's Job," *Editor and Publisher*, May 30, 1942. 7. It is interesting, considering the soap manufacturers' enthusiasm for this salvage campaign, that by the end of the year three of the major soap companies (accounting for approximately 80 percent of all soap products sold in the United States) would plead no contest to the charge of price fixing and be fined $10,000 each. The firms were Procter and Gamble, Colgate-Palmolive-Peet, and Lever Brothers. Department of Justice, "For Immediate Release," Thursday, December 17, 1942, TWAC, Box 104, Folder: Professional File, 1941–1942, General Antitrust Policies. Thus it was suggested that the soap companies' willingness to cooperate with

the salvage campaign was motivated more by self-interest than by patriotism, and that by 1945 Kenyon and Eckhardt was collecting commissions from the industry. Alfred Stanford to Maury Hanson, March 27, 1945, NA2, RG 188, Records of the Office of Price Administration, Entry 3, Office of Information, Office of the Director, Correspondence with Other OPA Departments and the OWI, 1943–1947, Box A4, Folder: Hanson, Maury. For an excellent discussion of how health and hygiene were treated in World War II advertising, see Henthorn, *From Submarines to Suburbs*.

52. "The Advertising Council," *Advertising and Selling*, July 1942, 9–10; "Huge Salvage Campaign Begins to Take Shape," *Advertising Age*, May 4, 1942, 1; "Government and Industry Form Partnership to Promote National Nutrition Plan," *Printers' Ink*, June 5, 1942, 17–19; "Campaign to Salvage Grease," *Printers' Ink*, July 24, 1942, 27; "The U.S. Nutrition Project," *Advertising and Selling*, July 1942, 17–18. For a detailed explanation of the considerations involved in carrying out the salvage campaign, see "Big Push on Scraps," *Business Week*, June 27, 1942, 20.

53. "Advertisers Mustered for War Campaign," *Broadcasting*, November 16, 1942, 9–10+.

54. Seymour Morris to Miller McClintock, July 16, 1942, NA2, RG 208, Entry 103, Records of the Radio Bureau, Records of the Allocation Division, General Correspondence, March 1942–January 1946, Box 602, Folder: Advertising Council; Spencer G. McNary to Seymour Morris, June 10, 1942, ibid., Box 641, Folder: Advertising Council.

55. Advertising Federation of America, "Special Bulletin," March 17, 1942, NA2, RG 214, Records of the Office for Emergency Management, Entry 1, Liaison Officer for Emergency Management: General Records, 1941–43, Box 16, Folder: AB–AK; Advertising Federation of America, *Guide for Wartime Advertising Policies*, ibid.

56. "Home-Front War Problems Challenge Advertising Clubs through the A.F.A." (eighth draft of copy for presentation booklet to local advertising clubs), n.d. [October 1942], CBC, Entry 39, Box 140, Folder: Advertising Council, 3.

57. James M. Landis to Chester J. LaRoche, January 1, 1943, CBC, Entry 39, Box 140, Folder: Advertising Council, 3.

58. Ibid.; "Advertising's Wartime Service," *Advertising Age*, December 14, 1942, 12; "All Out for War Is Brief Story of Advertising's Year," *Advertising Age*, December 21, 1942, 12.

59. "260 Ad Agencies Volunteer Services"; "Ad Council Conducting Many Projects," *Broadcasting*, October 12, 1942, 14; "Government Advertising Projects," *Printers' Ink*, October 9, 1942, 54.

60. "An Unnecessary Publication?," *Advertising Age*, November 2, 1942, 12. The Advertising Council's *Guide to War-Time Advertising* explained how advertisers, agencies, and the media could help in the war advertising effort. It listed government tasks with priority ratings for each, presented detailed background information on the most important tasks, and included bibliographic information on all tasks for those who desired further information. It also provided information on good advertising

tie-ins and suggested copy and layouts for guidance. See memo dated June 1942, OWI AD, Box 3, Entry 3B, Folder: Advertising Division—Monthly Report, June 1942.

61. "War Record Silences Advertising Critics," *Broadcasting,* August 10, 1942, 12, 44; "Washington Gets Our Story," *Advertising Age,* June 22, 1942, 12; "Advertisers Mustered," 9–10.

62. Larrabee, "Thing of Peace"; see also "Anti-Advertising Fears Allayed."

63. See Advertising Federation of America, "Highlights of the Thirty-Eighth Annual Convention and Advertising Exposition," June 21–24, 1942, FDR PPF, Box 602, Folder: Advertising Federation of America, 1939–43. See also "Advertising in Wartime," *Newsweek,* July 6, 1942, 49; "Waiving of Rights Is Held Temporary," *New York Times,* June 23, 1942, 29; "AFA Dedicates Industry to War Effort," *Broadcasting,* June 29, 1942, 11–12.

64. "Washington Gets Our Story."

65. "Minutes of the Executive Committee of the Advertising Council, Inc., October 16, 1942," ACA, RG 13/2/201, Box 1, Folder: Advertising Council Executive Committee Board of Directors Minutes, September–October 1942. *Advertising Age* criticized the council for not doing enough to include local salvage committees. See "Salvage Advertising Results," *Advertising Age,* September 7, 1942, 12.

66. Elmer Davis to Paul B. West, September 25, 1942, Bureau of Campaigns Chief, Box 140, Folder: Association of National Advertisers, RG 208, Office of War Information, Entry 39, Bureau of Campaigns Chief; Paul B. West to K. R. Dyke, September 24, 1942, ibid.

67. Paul B. West to Henry A. Wallace, October 7, 1942, CBC, Box 140, Folder: ANA.

68. Ken R. Dyke to Paul B. West, November 13, 1942, CBC, Box 140, Folder: ANA.

69. Paul B. West to A.N.A. Member(s), November 2, 1942, CBC, Box 140, Folder: ANA; Association of National Advertisers, *Legal-Legislative-Government Bulletin* 10, no. 44 (November 3, 1942), NA2, RG 208, Records of the Deputy Chief, Bureau of Campaigns, September 1941–February 1943, Box 142, Folder: A.N.A. Confidential Bulletins.

70. "McClintock, Ad Council Chief, a Skillful Organizer, Diplomat," *Editor and Publisher,* June 27, 1942, 1, POP, Box 8, Folder: Advertising, 1942, n.p. See, for example, "The Advertising Council U.S.A.," *Advertising Age,* February 23, 1942, 12; "On Going Forward/On Going Backward," *Space and Time,* no. 251 (February 23, 1942), NA2, RG 208, Entry 93, Records of the Radio Bureau, Records of the Office of the Chief, General Records of the Chief, William B. Lewis, July 1941–April 1943, Box 601, Folder: National Broadcasting Co., 2.

71. Emil Schram, "If American Business Wants to Run Its Own Show When This War Is Over," *Printers' Ink,* January 16, 1942, 38.

72. "Minutes of Meeting of Board of Directors of the Advertising Council, Inc., October 9, 1942," ACA, RG 13/2/201, Box 1, Folder: Advertising Council Executive Board of Directors Minutes, September–October 1942.

73. "Minutes of the Meeting of the Board of Directors of the Advertising Council,

Inc., August 25, 1942," ACA, RG 13/2/201, Box 1, Folder: Advertising Council Executive Committee and Board of Directors Minutes, July–August 1942, 9.

74. "Advertising Council U.S.A.," *Advertising Age*, February 23, 1942, 12.

75. "U.S. Needs an Advertising Manager," 30.

76. "Constructive Consumer Help Is Wartime Copy Theme," *Printers' Ink*, April 10, 1942, 15; "Advertising Council U.S.A."

77. "Advertising Given Unusual Tribute by Sec. Morgenthau," *Advertising Age*, January 4, 1943, 1.

78. "Department of Commerce Again Boosts Advertising," *Advertising and Selling*, September, 1942, 20. See also "Why Department of Commerce Believes in Wartime Advertising," *Industrial Marketing*, August 1942, 35–36; "Jesse Jones Tells NIAA of Belief in Advertising," *Advertising Age*, July 6, 1942, 4; "Vital Need of Advertising during War Shown in Summary by Commerce Dept.," *Broadcasting*, September 27, 1943, 59.

79. "Government Attitude on Advertising," Association of National Advertisers, Inc., *News Bulletin* 26, no. 36 (July 29, 1942), Deputy Bureau of Campaigns Chief, Box 142, Folder: A.N.A. Confidential Bulletins 239.

80. "War Dissolves Most Supposed Areas of Disagreement," *Advertising and Selling*, October 1942, 21; "The Critics' Showdown," *Advertising and Selling*, February 1943, 116.

81. "Nelson Reviews Advertising's War Role," *Broadcasting*, November 16, 1942, 11. See also "Advertising's Vital Role Told at ANA War Meet," *Advertising Age*, November 16, 1942, 1; "Donald Nelson on Advertising," *Advertising and Selling*, December 1942, 21; "Advertisers Mustered," 9–10.

82. See "Minutes of Meeting of Advertising Council, January 14, 1942," ACA, RG 13/2/201, Box 1, Folder: Advertising Council Minutes, January–February 1942; "Minutes of the Executive Committee of the Advertising Council, Inc., October 30, 1942," ibid., Folder: Advertising Council Executive Board of Directors Minutes, September–October 1942; "Meeting of the Board of Directors of the Advertising Council, Inc., July 31, 1942," ibid., Folder: Advertising Council Executive Committee and Board of Directors Minutes, July–August 1942.

83. "Preliminary Organization Report," n.d., ACA, RG 13/2/201, Box 1; "Minutes of the Executive Committee of the Advertising Council, April 6, 1942," ibid., Folder: Advertising Council and Executive Minutes, March–April 1942. The appointment of council member Charles M. Mortimer Jr. as consultant to the Office of Price Administration in early 1943 was duly noted by the council. See "Minutes of the Executive Council of the Advertising Council, Inc., April 30, 1943," 3, ibid., Folder: War Advertising Council Executive Committee and Board of Directors Minutes, March–April 1943.

Chapter 4. The Consumer Movement's Return

1. Stole, *Advertising on Trial*, chap. 2.

2. Norman Isaac Silber, *Test and Protest: The Influence of Consumers Union* (New

York: Holmes and Meier, 1983), 29. This investigation is covered in detail in Stole, *Advertising on Trial*, chap. 7.

3. "Reminiscences of Colston E. Warne: Oral History, 1971–1981," http://oralhistoryportal.cul.columbia.edu/document.php?id=ldpd_5037055 (accessed July 15, 2011).

4. Richard L. D. Morse, *The Consumer Movement: Lectures by Colston E. Warne* (Manhattan, Kans.: Family Economics Trust, 1993), chap. 4.

5. Historical Records Office, Robert E. Stone, director, Office of Price Administration, "Chronological Outline of Events and Situations in OPA History to July 1943," January 1944, John Kenneth Galbraith Papers, 1930–1989, John F. Kennedy Presidential Library and Museum, Harvard University, Cambridge, Mass. (hereafter JKGP), Box 2, Folder: Agency History Chronological History, cover page.

6. Cohen, *Consumers' Republic*, 65. See also Meg Jacobs, *Pocketbook Politics: Economic Citizenship in Twentieth-Century America* (Princeton, N.J.: Princeton University Press, 2005), chap. 5.

7. Jacobs, *Pocketbook Politics*, 192.

8. [Author not indicated; probably Colston E. Warne], "Private Companies Use Tax Money for Self-Glorification and Inflation," 1942–43, CEWP, Box 63, Folder 4, 3.

9. "Bread and Butter: Facts You Need before You Buy," *Consumers Union Reports*, March 1941, 80.

10. Consumers Union of U.S., "A Consumer Program for Victory," August and September 1942, CUA, Group 3E; ConsumerReports.org, "Our History: 1940s," http://www.consumerreports.org/cro/aboutus/history/printable/1940/index.htm (accessed January 4, 2009).

11. "Getting Your Money's Worth" (discussion outline, n.d.), CUA, Education Service Division, Group 3E, Box 1, Folder 4: Discussion Outlines, 1938–1942, Consumers Union of U.S.

12. Ibid.; Consumers Union of U.S., "The Consumer and the War" (discussion outline, January 1942), CUA, Education Service Division, Group 3E, Box 1, Folder 4: Discussion Outlines, 1938–1942, Consumers Union of U.S., 11.

13. An online ProQuest search of *New York Times* articles from January 1, 1940, to December 31, 1945, did not yield any entries for *Bread and Butter*.

14. [Author not indicated; probably Colston E. Warne], Memo to "Dear Friend," November 25, 1942, CEWP, Box 62, Folder 4.

15. Colston E. Warne, "Private Companies Use Tax Money for Self-Glorification and Inflation," n.d. [ca. 1942–43], CEWP, Box 63, Folder 4, 3–4.

16. Memo to "Dear Friend," November 25, 1942.

17. See, for example, Colston E. Warne to Henry Morgenthau, January 23, 1943, CEWP, Box 63, Folder 2; Elizabeth E. Hoyt to Professor Warne, January 7, 1943, ibid., Box 62, Folder 6; Colston (Warne) to Leland (Gordon), Thursday, (no month) 11, (1943), ibid., Box 63, Folder 2.

18. "Text of Open Letter Urging Limitation of War-Time Advertising," *Printers' Ink*, January 1, 1943, 16. For a list of those who signed the letter, see "Now for the Names . . .," *Printers' Ink*, January 8, 1943, 52–53+; "Gentlemen! Gentlemen! Professor Warne Has the Floor," *Printers' Ink*, January 29, 1943, 20; "The Critics' Showdown," *Advertising and Selling*, February 1943, 114–15. Private citizens expressed similar concerns. See C. L. Tierney to Franklin D. Roosevelt, January 17, 1943, The President's Official Files, Franklin D. Roosevelt Library, Hyde Park, N.Y. (hereafter FDR OF), Box 196, Folder: Advertising, 1943.

19. Colston E. Warne to Miss Thurman, December 23, 1942, CEWP, Box 62, Folder 1.

20. Colston E. Warne to G. R. Schmeidler, February 6, 1943, CEWP., Folder 6; Colston E. Warne to "Sir," January 1, 1942, ibid., Folder 1; James Rorty, "Pistol Packin' Adman," n.d., UAW Washington Office Legislative Department: Donald Montgomery Records, Walter Reuther Library, Wayne State University, Detroit, Mich. (hereafter DMR), Box 27, Folder 6.

21. C. B. Larrabee to Colston E. Warne, March 22, 1943, CEWP, Box 8, Folder 12, 2.

22. James W. Martin to J. W. Brown, February 3, 1943, CEWP, Box 63, Folder 2; "The Professors Do Their Bit," *Printers' Ink*, January 1, 1943 (written memo, not actual clipping), ibid., Box 62, Folder 6; James W. Brown to Leland Gordon, January 28, 1943, ibid.; James O. Peck to Leonard J. Gordon, February 19, 1943, ibid.

23. George Burton Hotchkiss, "A Professor (*Who Didn't Sign*) Replies," *Printers' Ink*, February 19, 1943, 52.

24. Advertising Federation of America, Memorandum, March 25, 1943, CEWP, Box 62, Folder 6.

25. C. E. Griffin, "The Place of Advertising in War Time" (written for the Advertising Federation of America), n.d. (probably early 1943), CEWP, Box 62, Folder 6. Parts of this letter were quoted in "Letter Contains Inconsistencies," an editorial in *Editor and Publisher*, March 20, 1943, 44.

26. "Advertising News and Notes," *New York Times*, January 22, 1943, 34.

27. H. W. Hailey, "The Considerations Involving the Freedom of the Press and Free Enterprise," n.d. (probably 1943), CEWP, Box 62, Folder 5; Morris D. Townshend, "Our Interpretation of the Colston Warne Petition," n.d. (probably 1943), ibid. For more and similar comments, see Warne correspondence, ibid.

28. C. E. Warne to E. S. Wilson, n.d. (probably 1943), CEWP, Box 62, Folder 6; A. H. Patterson to Mr. Warne, March 26, 1943, ibid.; A. H. Patterson to Mr. Warne, marked "about February 1943," ibid.; F. H. Seidel to "Professor Warne," March 2, 1943, ibid. See also David Levy to Colston E. Warne, January 22, 1943, ibid., Box 63, Folder 2; Colston E. Warne, "Should Advertising Be Drastically Curtailed in War-Time?" (address before the First District, Advertising Federation of America, Hotel Statler, Boston, April 19, 1943), ibid., Box 117, Folder 5, 6.

29. C. E. Warne to E. S. Wilson, n.d. (probably 1943), CEWP, Box 62, Folder 6.

30. Peck to Gordon, February 19, 1943, CEWP; Irwin Robinson to Colston E. Warne, January 13, 1943, ibid., Folder 2.

31. "Plan to Curtail Ads for 'Economy' Leaves Davis Cold," *Editor and Publisher*, January 2, 1943, 9.

32. J. K. Galbraith to Colston E. Warne, February 8, 1943, CEWP, Box 63, Folder 2; Warne to Schmeidler, February 6, 1943, ibid., Box 62, Folder 6; Colston E. Warne to "Sir," February (1943?), ibid., Box 62, Folder 1.

33. Warne to Schmeidler, February 6, 1943.

34. Colston E. Warne to Leon Henderson, September 11, 1942, CEWP, Box 52, Folder 3 (letter quotes Henderson).

35. [Consumers Union?], "A Brief Urging the Curtailment of Unessential Advertising Which, in War-Time, Is Wasteful of Critical Resources, Inflationary, and a Means of Tax Evasion" (marked "1942 or 1943"), CEWP, Box 62, Folder 5.

36. "Advertising and Waste," *Bread and Butter*, December 11, 1943, 3; Colston E. Warne, "Advertising vs Aluminum," *Consumers Union Reports*, June 1942, 167.

37. Warne, "Should Advertising Be Drastically Curtailed?"

38. "It Pays to Advertise," *Bread and Butter*, October 9, 1943, 3. See also "Wasting Paper and Money," *Bread and Butter*, April 8, 1944, 2.

39. Frederick L. Schuster, "Some Aspects of Our Present Business Situation and the War Effort" (talk before the Association of National Advertisers, May 3, 4, 5, 1942), DCBC, Box 142, Folder: A.N.A. Confidential Bulletins II.

40. John W. Hanes, "Corporations Urged to Use Ads Interpreting Wartime Profits," *Editor and Publisher*, January 23, 1943, 30.

41. Colston E. Warne to "Mr. Smith," March 10, 1943, CEWP, Box 63, Folder 2.

42. George Gallup, "An Analysis of the Study of Consumer Agitation," February 9, 1940, NBCP, Box 76, Folder 11.

43. Cohen, *Consumers' Republic*, 131.

44. Stole, *Advertising on Trial*. See also Testimony of Dexter Masters, director of publications, Consumers Union of U.S., New York City, in United States, Temporary National Economic Committee, *Investigation of Concentration of Economic Power: Hearings before the Temporary National Economic Committee, Congress of the United States, Seventy-Sixth Congress, First Session, Pursuant to Public Resolution No. 113 (Seventy-Fifth Congress)*, pt. 8: *Problems of the Consumer, May 10, 11, and 12, 1939* (Washington, D.C.: USGPO, 1939), 3341–42.

45. I base this statement on extensive research in both the consumer and industry archives. Both sides kept detailed records of press coverage that gave attention to criticism of the industry, and there was precious little of it, much to the chagrin of the consumer movement. An online ProQuest search of *New York Times* articles from January 1, 1942, to December 31, 1945, produced 265 entries for "Advertising Council" but only 2 entries for "Advertising Council +criticism." It yielded 224 entries for "Advertising +Patriotic" but only 9 entries for "Advertising +Un-Patriotic."

46. Robert W. McChesney, *Telecommunications, Mass Media, and Democracy: The Battle for the Control of U.S. Broadcasting, 1928–1935* (New York: Oxford University Press, 1995).

47. "AFA Finds Voorhis Is 'Firm Believer' in Advertising," *Advertising Age*, January 20, 1941, 1.

48. Inger L. Stole, "Selling Advertising: The U.S. Advertising Industry and Its Public Relations Activities, 1932–1945" (Ph.D. diss., University of Wisconsin–Madison, 1998); McChesney, *Telecommunications, Mass Media, and Democracy*; Liz Fones-Wolf, *Waves of Opposition: Labor and the Struggle for Democratic Radio* (Urbana: University of Illinois Press, 2006).

49. Helen J. Sionssat to Arthur Kallet, December 16, 1941, CEWP, Box 108, Folder 7 (censor issue); Colston E. Warne to Federal Communications Commission, January 5, 1942, ibid. For a discussion of FTC investigations into false advertising in the late 1930s and early 1940s, see Stole, *Advertising on Trial*, 152–57.

50. For a transcript of Warne's talk, see Colston E. Warne, "The Consumer Looks at Advertising, WABC 10:15 p.m., December 27, 1941," CEWP, Box 117, Folder 5. For examples of letters in response to the broadcast, see ibid., Box 108, Folder 2. For a much rarer critical response, see Caroline Williams Carter to "Attention of Program Announcer" on the CU Broadcast by Colston Warne, January 6, 1942, ibid., Box 62, Folder 6.

51. "Statement of Dr. Colston E. Warne, President of Consumers Union of the United States, Concerning Broadcast over the Columbia Broadcast System 10:15 p.m., December 27, 1941," CEWP, Box 117, Folder 5.

52. "Advertising Flaws Outlined on CBS," *Broadcasting*, January 5, 1942, 17; "CBS Gives Consumers Union Free Time to Attack Advertising," *Sales Management*, January 15, 1942, 47–48; Colston E. Warne to Secretary, Federal Trade Commission, February 23, 1942, CEWP, Box 52, Folder 1: Government FTC, 1942–71.

53. Stole, *Advertising on Trial*, chap. 5.

54. "Advertising and the Public Interest," *Consumers Union Reports*, September 1942, 227.

55. "Our Mistake," *Consumers Union Reports*, October 1942, 255.

56. Helen J. Sionssat to Warne, December 22, 1942, CEWP, Box 62, Folder 1.

57. T. J. Slowie to Colston E. Warne, February 10, 1943, CEWP, Box 63, Folder 2.

58. "Consumer Groups," *Tide*, February 1934, 10–11.

59. Stole, *Advertising on Trial*, chap. 2.

60. "Safeguard against the 'Monopolies,'" *Newsgram*, n.d., TNEC, Public Relations, Box 443, Folder: Clippings re: Monopoly Prior to November 1, 1938.

61. "Committee Upholds Advertising Role," *New York Times*, May 12, 1939, TNEC, Public Relations, Box 443, Folder: Clippings re: Monopoly, January 1, 1939–December 31, 1939.

62. "Outline of Testimony, Dr. Ruth Ayres," TNEC, Statements and Reports Submitted to the Committee, Box 26, Folder: Consumers; "Outline of Testimony, Mr. Dexter Masters," ibid.; "Outline of Testimony, Mrs. Alice S. Belester," ibid.; "Outline of Testimony, Mrs. Paul S. Roller," ibid.

63. "Statement by Donald E. Montgomery, Consumers' Counsel, Agricultural Ad-

justment Administration, at the Conclusion of Hearings before the Temporary National Economic Committee, on Consumers' Problems," May 12, 1939, TNEC, Department of Treasury Hearings, Box 431, Folder: TNEC Hearings on Consumer Problems; Herman Oliphant to Hatten W. Summers, September 7, 1938, ibid., Department of the Treasury, Correspondence, Box 430, Folder: Miscellaneous 'crank' letters, pamphlets. For these and other similar statements, see Temporary National Economic Committee, *Investigation of Concentration of Economic Power: Description of Hearings and Monographs of the Temporary National Economic Committee* (Washington, D.C.: USGPO, 1941).

64. "Consumers Enter Monopoly Inquiry," *New York Times*, May 11, 1939, TNEC, Public Relations, Box 443, Folder: Clippings re: Monopoly, January 1, 1939–December 31, 1939.

65. "Grade Labeling—or Inflation?," *Bread and Butter*, April 10, 1943, 2.

66. "Grade Labeling in Canada," TNEC, Box 431, Folder: TNEC Hearings on Consumer Problems.

67. Gallup, "Analysis of the Study"; "FTC Asks Probe of Advertising Relationship to the Consumer," *Advertising Age*, January 22, 1940, 1; "Hearings on Consumer Standards Marked by Official Apathy," *Advertising Age*, January 29, 1940, 1; "Would Make FTC Arbiter of All Seals of Approval," *Advertising Age*, March 4, 1940, 1; "Not Anti-Advertising, Montgomery Tells Meeting," *Advertising Age*, March 4, 1940, 26.

68. "Grade Labeling—or Inflation?"

69. "Memorandum to Members of the Staff of the Antitrust Division, re: Effect of General Price Ceiling upon Antitrust Proceedings," June 15, 1942, TWAC, Box 104, Folder: Professional File, 1941–1942, General Antitrust Policies. Congress recognized these dangers in the Emergency Price Control Act of 1942, which, in addition to vesting in OPA the power to set the maximum price, gave it power to regulate and prohibit "practices relating to changes in form and quality." "O.P.A. to Set Up Mandatory Standards on Consumer Goods?," Association of National Advertisers, *News Bulletin* 26, no. 42 (September 11, 1942), DCBC, Box 142, Folder: A.N.A. Confidential Bulletins, 289.

70. Donald Montgomery, "Will Grade Labeling Benefit the Consumer, WEVD—8:15 p.m. EWT, April 29, 1944," DMR, Box 6, Folder 11: Grade Labelling—Radio Talks and Symposium in New York City, 1944–1945.

71. "The Coming Victory Label," *Advertising and Selling*, June 1942, 19–20; "Grade Labeling to Halt, OPA Spokesman Discloses," *Advertising Age*, March 29, 1943, 1; "Ad Men Condemn Grade Label Plan," *New York Times*, June 30, 1943, 29.

72. "An Industry as Old as Private Enterprise Fights for Its Life," *Wall Street Journal*, August 13, 1942, UD5, Box 2.

73. "Care Is Urged in Placing of Brand Names," *New York Herald Tribune*, November 13, 1942, UD5, Box 2.

74. "Excerpts from Address by Leon Henderson, Administrator, Office of Price Administration, before Joint Meeting Sponsored by New England Council and Boston

Advertising Club, Statler Hotel, Boston, November 19, 1942, 1:00 P.P. EWT," DMR, Box 15, Folder 5.

75. "Byrnes Wants Consumer Goods Standards," Association of National Advertisers, *News Bulletin* 26, no. 53 (November 20, 1942), CBC, Box 140, Folder: Association of National Advertisers.

76. Memorandum from H. S. Schenker, Benjamin Jurist, and H. J. Wollner to W. S. Macleod, December 3, 1942, DMR, Box 4, Folder 16.

77. "One Government Brand, Minus All Promotion, Urged," March 10, 1942, CEWP, Box 63, Folder 4.

78. "Suggestions for Program" (no author; n.d., although probably fall 1942), CBC, Box 140, Folder: Association of National Advertisers.

79. "O.P.A. Consumer Division Absorbed by Information Unit," Association of National Advertisers, Inc., *News Bulletin* 26, no. 44 (September 11, 1942), DCBC, Box 142, Folder: A.N.A. Confidential Bulletins, 301–2.

80. "What Will Government-Imposed Standardization Mean to Advertising?" *Printers' Ink*, January 15, 1943, 64–67; "Grade Labeling down the Wind, Food Men Told," *Advertising Age*, December 21, 1921, 1–2, 1942.

81. Gordon H. Cole, "Canners Open Drive to Wreck OPA Grade-Labeling Program," PM's Bureau, March 18, 1943, NA2, RG 122, Records of the Federal Trade Commission, Entry UD5, Division of Legal and Public Records: Press Clippings, Notices and Releases, 1918–1959, Box 3, ring-bound volume labeled "Federal Trade Commission Library, Advertising: 1943–" (hereafter UD5, Box 3).

82. "Grade Labeling and Buck Passing," *Bread and Butter*, April 24, 1943, CEWP 2, Box 3, Folder 17, CEWP.

83. "Standardized Labeling Gets Start in New Grapefruit Juice Ceiling," unidentified newspaper clipping, January 23, 1943, UD5, Box 3, "FTC Library 1943–"; "Grade Labeling Termed Threat to War Food Production," *Nash[ville] Post*, March 31, 1943, ibid.

84. "Brand Advertising Seen, Grade Label Campaign 'Target,'" December 12, 1942, "N.Y.J.J.C.," UD5, Box 2.

85. "Grade Labeling," *Minneapolis Tribune*, March 22, 1943, UD5, Box 3; "OPA Ruling Starts Grade Labeling," *Editor and Publisher*, January 30, 1943, 32.

86. "Bid for More Jobs," *Gadsden (Ala.) Times*, March 17, 1943, UD5, Box 3, "FTC Library 1943–."

87. "Ad Men Condemn Grade Level Plan," *New York Times*, June 30, 1943, NA2, RG 122, Records of the Federal Trade Commission, UD5, Box 3, ring-bound volume labeled "Advertising 1943"; "Statement of Prentiss M. Brown, Administrator OPA, before the Special Subcommittee on Investigation of Restrictions on Brand Names and Newsprint of the Committee on Interstate and Foreign Commerce (Honorable Lyle H. Boren, Chairman)," n.d., NA2, RG 188, Records of the Office of Price Administration, Entry 93, Information Dept: Speeches Delivered by OPA Administrators, 1941–1946, Box 2, Folder: "Misc. Material by Prentiss Brown," 3.

88. Warren L. Bassett, "ANA Issues Study on Grade Labeling," *Editor and Publisher*, December 13, 1941, 22. See also George Burton Hotchkiss, "Grade Labeling Will Not Benefit the Consumer," DMR, Box 6, Folder 11.

89. Jacobs, *Pocketbook Politics*, chap. 5.

90. Elisabeth Dryden, "You Can Strengthen Grade Label Order," P.M., February 15, 1943, UD5, Box 3; Warren L. Bassett, "ANA Issues Study on Grade Labeling," *Editor and Publisher*, December 13, 1941, 22.

91. J. K. Galbraith to Mr. Brown, January 21, 1943, JKGP, Box 3, Folder: Correspondence 1/19–31/43.

92. "Grade Must Be Put on Label," *Boston Post*, December 13, 1942, UD5, Box 2.

93. "Salient Facts about the Brand Names Foundation," n.d., CEWP, Box 62, Folder 3.

94. "Senseless and Frightening," reprinted from Hearst papers, March 1943, DMR, Box 15, Folder 5; B. E. (?) Berlin to Elizabeth W. Goldschmidt, April 30, 1943, ibid.; Gordon H. Cole, "Labor Demands Grade-Labeling," PM's Bureau, March 19, 1943, UD5, Box 3; "Grade Labeling," *Chicago Tribune*, March 2, 1943, UD5, Box 3.

95. "Social Uses of Advertising," *Wall Street Journal*, August 14, 1941, UD5, Box 2.

96. "Senseless and Frightening"; Berlin to Goldschmidt, April 30, 1943; Cole, "Labor Demands Grade-Labeling"; "Grade Labeling."

97. Montgomery, "Will Grade Labeling Benefit?" For a discussion of the communist attack on the consumer movement by ultra-right-wing forces in the late 1930s, see Stole, *Advertising on Trial*, chap. 7.

98. "Charge OPA Policy Hits Trade Marks," *New York Times*, March 26, 1943, UD5, Box 3; "C.I.O. Opposes Grade Label Abandonment," *Post*, March 29, 1943, ibid.; M. F. Lam, "Abandonment of Grade Labeling Program Looms after Congress Parley with Brown," *Journal of Commerce*, March 26, 1943, ibid.

99. Gordon H. Cole, "CIO Warns Inflation Lurks in Anti-Grade Label Fight," P.M. Bureau, March 29, 1943, UD5, Box 3.

100. "Grade-Labeling—or Inflation?"

101. Clipping from *Denver Post*, March 19, 1943, UD5, Box 3.

102. Cole, "Labor Demands Grade-Labeling."

103. Lou Maxon to Bruce Barton, August 23, 1943, BBP, Box 1, Folder: Advertising Federation of America, 1942–1955, 2; "Department Ready to Protect Postwar Free Trade," *Advertising Age*, April 10, 1944, 36–37; "AFA Calls for Communications Freedom," *Broadcasting*, July 5, 1943, 14+; "The Public and Grade Labeling," *Advertising Age*, June 7, 1943, 12.

104. "Brown Likely to Drop Rule on Grade Labeling," *New York Herald Tribune*, March 31, 1943, UD5, Box 3. For a response from Consumers Union, see "Grade Labeling: CU's Reply," *Consumer Reports*, March 1944, 59. For a discussion of the ongoing debate over grade labeling in the 1930s see, for example, Stole, *Advertising on Trial*, chaps. 3 and 6; Jacobs, *Pocketbook Politics*.

105. "Victories for the People," *Bread and Butter*, April 10, 1943, CEWP, Box 3, Folder 15, 3; Gordon H. Cole, "Anti-Labeling," PM's Bureau, April 2, 1943, UD5, Box

3; Adam Lapin, "Wouldn't Grade Cans, Sells Rotten Peaches to Tots," *Daily Worker*, April 1, 1943, UD5, Box 3. Concerns that OPA members recruited from business circles might have a strong, and in some respects adverse, reaction to the agency's mission arose in other contexts as well. See Burton E. Oppenheim to J. K. Galbraith, November 16, 1942, JKGP, Box 3, Folder: Correspondence 11/2–30/42.

106. Gordon H. Cole, "President Will Intervene in Labeling Fight If Veto Is Sustained," PM's Bureau, April 6, 1943, UD5, Box 3.

107. "Grade Labeling under Fire," *Star*, March 19, 1943, UD5, Box 3.

108. "OPA Gets New Plea on Grade Labeling," *Star*, March 23, 1943, UD5, Box 3. The leading groups behind this claim were the American Association of University Women, the American Home Economics Association, the National League of Women Shoppers, the National Federation of Settlement Houses, the National Farmers Union, the Co-operative League of the United States, the National Council of Jewish Women, the National Council of Negro Women, the National Council of Catholic Women, Consumers Union, the Congress of Women's Auxiliaries of the CIO, and the Ladies' Auxiliary of the Brotherhood of Sleeping Car Porters, AFL; Ann Cottrell, "Grade Labeling Gets Consumer, Labor Support," *New York Herald Tribune*, April 1, 1943, UD5, Box 3.

109. Robert Devore, "House Votes Probe of Food" (newsprint), *Post*, April 11, 1943, UD5, Box 3; "House Inquiry on Grade-Label Plan Ordered," *New York Herald Tribune*, April 11, 1943, ibid.

110. "Willis Dec[lares] Grade Labeling as Impractical," *New York Herald Tribune*, April 30, 1943, UD5, Box 3.

111. "Hold Grade Label Plan Detrimental to Food Quality," *New York Journal of Commerce*, April 30, 1943, UD5, Box 3. See also "Let's See the Brands," *El Paso (Tex.) Times,* June 3, 1943, ibid.; "Lowering Food Standards," *Plainfield (N.J.) Courier-News*, June 8, 1943, ibid.

112. "Grade Labeling Hit as Quality Ceiling," *Bureau of Journal of Commerce*, June 3, 1943, UD5, Box 3.

113. "Brown Doubts OPA Labeling Order's Legality," *Times Herald*, April 15, 1943, UD5, Box 3.

114. Lew Hahn to J. Kenneth Galbraith, May 18, 1943, JKGP, Box 3, Folder: Correspondence, 5/1–31/43.

115. J. K. Galbraith to Kenneth W. Rowe, May 4, 1943, JKGP; "OPA Holds Up Death of 1934 Grade Labeling," *Nashville Post*, April 28, 1943, UD5, Box 3; "Lend-Lease Grade Labeling Program under Trade Fire," *New York Journal of Commerce*, April 16, 1943, ibid.; "Grade Labeling Urged by Women," *New York Times*, April 26, 1943, ibid.; Kathryn McHale et al. to Prentiss Brown, April 23, 1943, CEWP, Box 52, Folder 3. A copy of this letter was also sent to the president; see "To Honorable Franklin D. Roosevelt," April 23, 1943, CEWP, Box 52.

116. "OPA Gives Up Fight to Force Grade Labeling," *[Wash]ington Post*, May 19, 1943, UD5, Box 3.

117. "Grade Labeling Effective on '43 Fruit Pack," *Editor and Publisher*, May 22, 1943, 12.

118. Carl A. Auerbach, "Quality Standards, Informative Labeling, and Grade Labeling as Guides to Consumer Buying," *Law and Contemporary Problems* 14, no. 2 (1949): 362–93; Congress, House of Representatives, *Brand Names and Newsprint: Hearings before a Subcommittee of the Committee on Interstate and Foreign Commerce, House of Representatives, Seventy-Eighth Congress, First Session, Pursuant to H. Res. 98, a Resolution to Investigate Federal Grade Labeling of Articles or Commodities, and the Discarding of Private Brand Names, Curtailing the Production or Consumption of Newsprint or Papers, and Any Requirements Intending to Bring About Simplification and Standardization of Production, Marketing, and Distribution of Articles of Commodities, as Well as Concentration of Industry or Production*, pt. 1: Hearings, *May 10–June 8, 1943*; pt. 2: Hearings, *June 14–30, 1943* (Washington, D.C.: USGPO, 1943); "House Committee Asked O.P.A. to Suspend Grade Labeling Orders," Association of National Advertisers, *Legal-Legislative-Government Bulletin* 11, no. 20 (May 12, 1943): 123, DCBC, Entry 40, Box 142, Folder: A.N.A. Confidential Bulletins; "Delay Is Asked on Labeling, Standardization," *New York Herald Tribune*, May 7, 1943, UD5, Box 3, "FTC Library 1943–."

119. "Boren Denounces Grade Labeling as 'Whim and Caprice,'" *New York World-Telegram*, May 29, 1943, UD5, Box 3.

120. "Pledges Defense of Trade Marks," *New York Herald Journal*, June 23, 1943, UD5, Box 3.

121. Ibid., 3.

122. "Statement of Prentiss M. Brown," 18–19.

123. "Limitations on OPA Power," *New York Journal of Commerce*, July 8, 1943, UD5, Box 3; Office of War Information, Office of Price Administration (OPA-2870), "For Immediate Release," August 5, 1943, DMR, Box 15, Folder 10, 1; "Grade Labeling Dropped on Score of Products," *New York Herald Tribune*, August 25, 1943, UD5, Box 3, "FTC Library 1943–"; Johnson Kanady, "OPA's 'Flaunting' of Grade Label Edict Revealed," *Times-Herald*, August 25, 1943, ibid.

124. "Maxon Resigns from OPA; Blasts Theorists," *Editor and Publisher*, July 17, 1943.

125. "Says Grade Labeling Threat to Freedom," *Editor and Publisher*, November 27, 1943, 13.

126. Colston E. Warne, "Grade Labels or Trade Labels?" *Current History*, February 1944, 104–9.

127. "Consumers Ask Vinson to Restore Grade Labels, For Release Monday AM papers, November 15, 1943," DMR, Box 15, Folder 5.

128. "Inside Washington: 40 Fighting Congressmen," *Printers Ink*, August 13, 1943, Montgomery Papers, Box 15, Folder 5, 8.

129. Alan Brinkley, *The End of Reform: New Deal Liberalism in Recession and War* (New York: Vintage Books, 1996), 118; Warne, "Grade Labels or Trade Labels?"

130. Colston E. Warne, "Government Control of Price and Quality," CEWP, Box 117, Folder 5.

Chapter 5. Advertising, Washington, and the Renamed War Advertising Council

1. "Minutes of Meeting of Advertising Council, Inc., February 2, 1943," ACA, RG 13/2/201: Meeting Minutes, 1942–68, Box 1, Folder: Advertising Council Minutes, January–February 1942. For information on the lack of an official policy on the matter, see Office of Facts and Figures, "Wartime Paid Government Advertising Policy and Practices," to the Director from Bureau of Intelligence, February 25, 1942, OWI AD, Entry 3B, Box 3, Folder: Advertising Division War-Time Paid Advertising—Policy and Practice, 1942.

2. "Union Gov't Used Paid Ads during the Civil War," *Editor and Publisher*, May 8, 1942, 12.

3. For a discussion of advertising during World War I, see, for example, Stephen L. Vaughn, *Holding Fast the Inner Lines: Democracy, Nationalism, and the Committee on Public Information* (Chapel Hill: University of North Carolina Press, 1980), chap. 8. For a treatment of the National Industrial Recovery Administration's use of advertising, see, for example, "Advertising Displaces Ballyhoo in NRA Program," *Printers' Ink*, October 12, 1933, 3; "Roosevelt Administration Approves Advertising," *Advertising Age*, July 29, 1933, 4; "Advertising Is Called an Aid to Government," *Advertising Age*, June 23, 1934, 20; "House Tables Gov't Ad Bill; Measure Seen Doomed," *Editor and Publisher*, December 11, 1943, 7; "Advertising Plan for Defense Saving Bonds and Stamps," POP, Box 11, Folder: Advertising—Paid Space.

4. "Ad Standards Raised by British Government," *Editor and Publisher*, July 11, 1941, 8; "British Advertising Continues to Function," *Wall Street Journal*, February 4, 1942, UD5, Box 2; "£2,000,000 Will Be Spent by Britain for War Advertising This Year," *Printers' Ink*, March 6, 1942, 13–14+; J. P. McNulty, "Letter from London: Britain's Biggest Advertiser," *Advertising and Selling*, December 1942, 56+.

5. Roy Dickinson, "How U.S. Could Use Paid Advertising NOW," *Printers' Ink*, June 11, 1941, 10.

6. Ian Macdonald, "Government Advertising Is Part of Canada's War Program," *Printers' Ink*, October 24, 1941, 22. See also "42 Ideas for War Advertising That U.S. Might Adapt . . . A List Built out of Experience (and Mistakes) of Britain and Canada," *Printers' Ink*, March 6, 1942, 15+; C. V. Charters, "Canada Has Found Paid Space Promotes Its War Effort," *Editor and Publisher*, January 24, 1942, 5; "Canadian Advertisers Had Two-Year Start on U.S.," *Editor and Publisher*, February 14, 1942, 5. For a discussion of paid government advertising in Britain, Canada, and Australia, see also Office of Facts and Figures, "Wartime Paid Government Advertising."

7. Macdonald, "Government Advertising," 21.

8. Ibid., 66; D. H. Weld, "Advertising Costs Drop to 2% of National Income," *Printers' Ink*, October 31, 1941, 9–12.

9. "Little Left for Advertising in U.S. Bond Budget," *Advertising Age*, March 31, 1941, 18. In addition to paid savings bonds promotions, both the U.S. Army and the Navy used paid advertising as part of their recruitment efforts during the early phases of the war. See, for example, Advertising Council, "The Advertising Council: A Six Months' Record," TABP, Box 4, Folder 7.

10. Office of Facts and Figures, "Wartime Paid Government Advertising," 5.

11. "Report from March 29, 1943, Meeting," Henry Morgenthau Diaries, Franklin D. Roosevelt Library, Hyde Park, N.Y., Box 620, 12.

12. "U.S. Use of Paid Space Advocated by Alleman," *Editor and Publisher*, February 2, 1942, 30.

13. "Should the U.S. Advertise?," *Advertising Age*, April 6, 1942, 12; "Inland Tables Petition for Paid Government Space," *Advertising Age*, February 23, 1942, 1; "Should the U.S. Get Free Space and Time?," *Advertising and Selling*, July 1941, 22; "The Department of Commerce Comments on the Report 'War-Time Paid Government Advertising,'" OWI AD, Box 2, Entry 3, Folder: Advertising Division Correspondence, 1942, 4; Dorothy Ducas to Elmer Davis, September 3, 1942, National Archives, Suitland, Md., RG 208, Records of the Director, Records of the Director, 1942–43, Folder A-C, Entry 1.

14. "ANPA Canvasses U.S. Paid Advertising," *Broadcasting*, April 27, 1942, 12; "U.S. Urged to Buy War Advertising," *New York Times*, n.d., POP, Box 8, Folder: Advertising, 1942; "Paid Advertising by Government Urged in War Bond Sale at ANPA Convention," *Commercial and Financial Chronicle*, April 30, 1942, 1712; "Advertising Brains Available for Defense," *Printers' Ink*, June 6, 1941, 37–38; "Who Should Pay for War Advertising?," *Advertising and Selling*, June 1942, 13–14.

15. "Government Advertising," *Editor and Publisher*, January 3, 1942, 22. See also "Advertising Brains Available"; "Who Should Pay for War Advertising?"

16. "No Subsidy!" *Editor and Publisher*, April 11, 1942, 20; "Not a Subsidy," *Editor and Publisher*, February 14, 1942, 22.

17. "ANPA Canvasses U.S. Paid Advertising"; "U.S. Urged to Buy War Advertising"; "Paid Advertising by Government."

18. "Advertising for U.S.A.," *Editor and Publisher*, January 17, 1942, 18; "Gannett Endorses Paid Advertising by U.S.," *Editor and Publisher*, January, 31, 1942, 4.

19. "AAAA Shows Government What War Ads Can Do," *Editor and Publisher*, October 3, 1942, 10. See also "Stuart Sherman Believes in Gov't Use of Paid Space," *Editor and Publisher*, April 4, 1942, 3.

20. "Two State Groups Urge U.S. to Use Paid Advertising," *Editor and Publisher*, February 28, 1942, 8; George A. Brandenburg, "Wartime Publishing Problems at Inland Meeting," *Editor and Publisher*, February 21, 1942, 5; "La. Press Group Urges Gov't Paid Advertising," *Editor and Publisher*, May 9, 1942, 37; "U.S.A.—Propagandist," *Editor and Publisher*, March 21, 1942, 22; "Paid Advertising by Government."

21. "Morgenthau Says But One Publisher Protested to Him," *Editor and Publisher*, February 14, 1942, 4.

22. "ASNE to Vote on Question of Gov't Paid Advertising," *Editor and Publisher*, April 25, 1942, 17.

23. Ibid.; James Rorty, *Our Master's Voice: Advertising* (New York: John Day, 1934); George Seldes, *Freedom of the Press* (New York: Garden City, 1937); "Should the U.S. Advertise?"; "Inland Tables Petition"; "Should the U.S. Get Free Space?"; "Department of Commerce Comments."

24. Colston E. Warne, "Should Advertising Be Drastically Curtailed in War-Time?" (address before the First District, Advertising Federation of America, Hotel Statler, Boston, April 19, 1943), CEWP, Box 117, Folder 5, 5.

25. Arthur Robb, "Shop Talk at Thirty," *Editor and Publisher*, May 16, 1942, 36.

26. "To Stop to Debate Paid Government Advertising," *Printers' Ink*, November 27, 1942, 26. See also "Davis Given Free Hand as Boss of War Information," *Advertising Age*, June 22, 1942, 16.

27. Neville Miller to William Lewis, June 4, 1942, NA2, RG 208, Entry 93, Records of the Radio Bureau, Records of the Office of the Chief, General Records of the Office of the Chief, General Records of the Chief, William B. Lewis, July 1941–April 1943, Box 602, Folder: National Association of Broadcasters (pink label).

28. "Advertising and Politics," *Editor and Publisher*, November 14, 1942, 28.

29. An early advertising concern had been that the advertising industry would be unable to organize a system of free help to the government. Many believed that the government would be better served through advertising efforts that the government itself paid for and organized. See "Advertising and War," *Advertising and Selling*, November 1942, 19–20; "War-Time Radio Advertising," February 1, 1942, Box 130, Folder 5, National Broadcasters Association Papers, Wisconsin Center for Historical Research, State Historical Society of Wisconsin, Madison.

30. Peter H. Odegard, "The Place of the War Bond Program in the Newspaper at War" (talk to the Newspaper Advertising Executives Association, October 13, 1942), NA2, RG 56, General Records of the Department of the Treasury, Entry 405-G, Records of the Savings Bond Division (including records of its predecessor, the War Finance Division), Historical and Promotional Records, 1941–60, Box 2, Speech Files, Hannegan-Wallace, Folder: Odegard, Peter, Special Consultant, 6; "Fat Drive Delayed by Request for Free Ad," *Editor and Publisher*, July 18, 1942, 9; "NAEA Hears of Appreciation in Washington for Advertising," *Editor and Publisher*, October 17, 1942, POP, Box 8, Folder: Advertising, 1942; "MacLeish, Phrase Maker, Sees Fate of U.S. as War in 'Words,'" *Editor and Publisher*, April 18, 1942, 12; "Morgenthau Stresses Role of Sponsored Bond Ads," *Editor and Publisher*, April 3, 1943, 3.

31. Odegard, "Place of the War Bond."

32. Elmer Davis to OWI Employees, "OWI Policy on Paid Advertising," August 12, 1943, NA2, RG 208, Entry 94, Records of the Radio Bureau, Records of the Chief, George Ludlam (hereafter GLR), Box 619, Folder: Paid Advertising.

33. "Davis Opposes Advertising by U.S.," *Broadcasting*, April 19, 1943, 12.

34. "ANA Told Future Holds More War Problems for Business," *Editor and Publisher*, November 14, 1942, 11.

35. See, for example, Dickinson, "How U.S. Could Use Paid Advertising"; "Britain Buys Space," *Advertising and Selling*, August, 1942, 26; "Who Should Pay?"; "War-Time Paid Government Advertising"; Chester J. LaRoche, Arthur Price, Arthur T. Robb, Ralph Coghlan, and Leonard Dreyfuss, "Should the Government Advertise?," *Public Opinion Quarterly* 9, no. 4 (Winter 1942): 511–36.

36. "Advertisers Mustered for War Campaign," *Broadcasting*, November 16, 1942, 10; "To Stop to Debate"; "ANA Told Future Holds More," 11.

37. "Who Should Pay?," 13.

38. "Publishers Want No Ad Subsidy, ANPA Is Told," *Advertising Age*, April 26, 1943, 1. For the Bankhead bill's full text, see "Here's Text of Bankhead Government Advertising Bill," *Printers' Ink*, May 14, 1943, 80. See also "House Committee Pigeon-holes Paid Gov't Ad Bills," *Advertising Age*, December 13, 1943, 1; War Advertising Council, "War Advertising Council Terms Bankhead-Cannon Bill Hindrance to War Effort," December 3, 1943, ACA, RG 13/2/305, Washington Office Subject File 1942–81, Box 1, Folder: Bankhead Bill 1943;"Bankhead Readies Paid Advertising Bill for Congress," *Advertising Age*, April 5, 1943, 7; "That Treasury Advertising Bill," *Advertising Age*, April 12, 1943, 12; "Publishers Want No Ad Subsidy"; "Advertising as a Subsidy," *Advertising Age*, May 17, 1943, 12; "Ad Groups 'Gang Up' on Bankhead Bill in House," *Advertising Age*, December 6, 1943, 1; "Gov't Advertising Bill Given Okay by Senate Group," *Advertising Age*, November 3, 1943, 8; "War-Time Paid Government Advertising."

39. W. M. Dear, "Publishers Must Maintain Eternal Vigilance against Government Restrictions and Control; Government Advertising Smacks of Subsidy," *Commercial and Financial Chronicle*, May 6, 1943, 1688; "Straight Thinking Needed," *Editor and Publisher*, April 17, 1943, 44.

40. "Frank Tripp Replies to E and P on Bankhead Bill," *Editor and Publisher*, November 13, 1943, 10.

41. "Senate Banking Group Okays Bankhead Bill," *Editor and Publisher*, October 19, 1943, 6.

42. Joe B. Carrigan to Elmer Thomas, March 26, 1943, GLR, Box 619, Folder: Paid Advertising. Supporters of the Bankhead bill and the related Cannon bill did not give up the fight. They kept reintroducing revised versions of the bills until those were defeated as well. See, for example, "Bankhead Bill to Emerge Anew as Congress Gathers," *Advertising Age*, January 10, 1944, 47; "Revised Version of Bankhead Bill Goes to House," *Advertising Age*, February 7, 1944, 8; "War Bond Ad Bill Faces Showdown in House Soon," *Advertising Age*, February 14, 1944, 1; "New Delays Balk Devotees of U.S. Paid Advertising," *Advertising Age*, April 3, 1944, 1.

43. NA2, RG 208, Entry 42, General Records of the Office of Program Coordination, July 1943–May 1944 (hereafter OPC), Box 149, Folder: Association of National Advertisers, 381; "NEA Backs Bankhead Gov't Advertising Bill," *Editor and Publisher*, October 23, 1943, 10.

44. "Bankhead Bill Cut in Half Passed by Senate," *Editor and Publisher*, November

20, 1943, 7; "This Bill Should Be Beaten," *Editor and Publisher*, November 20, 1943, 28.

45. Statement of Ted R. Gamble, National Director of the War Finance Division of the Treasury Department, before the Committee on Ways and Means of the House of Representatives, December 3, 1943, NA2, RG56, General Records of the Department of the Treasury, Entry 405-G, Records of the Savings Brands Division (including records of the "Predecessor, the War Finance Division"), Office of the National Director, Historical and Promotional records, 1941–60, Box 1, Speech Files, Boyle-Graves, Folder: Gamble T.R., 1943, 1 of 2, 5.

46. Ibid., 4.

47. "House Tables Gov't Ad Bill," 18; Esther M. Coppock to Madeline Ross, June 1, 1944, WP, Box 15, Folder 7.

48. Allen Grover to Miller [McClintock], April 28, 1942, OWI AD, Box 2, Entry 3B, Folder: Advertising Division Correspondence, 1942 (part 2).

49. C. B. Larrabee, "*A Challenge* to the Decent and Patriotic Elements in Advertising," *Printers' Ink*, April 23, 1943, 13.

50. Arthur Price, "Advertising Is Far from All-Out!" *Advertising and Selling*, April 1942, 16, emphasis in the original.

51. "Asks Greater War Effort on Part of Admen," *Advertising Age*, March 15, 1943, 8.

52. "War Theme Is Tops Again in National Copy, Study Shows," *Advertising Age*, June 28, 1943, 38.

53. "Qualms about Advertising in Wartime," *Advertising and Selling*, June 1942, 26; "Advertising News and Notes," *New York Times*, May 8, 1942, 31; "War Advertising Wins O.K., but Boasting Is Out," *Advertising Age*, May 11, 1942, 4. The public's confidence in advertising was quite high. Their aversion to boasting war advertisements continued throughout the war, however. See, for example, "Advertisers' War Effort," *Business Week*, November 21, 1942, 92; "Boasting Decried in War Advertising," *New York Times*, November 13, 1942, 33. In July 1942, *Printers' Ink* reported that 58 percent of 1,120 consumers in a survey believed that advertising provided specific benefits. Slightly more women than men fell into this category. See Daniel Starch, "What Consumers Really Think about Advertising," *Printers' Ink*, July 24, 1942, 26–27; R. M. Dobie, "Public Wants War Advertising to Continue, ANA Survey Shows," *Editor and Publisher*, May 9, 1942, 5. For a copy of the survey, see Psychological Corporation, "What the Public Is Thinking about Advertising: A Nation-Wide Survey Made for the Association of National Advertisers, Inc.," Bureau of Campaigns Chief, Box 140, Folder: Association of National Advertisers. For a copy of the detailed responses, see Association of National Advertisers, "What the Public Is Thinking about Advertising and Business," DCBC, Folder: A.N.A. Confidential Bulletin.

54. T. Mills Shepard, "What the War Theme Is Doing to Advertising Readership," *Advertising and Selling*, October 1942, 13.

55. "Advertising at Work," *Business Week*, June 19, 1943, 96; "ANA Finds Public Appreciates War Advertising," *Printers' Ink*, June 11, 1943, 24.

56. "Advertisers Take Stock of Themselves at A.N.A. Meeting," *Printers' Ink*, November 20, 1942, 16. See also "Advertisers' War Effort," *Business Week*, November 21, 1942, 92.

57. "Ad Men Condemn Grade Level Plan," *New York Times*, June 30, 1943, UD5, Box 3.

58. Roland Marchand, *Creating the Corporate Soul: The Rise of Public Relations and Corporate Imagery in American Big Business* (Berkeley: University of California Press, 1998), 313, 315.

59. James Playsted Wood, *The Story of Advertising* (New York: Ronald Press, 1958), 444. In contrast to the U.S. Army, which banned advertising in its service publications, the Navy allowed ads in some of its publications. See, for example, "Message to Joe," *Business Week*, April 29, 1944, 90. For additional information on soldiers' interest in advertisements, see William L. O'Neill, *A Democracy at War: America's Fight at Home and Abroad in World War II* (New York: Free Press, 1993), 255.

60. "Fighters Tell ANA They Resent Exaggerated Claims in Ad Copy," *Printers' Ink*, June 11, 1943, 26.

61. Charles G. Mortimer, "A Careful and Courageous 'Good and Bad' Wartime Advertising Study," in American Management Association, *Wartime Adjustments in the Sales Structure: With a Symposium on Wartime Advertising* (New York: AMA, 1943), ACA, RG 13/2/305, Box 1, Folder: ANA File, 1943–44, 11.

62. Richard R. Lingeman, *Don't You Know There's a War On? The American Home Front, 1941–1945* (New York: G. P. Putnam's Sons, 1970), 294; Wood, *Story of Advertising*, 444; O'Neill, *Democracy at War*, 254; "How to Lose Customers," *Time*, February 21, 1944, 79, CEWP, Box 62, Folder 1. For soldiers' objections to war-theme advertising and the industry's response to them, see "Government Seeks Aid of Advertisers," *New York Times*, February 11, 1944, 23; Eric Sevareid, "Super-Dupering the War," *Saturday Review of Literature*, February 12, 1944, 9–10; "Healy Asks Advertisers to Make War Messages 'More Vital, More Dynamic,'" *Broadcasting*, February 14, 1944, 13.

63. "Fighters Tell ANA," 24.

64. "Ad-vice from Guadalcanal," *Printers' Ink*, June 4, 1943, 16; "Spanking of the Week," *Time*, August 30, 1943, 47, CEWP, Box 62, Folder 1; Sevareid, "Super-Dupering the War," 9; Ric Jensen and Christopher Thomas, "To What Extent Did American Corporations Publish 'Brag Ads' during World War II?," *Advertising and Society Review* 10, no. 2 (2009), http://muse.jhu.edu/journals/advertising_and_society_review/summary/v010/10.2.jensen.html (accessed August 15, 2011). For a particularly critical view on the use of soldiers and the armed forces in advertisements, see Major Knox Manning, "Speech at U.S. Army Force, at PAA Conference at Fresno, June 14 [probably 1944]," TDBP, Box 5, Folder 6. For a satirical take on the issue, see "Advertising Has Gone to War," *Advertising Age*, December 4, 1944, 41.

65. "Educational Role of Advertising Charted by Industrial Conference," *Printers' Ink*, January 29, 1943, 56; "Advertising Shift Urged by Experts," *New York Times*, March 14, 1942, 28.

66. "Beck Outlines Wartime Tasks for Advertising," *Advertising Age*, February 23, 1942, 33.

67. "'Reason Why' Copy Stressed in New War Bond Series," *Advertising Age*, July 6, 1942, 26. Advertisements promoting war bonds to "the farm market" emphasized this angle as well. See memo to "All Advertising Agencies Placing Advertising in Farm Papers for the Farm Market" from Guy Lemmon, coordinator of the U.S. Treasury Project for the AAAA, May 19, 1943, TDBP, Box 3, Folder 5.

68. "New Haven Railroad Series Received So Well, It Goes National," *Printers' Ink*, December 11, 1942, 19. This advertisement received one of *Advertising & Selling*'s Annual Advertisement Awards for 1942. See "Kudos for Ads," *Business Week*, February 6, 1943, 68.

69. Quoted in Lingeman, *Don't You Know?*, 296. See also Richard Polenberg, *America at War: The Home Front, 1941–1945* (Englewood Cliffs, N.J.: Prentice-Hall, 1968).

70. "1943 Sets New Marketing Trends," *Printers' Ink*, January 7, 1944, 19.

71. "'Reason Why' Copy Stressed." For an excellent treatment of this subject, see Henthorn, *From Submarines to Suburbs*; Marchand, *Creating the Corporate Soul*, chap. 8.

72. "Give Her a War Bond and You Give Her the Best," advertisement in *Life*, December 6, 1943, 11 (see fig. 11 in chap. 6).

73. "Public Service Advertising," *Advertising Age*, February 2, 1942, 12.

74. "House Orders OWI to Quit Domestic Operations," *Editor and Publisher*, June 26, 1943, 20; Allan M. Winkler, *The Politics of Propaganda: The Office of War Information, 1942–1945* (New Haven, Conn.: Yale University Press, 1978), 66–72; "OWI Chief Answers Jibes of Congress; Defends Position," *Advertising Age*, March 29, 1943, 1. The reaction against the OWI was symptomatic of a more general hostility toward the New Deal. As the war wore on, argues Alan Brinkley, conservative attacks on the Roosevelt administration's domestic policies increased while liberal support for the same programs declined. Many of the New Deal's previous supporters were disappointed with what they perceived as Roosevelt's failure to provide domestic leadership. By the end of 1943, the liberal diaspora was nearly complete, as most war agencies replaced old "New Dealers" with more conservative individuals. The latter, often referred to as dollar-a-year men, were paid by major business interests and expressed their loyalties accordingly. For a treatment of these issues, see Alan Brinkley, *The End of Reform: New Deal Liberalism in Recession and War* (New York: Alfred A. Knopf, 1995), 137–54; Malcolm Cowley, "The End of the New Deal," in Polenberg, *America at War*, 80–85. See also "Report to the President," NA2, RG 208, Records of the Historian, Subject File 1941–46, Box 13, Entry 6E, Folder: Final Report by Elmer Davis to the President Concerning OWI 9/15–1945, 60–62.

75. "Willkie Influence in Office of War Information," The President's Secretary's Files, Franklin D. Roosevelt Library, Hyde Park, N.Y., Box 8, Folder: Office of War Information; Sidney Weinberg, "What to Tell America: The Writers' Quarrel in the Office of War Information," *Journal of American History* 55, no. 1 (June 1968): 82.

76. "Willkie Influence." See also Winkler, *Politics of Propaganda*, 63–66; Weinberg, "What to Tell America," 87.

77. Weinberg, "What to Tell America," 86; Winkler, *Politics of Propaganda*, 64. See also John Morton Blum, *V Was for Victory: Politics and American Culture during World War II* (San Diego: Harcourt Brace Jovanovich, 1976), 39, for a variation on this slogan. The fictitious Coca-Cola slogan spoofed the Four Freedoms outlined in President Roosevelt's 1941 State of the Union Address ("freedom of speech and expression," "freedom of every person to worship God in his own way," "freedom from want," and "freedom from fear"). See Brinkley, *End of Reform*, 143. For a discussion of advertisers' tendency to undermine their audiences' intelligence, see Roland Marchand, *Advertising the American Dream: Making Way for Modernity, 1920–1940* (Berkeley: University of California Press, 1985), 67.

78. Quoted in Weinberg, "What to Tell America," 86.

79. Ibid.; Dannagal Goldthwaite Young, "Sacrifice, Consumption, and the American Way of Life: Advertising and Domestic Propaganda during World War II," *Communication Review* 8, no. 1 (2005): 29.

80. Weinberg, "What to Tell America," 89. With the Domestic Branch cut down and circumscribed, Cowles resigned. He was elected president of the AFA soon thereafter. Cowles's resignation influenced his assistant, William Lewis, to follow suit. E. Palmer Hoyt, publisher of the *Portland Oregonian*, became the new head of the Domestic Branch. See Advertising Federation of America, "Officers for One Year, Elected June 29, 1943," BBP, Box 1, Folder: Advertising Federation of America; "Wm. B. Lewis, Ex-CBS Executive, Resigns from OWI," *Advertising Age*, June 21, 1943, 20; "OWI Names Editors to Advise on Operations," *Advertising Age*, July 12, 1943, 4; "Capital Given Quick Defense of OWI Division," *Advertising Age*, June 29, 1943, 4.

81. "The Impact of War on Advertising," *Advertising and Selling*, July 1943, 21.

82. "Testimony of Chester J. LaRoche, Chairman, War Advertising Council, on HR 2968 as It Concerns the Appropriations for the Office of War Information before the Senate Appropriations Committee," June 26, 1943, NA2, RG 208, Entry 28, Records of the Domestic Operations Branch, 1926–46, Records of the Director, General Records of Assistant Director James Rogers and William Lewis (hereafter JRWL), Box 46, Folder: War Advertising Council, Inc., 2, 5, 11; "Advertising Leaders Rally for OWI," *Broadcasting*, July 5, 1943, 20.

83. "Budget Cut 'Simplifies' Grandiose Plans for OWI," *Editor and Publisher*, August 21, 1943, 5, quote from 42.

84. "Admen Appointed to New Posts in Reorganized OWI," *Advertising Age*, March 15, 1943, 1; "Full Text of Statement by OWI and Its Operations," *Advertising Age*, March 29, 1943, 36; "OWI Tells Its Story," *Advertising Age*, April 5, 1943, 12; "OWI Ad Unit Adds Three New Members to Staff," *Advertising Age*, June 7, 1943, 6; "OWI 'Advertising' Unit Evades Lethal Blows of Congress," *Advertising Age*, July 5, 1943, 1; "Don't Hamstring OWI," *Advertising Age*, June 28, 1943, 12; David Lloyd Jones, "U.S. Office of War Information," 217.

85. War Advertising Council, "For Immediate Release," October 8, 1943, NA2, RG 208, Entry 27, Records of the Domestic Operations Branch, Records of the Assistant Director, General Records of Assistant Director James Allen, 1941–43, Box 427, Folder: War Advertising Council, 4.

86. Palmer Hoyt to Chester J. LaRoche, June 29, 1943, NA2, RG 208, Entry 23, Records of the Domestic Operations Branch, Correspondence of Director Neil Dalton, Box 27, Folder: War Advertising Council. See also "OWI: Advertising Agency," *Tide*, July 15, 1944, 20, OPC, Box 153, Folder: TIDE Reprint on OWI.

87. For a list and description of the Advertising Council's campaigns through its first eighteen months of existence, see "Memorandum on the Work of the War Advertising Council, 1942–1943," ACA, RG 13/2/202: Annual Reports, 1943–, Box 1, Folder: Ad Council Annual Report, 1942–43.

88. "OWI 'Advertising' Unit Evades," 41.

89. "War Advertising Council Opening Drive for War Advertising Message in Every Ad," *Broadcasting*, July 5, 1943, 18; "'War Advertising Council' New Name for Liaison Group," *Advertising Age*, June 7, 1943, 2; "'War Message in Every Ad.' Set Up as Goal of Field," *Advertising Age*, June 14, 1943, 8; "What Is War Advertising?," *Advertising Age*, June 21, 1943, 12; "Advertising News," *New York Times*, June 9, 1943, 28; "$500,000,000 Goal Set by Ad Council," *New York Times*, June 3, 1943, 29; "War Advertising Council Incorporated Memorandum," July 10, 1943, TDBP, Box 4, Folder 9. "Don't Hamstring OWI, An Editorial Appearing in the June 28 Issue of *Advertising Age*," JRWL, Box 46, Folder: War Advertising Council, Inc.; "Advertising Leaders Rally for OWI," *Broadcasting*, July 5, 1943, 20; T. S. Repplier to Gardner Cowles Jr., May 24, 1943, NA2, RG 208, Entry 20, Records of the Domestic Operations Branch, Correspondence of Director Gardner Cowles Jr., 1942–43, Box 12, Folder: War Advertising Council, Inc.

90. Chester J. LaRoche, "This Is Good War Advertising," *Printers' Ink*, July 9, 1943, 16–17; T. S. Repplier to Gardner Cowles Jr., June 18, 1943, JRWL, Box 46, Folder: War Advertising Council, Inc.

91. Elmer Davis to Chester J. LaRoche, June 29, 1943, JRWL, Box 46, Folder: War Advertising Council, Inc.; "Wartime Advertising Awards," *Advertising and Selling*, March 1944, 34.

92. "New War Ad Drive Gets Under Way," *Broadcasting*, July 19, 1943, 10; "Double Ad Support to the War Effort Urged by LaRoche on Closed Circuit," *Broadcasting*, July 12, 1943, 52; "War Advertising Council Opening Drive"; "Government Leaders Broadcast 'War Message in Every Ad' Plea," *Printers' Ink*, July 23, 1943, 86. Participating in the broadcast were Judge Fred M. Vinson, head of the Office of Economic Stabilization; Elmer Davis, director of the OWI; Marvin Jones from the War Food Administration; Donald Nelson, chairman of the War Production Board; and Chester LaRoche, chairman of the War Advertising Council. For reprints of their speeches, see "An Appeal to Business from the Country's War Leaders," ACA, RG 13/2/300, Box 1, Folder: War Advertising Council; Published Reports; Results of Campaigns;

War Theme Digest, February–March 1944, Carleton D. Smith to Don Stauffer, July 9, 1943, GLR, Box 619, Folder: National Broadcasting Company.

93. "War Leaders Appeal for a 'War Message in Every Ad,'" *War Advertising*, August 1, 1943, 1, TDBP, Box 4, Folder 9. See also "A War Message in Every Ad," *Advertising and Selling*, August 1943, 24; "The Council's 'Broadcast to Business,'" *Washington Newsletter*, no. 2 (August 20, 1943), OPC, Box 149, Folder: Advertising Council Newsletter, 4.

94. "War Ad Council to Ask Advertisers for Space," *Printers' Ink*, June 18, 1943, 61. See also "'A War Message in Every Ad,'" *Advertising and Selling*, July 1943, 26.

95. Office of War Information, "Text of Address by Chester J. LaRoche, Office of War Information Consultant and Chairman of the War Advertising Council, in a Broadcast over the NBC Network Originating in Washington, D.C., at 1:15 p.m., Wednesday, July 14, 1943," CEWP, Box 63, Folder 2.

96. *Washington Newsletter*, no. 3 (September 15, 1943), OPC, Folder: Advertising Council, 1.

97. Harry S. Truman, "I Believe in Advertising," *Printers' Ink*, November 19, 1943, 87. For a copy of the speech, see also "Address by Senator Harry S. Truman of Missouri at Annual Meeting of Central Council A.A.A.A. Lake Shore Club, Chicago— Thursday, November 11, 1943," TDBP, Box 7, Folder 10. The speech was reprinted in *Printers' Ink* after Roosevelt's death and Truman's ascent to the presidency. See "What President Truman Had to Say about Advertising," *Printers' Ink*, April 20, 1945, 23. Truman repeated his charges in a speech before the Milwaukee Advertising Club in March 1944. See "Deductions for Advertising Win Truman's Approval," *Advertising Age*, March 27, 1944, 1.

98. Harry S. Truman, "Big Business Advertises at Your Expense," *Progressive: La Follette's Magazine*, September 20, 1943, 1; Truman, "I Believe in Advertising," 87.

99. "A Senator on Advertising," *Business Week*, November 20, 1943, 111; "Loose Talk by Senator Truman," *Advertising and Selling*, October, 1943, 30.

100. "Suggested Letter from President Roosevelt," FDR PPF, Box 602 (2), Folder: Advertising Federation of America, 1939–1943.

101. Franklin D. Roosevelt to Elon Borton, June 15, 1943, FDR PPF, Box 602 (2), Folder: Advertising Federation of America, 1939–1943.

102. T. S. Repplier to Frederic R. Gamble, October, 25, 1943, TDBP, Box 4, Folder 9.

103. Ibid.

104. "OWI: Advertising Agency," *Tide*, July 15, 1944, OPC, Box 153, Folder: TIDE Reprint on OWI, 20.

105. Elmer Davis to Irwin Robinson, April 7, 1944, OPC, Box 151, Folder: War Advertising Council.

106. "Memorandum for General Watson and Grace Tully," February 16, 1944, and "Memorandum for the President," March 6, 1944, both FDR OF, Box 196, Folder: Advertising, 1944.

107. "Minutes of Meeting of the Board of Directors—War Advertising Council, Inc.,

January 28, 1944" and "Minutes of the Meeting of the War Advertising Council, Inc., February 18, 1944," both ACA, RG 13/2/201, Box 1, Folder: War Advertising Council—Board of Directors Minutes, January–February 1944. For an outline of the program, see "Minutes of Meetings of Sponsor Members and Board of Directors of War Advertising Council, March 3, 1944," ibid., Folder: War Advertising Council—Minutes, March–April 1944; "Words That Work for Victory," ibid., RG 13/2/202: Annual Reports, 1943–, Box 1, Folder: Ad Council Annual Report, 1944–45, 5. For a summary of Nelson's speech, see "WPB Warning Given on Civilian Output," *New York Times*, March 9, 1944, 23.

108. "Background Information for the White House Conference," FDR OF, Box 196, Folder: Advertising, 1944, emphasis in the original.

109. "Words That Work for Victory," 4–5; Franklin D. Roosevelt to Harold B. Thomas, December 7, 1944, ACA, RG 13/2/305, Box 5, Folder: The President's Letter.

110. Paul West to Stephen Early, March 14, 1944, FDR OF, Box 196, Folder: Advertising, 1944.

111. Paul B. West to George Healy, March 16, 1944, FDR OF, Box 196, Folder: Advertising, 1944. Others expressed similar views. See, for example, Joseph E. Casey to Stephen Early, March 16, 1944, ibid.

112. "Minutes of Meeting—Board of Directors and Sponsor Members—War Advertising Council, Inc., March 17, 1944," ACA, RG 13/2/201, Box 1, Folder: War Advertising Council—Minutes, March–April 1944.

113. Advertising organizations continued to keep a close watch on members' activities to ensure that advertising kept building its reputation. For example, the theme of the AFA's June 1943 conference was "Advertising's Place in the War and After." It featured off-the-record sessions to discuss whether advertising was doing its utmost to aid the war effort. See "Advertising's Role in War Takes Spot at AFA Conference," *Advertising Age*, June 21, 1943, 28.

Chapter 6. The Increasing Role of the War Advertising Council

1. The War Advertising Council admitted that it was not until the food campaigns in January 1943 that the formula for effective cooperation between the government and the council was worked out in any measure. Memo to Harold Thomas from A. E. Winger, August 17, 1944, ACA, RG 13/2/201: Meeting Minutes, 1942–98, Box 1, Folder: War Advertising Council—Board of Directors and Sponsor Members—Minutes, July–August 1944; "R. M. Dobie, McClintock Ad Council Chief, a Skillful Organizer, Diplomat," *Editor and Publisher*, June 27, 1942, 3; "Advertising Has Big Job Now and after War, AFA Hears," *Editor and Publisher*, June 27, 1942, 7.

2. "Is It Time to Re-examine the Relationships of Government and Advertising?," *Advertising and Selling*, October 1942, 20. For a discussion of the OWI's Domestic Branch and its coordinating difficulties, see Sidney Weinberg, "What to Tell America: The Writers' Quarrel in the Office of War Information," *Journal of American History* 55, no. 1 (June 1968): 73–89.

3. "Helping Advertising Get 'on the Beam,'" January 25, 1943, TDBP, Box 4, Folder 1. See also letter to Thomas D'Arcy Brophy from unidentifiable individual at Pedlar and Ryan, Inc., Advertising, January 25, 1943, ibid., Box 1, Folder 6; "Minutes of the Executive Committee of the Advertising Council, Inc.," January 8, 1943, ACA, RG 13/2/201, Box 1, Folder: War Ad., January–February 1943; "Confidential Memo to Mr. Brophy from Ralph Allum," November 19, 1943, TDBP, Box 4, Folder 9. See also Advertising Council, "Report of the Committee to Coordinate War Advertising," January 28, 1943, ibid.

4. "LaRoche Becomes Full-Time Head of Ad Council," *Advertising Age*, February 15, 1943, 6. After his six-month leave expired, LaRoche permanently resigned his position with Young and Rubicam in order to devote himself to working for the Advertising Council. See "Chester LaRoche Resigns from Young & Rubicam," *Advertising Age*, August 9, 1943, 1. In February 1943, LaRoche received the Gold Medal for Distinguished Service to Advertising. See "To Chester J. LaRoche in Recognition of His Distinguished Services to Advertising," *Advertising and Selling*, February 1943, 6–7; Miller McClintock to Kenneth R. Dyke, November 13, 1942, CBC, Box 140, Folder: Advertising Council.

5. Chester J. LaRoche to Gardner Cowles Jr., January 13, 1943, JRWL, Box 46, Folder: War Advertising Council, Inc., 1, 2.

6. "Advertising Plan to Coordinate War Advertising," n.d., TDBP, Box 4, Folder 1.

7. "War Council Plans to Enlist All Advertisers in Campaign," *Broadcasting*, June 14, 1943, 58; "Advertising Council Community War Plan," ACA, RG 13/2/300, Box 1, Folder: War Advertising Council Community War Plan, April 1943; Advertising Council, "Note: This is revision number one of the Advertising Council's Community War Plan," May 10, 1943, NA2, RG 56, General Records of the Department of the Treasury, Entry 405-G, Records of the Savings Bond Division, Historical and Promotional Records Division, Box 1, Speech Files, Boyle-Graves, Folder: Gamble T.R., 1943 (2 of 2). For a detailed outline of the goals and strategies involved in the new cooperative effort between the Advertising Council and the OWI, see Advertising Council, "Supplementary Report of the Committee to Coordinate War Advertising," February 18, 1943 (date on p. 4), JRWL, Box 46, Folder: War Advertising Council, Inc.

8. Gardner Cowles Jr., "Advertising and the Home Front" (speech given at the Annual Advertising Awards Presentation Banquet, February 5, 1943), National Association of Broadcasters Papers, State Historical Society of Wisconsin, Madison, Box 10, Folder 7, 5, emphasis in the original.

9. American Association of Advertising Agencies, "Should Your Agency Contribute to the Financial Support of the War Advertising Council?," TDBP, Box 4, Folder 9. For a list of war campaigns needing advertising support in September 1943, see "Urgent War Campaigns Requiring Advertising Support," *Advertising Age*, September 27, 1943, 50. In 1944, the council's annual budget reached $180,000. See "Words That Work."

10. These preliminary numbers covered only advertisers who placed their ads

through advertising agencies. War Advertising Council, "A Report on War Theme Advertising Used Jan. 1st–May 31st, 1943," June 23, 1943, OPC, Box 149, Folder: Advertising Council.

11. "Advertisers Advertise to Preserve Brand Names," Association of National Advertisers, Inc., *News Bulletin* 27, no. 40 (September 24, 1943), NA2, RG 208, Records of the Office of War Information, Entry 40, Folder: Association of National Advertisers, 362; T. S. Repplier to Gardner Cowles Jr., June 18, 1943, JRWL, Box 46, Folder: War Advertising Council, Inc.

12. "Advertisers Advertise to Preserve Brand Names."

13. Frederic R. Gamble (managing director of the AAAA), "Address at Meeting of Southern California Chapter, A.A.A.A.," October 22, 1943, TDBP, Box 7, Folder 10, 4.

14. Fox, *Madison Avenue Goes to War*, 33.

15. Henry Morgenthau Jr., "The Job Has Just Begun," *Advertising and Selling*, December 1943, 60.

16. "War Advertising Exhibit," *Washington Newsletter*, no. 2 (August 20, 1943), NA2, RG 208, Entry 42, OPC, Box 149, Folder: Advertising Council Newsletter, 4.

17. C. G. Mortimer to A.N.A. Members, September 12, 1943, TDBP, Box 23, Folder 1, 2. See also "Minutes of the Meeting of the Board of Directors of the War Advertising Council, Inc., September 10, 1943," ACA, RG 13/2/201, Box 1, Folder: War Advertising Council—Council and Board of Directors Minutes, September–October 1943, 2.

18. "People Think Manufacturers Are Doing a Good Job," *Consumer News Digest*, November 30, 1943, 4, CEWP, Box 62, Folder 1, 4.

19. Irwin Robinson to C. J. LaRoche, August 25, 1943, OPC, Box 149, Folder: War Advertising Council Conference Report.

20. Gamble, "Address at Meeting," 3; Mortimer to A.N.A. Members, September 12, 1943, 1.

21. Gamble, "Address at Meeting," 3.

22. "War Advertising Council Makes Appeal to Own Profession," *Editor and Publisher*, December 4, 1943, 22.

23. War Advertising Council, "For Immediate Release," October 8, 1943, NA2, RG 208, Entry 27, Records of the Domestic Operations Branch, Records of the Assistant Director, General Records of Assistant Director James Allen, 1942–43, Box 42, Folder: War Advertising Council.

24. George H. Roeder Jr., *The Censored War: American Visual Experience during World War Two* (New Haven, Conn.: Yale University Press, 1993), 24–25; Weinberg, "What to Tell America," 82. Cowles and LaRoche's official reason for turning down the request was that all available advertising space was committed to other campaigns such as war production and food rationing.

25. Roeder, *Censored War*, 24–25. For an excellent discussion of wartime advertisements, see Fox, *Madison Avenue Goes to War*, chap. 4.

26. "The Problem of the Big Drive," *Advertising and Selling*, May 1943, 21. See also "The Impact of War on Advertising," *Advertising and Selling*, May 1943, 21. Prior to

this change, *Life* magazine had shown horrible depictions of Japanese brutality and American retaliation. See "Ad-vice from Guadalcanal," *Printers' Ink*, June 4, 1943, 16.

27. War Advertising Council, "Guide for the Preparation of Campaign Folders," December 20, 1943, ACA, RG 13/2/305: Washington Office Subject File, 1942–81, Box 6, Folder: W.A.C. Presentations, 1943, 1944. For information about the OWI Program Book, see War Advertising Council, in Cooperation with the Office of War Information, "Your Advertising Can Save Lives," NA2, RG 208, Entry 6E, Records of the Office of War Information, Records of the Historian, Subject File 1941–46, Box 5, Entry 6E, Folder: Campaigns—War Advertising Council.

28. War Advertising Council, Inc., *War Theme Digest*, ACA, RG 13/2/300, Box 1, Folder: War Advertising Council; Published Reports; "Results of Campaigns"; *War Theme Digest* (February–March 1944), ACA, RG 13/2/300.

29. "Media Salesmen Urge Use of War Ads," *Sales Management*, March 1, 1944, 80; "Ad Council Record Outlined in Talk by John Sterling," *Advertising Age*, May 1, 1944, 45; "Words That Work," 5. The WAC also started to classify its campaigns according to their urgency. See, for example, "Council Assigns Emergency Rating to 5 Campaigns," *Advertising Age*, February 5, 1945, 51. See also "Home Front Campaigns of the War Advertising Council," *Advertising and Selling*, March 1945, 193, and May 1945, 169, for examples of such ratings.

30. War Advertising Council, *4 Ways to Show Your Colors*, ACA, RG 13/2/305, Box 3, Folder: Council Promotion 1944, 2.

31. "The (S)Word Is Mightier Than the Sword," ACA, RG 13/2/300: War Advertising Council File, 1941–45, Box 1, Folder: War Advertising Council, "The Word Is Mightier Than the Sword"; "Advertising News and Notes," *New York Times*, August 1, 1944, 20; "Full Steam for War Themes," *Advertising and Selling*, March 1944, 68. See War Advertising Council in Cooperation with the Office of War Information, "Your Advertising Can Save Lives," and War Advertising Council, *Facts You Should Know about the National War Fund* (New York: War Advertising Council, 1944), for examples of different forms of advertising tie-ins.

32. Don Wharton, "The Story Back of the War Ads," *Advertising and Selling*, June 1944, 146. The survey drew data from ten issues of three monthlies, two picture magazines, two women's magazines, two weeklies, and a newsmagazine.

33. "Advertisers to Play Big Postwar Role, ANA Told," *Advertising Age*, November 22, 1943, 2.

34. "Report of the War Advertising Survey Committee to the American Association of Advertising Agencies and the National Association of Better Business Bureaus," n.d., TDBP, Box 7, Folder 11, 4.

35. Ibid., 6. The committee instructed advertisers to (1) remind the public of U.S. objectives in the war and prepare them for the needed struggle and sacrifice; (2) encourage everyone to take part in the government's home-front activities; (3) promote the public health and encourage nutrition education; (4) make sure that war workers received due credit for doing their part to aid war production; (5) help align

consumers' buying habits with the wartime economic program; and (6) help maintain demand for consumer goods that were difficult to obtain during wartime, so as to guard against "economic shocks" as the nation returned to peacetime conditions.

36. Ibid., 5; William M. Farr to Allen L. Billingsley, n.d., TDBP, Box 7, Folder 11, 4.

37. "Work to Clean Up 'Objectionable' 2% of War-Efforts Ads," *Advertising Age*, June 19, 1944, 1; "Few Wartime Ads Objectionable, Is BBB Conclusion," *Advertising Age*, August 7, 1944, 44.

38. Thomas D'Arcy Brophy to Allen L. Billingsley, July 17, 1944, TDBP, Box 5, Folder 6, 1.

39. Letter to Thomas D'Arcy Brophy, July 12, 1944, TDBP, Box 7, Folder 11.

40. The womanpower campaign was designed to attract women to work in war-related industries. For an excellent treatment of this campaign, see Maureen Honey, *Creating Rosie the Riveter* (Amherst: University of Massachusetts Press, 1984), chap. 1.

41. Thomas D'Arcy Brophy to Allen L. Billingsley, June 28, 1944, TDBP, Box 7, Folder 11.

42. Brophy to Billingsley, July 17, 1944.

43. "A Tremendous Job Remains," *Advertising and Selling*, April 1944, 36. These findings contradicted an ANA survey from May 1943. Respondents in this survey reported that advertisements had provided them with helpful information about the various government campaigns. Association of National Advertisers, "Public Sentiments towards Wartime Advertising," Study No. 3, POP, Box 12, no folder.

44. "A Clean House for Advertising," *Advertising and Selling*, December 1944, 46.

45. Ibid.

46. *Washington Newsletter*, no. 3 (September 15, 1943), TDBP, Box 4, Folder 9, 1.

47. Allen L. Billingsley, Philip W. Lennen, William Reydel, and Guy C. Smith to Thomas D'Arcy Brophy, December 20, 1944, TDBP, Box 10, Folder 7, 2.

48. Ibid., 1.

49. Robinson Murray to Blake Clark, August 31, 1943, CEWP, Box 63, Folder 2, 2.

50. For a list of the WAC's campaigns between 1942 and 1945, see "Listing of Wartime Campaigns—1942–1945," TDBP, Box 1, Folder 5.

51. Allan M. Brandt, *No Magic Bullet: A Social History of Venereal Disease in the United States since 1880* (New York: Oxford University Press, 1987), 24.

52. Ibid., 77.

53. Ibid., chap. 2. The title of the film was later changed to *Fit to Fight*. It was declared obscene by the New York Board of Censors in 1919. Ibid., 69.

54. Ibid., 129.

55. Ibid., 143, 147.

56. H. Andrew Dudley to Chester J. LaRoche, May 14, 1943, NA2, RG 208, Entry 84, Records of the Deputy Director for Labor and Civilian Welfare, Records of Natalie Davisen, Program Manager for Homefront Campaigns, July 1943–August 1945 (hereafter NDR), Box 4, Folder: 1943—VD Correspondence, Letters, and Memos.

57. Charles Levitt to Gardner Cowles Jr., May 24, 1943, NDR, Box 4, Folder: 1943—

VD Correspondence, Letters, and Memos; "'Catholic News' Hits Ad Council for 'VD' Campaign," *Advertising Age*, September 4, 1944, 1; "Catholics vs. V.D. Frankness," *Newsweek*, September 18, 1944, 84. It is unclear how many of the five million people estimated to be infected with VD were soldiers. One of the largest censorship attempts by the Catholic Church focused on the movie industry. For an excellent treatment of the Catholic Church's efforts to censor the film industry, see Gregory D. Black, *Hollywood Censored: Morality Codes, Catholics, and the Movies* (New York: Cambridge University Press, 1994).

58. "Venereal Disease Program," undated memo, NA 2, RG 208, Office of War Information, Records of the Office of War Information, Entry 82, Records of the Deputy Director for Labor and Civilian Welfare, General Records of Deputy Director Herbert Little, October 1943–December 1944 (hereafter HLR), Box 558, Folder: V.D. Program, 9–10.

59. "Venereal Disease Program, Preliminary Draft," September 16, 1943, HLR, 8.

60. Paul B. West to C. J. LaRoche, July 1, 1943, NDR, Box 4, Folder: 1943—VD Correspondence, Letters, and Memos, 1–2; William B. Lewis to R. A. Vonderlehr, June 5, 1943, ibid.; Chester J. LaRoche to H. Andrew Dudley, June 10, 1943, ibid.; Noble Cathcart to James G. Rogers Jr., "VD Program," July 14, 1943, ibid.; Paul B. West to C. J. LaRoche, July 1, 1943, ibid., 1.

61. Allyn B. McIntire to Noble Cathcart, August 9, 1943, NDR, Box 4, Folder: 1943—VD Correspondence, Letters, and Memos.

62. Raymond Browne to Staff, "Conference Report," September 15, 1943, NDR, Box 4, Folder: 1943—VD Correspondence, Letters, and Memos; Andrew Dudley to James G. Rogers Jr., July 7, 1943, ibid.; Charles Levitt to James Rogers, July 15, 1943, ibid.

63. Levitt to Rogers, July 15, 1943; Dudley to Rogers, July 7, 1943.

64. Raymond Browne to Staff, "Conference Report," September 16, 1943, NDR, Box 4, Folder: 1943—VD Correspondence, Letters, and Memos; Robert Simpson to Robert Ferry, Crane Haussaman, and Herbert Little, November 2, 1943, NA2, RG 208, Entry 43, Records of the Office of the Director of War Programs, Materials for Information Campaigns, April–October 1943, Box 1, Folder: Program-V.D.C.

65. Robert Simpson to Phil Rogers, November 3, 1943, NDR, Box 4, Folder: 1943—VD Correspondence, Letters, and Memos.

66. Robert Simpson to Paul Warwick, December 13, 1943, NDR, Box 4, Folder: 1943—VD Correspondence, Letters, and Memos; Palmer Hoyt to Thomas Parran, December 2, 1943, ibid.

67. WAC Staff, "SUMMARY for the Use of Sponsorship Committees on the VD Information Campaign," January 17, 1944, NDR, Box 4, Folder: V.D. Mimeographed Releases, 3. For OWI guidelines to other media, see, for example, "Magazine War Guide for March–April 1944," December 10, 1943, ibid., Folder: 1943—VD Correspondence, Letters, and Memos; and United States Public Health Services, Office of War Information, "Venereal Diseases Control," January 1944, HLR, Box 558, Folder: V.D. Program.

68. "Advertisers Urged to Aid Campaign against 'V.D.,'" *Advertising Age*, August 7, 1944, 60; "Agencies Work to Rescue 'VD' Drive through Revisions," *Advertising Age*, September 18, 1944, 1, 60. Allyn McIntyre from the Pepperell Company was appointed as campaign manager. He received help from Douglas Meldrum, a WAC staff member. See "'Catholic News' Hits Ad Council."

69. "Shameless, Sinful," *Time*, October 16, 1944, 56. For WAC examples of how advertisers could incorporate VD themes into various forms of media and for different groups of audiences, see *Hidden Enemy: V.D.*, HLR, Box 558, Folder: V.D. Program. See also "Catholics vs. V.D. Frankness."

70. "Social Disgrace 'Ads' That Ignore Moral Considerations Scorned—Proposed Campaign to Bring 'VD' into the Open Would Shock Sense of Decency of Overwhelming Majority of Americans, Paper Says," N.C.W.C. News Service, August 21, 1944, HLR, Box 558, Folder: V.D. Program, 1; "War Advertising Council's V-D Campaign Criticized by Catholic Press and Laity," *Printers' Ink*, September 8, 1944, 54; "Controversy on the Venereal Disease Campaign," TDBP, Box 5, Folder 1.

71. "Paper Asks Steps to Oppose Proposed 'VD' Campaign," N.C.W.C. News Service, HLR, Box 558, Folder: V.D. Program, September 5, 1944, 8.

72. "War Advertising Council's V-D Campaign Criticized"; "Shameless, Sinful"; "Controversy on the Venereal Disease Campaign."

73. "K of C Protest Proposed 'VD' Campaign," N.C.W.C. News Service, September 4, 1944, HLR, Box 558, Folder: V.D. Program, 4; "Controversy on the Venereal Disease Campaign," 3.

74. "Campaign Advocating Respect for God's Laws Seen as Remedy," N.C.W.C. News Service, HLR, Box 558, Folder: V.D. Program, 4; "Controversy on the Venereal Disease Campaign," 8.

75. "V.D. Campaign," *America*, September 9, 1944, 555, HLR, Box 558, Folder: V.D. Program, 4; "Controversy on the Venereal Disease Campaign."

76. "Social Disease Drive Brings New Protest," *New York Times*, September 2, 1944, HLR, Box 558, Folder: V.D. Program.

77. John O'Hara, "Cannot the Same Power That Sells Toothpaste Sell Moral Ideas?," *Printers' Ink*, September 29, 1944, 26.

78. "Can Advertisers Fight VD?," *Advertising Age*, September 4, 1944, 12.

79. Quote from Thomas Parran to the War Advertising Council, September 16, 1944, HLR, Box 558, Folder: V.D. Program.

80. "Minutes of Meeting—Board of Directors and Sponsor Members—War Advertising Council, Inc., August 31, 1944," ACA, RG 13/2/201, Box 1, Folder: War Advertising Council—Board of Directors and Sponsor Members—Minutes, July–August 1944.

81. WAC Staff, "SUMMARY for the Use of Sponsorship Committees," 3. For OWI guidelines to other media, see, for example, "Magazine War Guide" for March–April 1944; and United States Public Health Services and Office of War Information, "Venereal Diseases Control."

82. "'Catholic News' Hits Ad Council"; "Catholics vs. V.D. Frankness." Herbert Little to George Healy, March 25, 1944, HLR, Box 558, Folder: V.D. Program; "To the People of the United States," n.d., ibid.

83. Thomas Parran to Walter Wagner, March 16, 1944, HLR, Box 558, Folder: V.D. Program, 1; Little to Healy, March 25, 1944. For a progress report on the general VD campaign, see "Changing Views on the VD Problem"; Parran to Wagner, March 16, 1944; Little to Healy, March 25, 1944; Healy to Parran, September 6, 1944; Parran to the War Advertising Council. For an excellent treatment of the Catholic Church's attempts at censoring the film industry, see Black, *Hollywood Censored*.

84. "Agencies Work to Rescue 'VD' Drive."

85. Healy to Parran, September 6, 1944; Parran to the War Advertising Council, September 16, 1944.

86. Herbert Little to David Frederick, "Suggested Statement for War Advertising Council," September 22, 1944, HLR, Box 558, Folder: V.D. Program.

87. Ibid.; "Shameless, Sinful"; "Controversy on the Venereal Disease Campaign"; "Parran Hopes for Admen's Support of VD Campaign," *Advertising Age*, September 25, 1944, 16.

88. "Controversy on the Venereal Disease Campaign," 4; "Council Drops Venereal Disease Campaign," *Printers' Ink*, September 29, 1944, 32; "Minutes of Meeting—Board of Directors and Sponsor Members—War Advertising Council, Inc., September 15 and September 22, 1944," ACA, RG 13/2/201, Box 1, Folder: War Advertising Council—Board of Directors—Minutes, September–October 1944. The *New Republic* was among those that regretted the campaign's demise. See "Catholics and Venereal Disease," *New Republic*, October 9, 1944, 446.

89. "Catholics and Venereal Disease," *New Republic*, October 9, 1944, 446; "Shameless, Sinful"; "Controversy on the Venereal Disease Campaign"; "Parran Hopes for Admen's Support."

90. War Advertising Council, "Controversy on the Venereal Disease Campaign, for Release in A.M. Papers, Wednesday, September 26, 1944," HLR, Box 558, Folder: V.D. Program.

91. Robert Merton's analysis of the entertainer Kate Smith's marathon broadcast over CBS during the third war bond drive in September 1943 shows how the council used its campaigns as a means to align itself with patriotism and patriotic causes. Robert K. Merton, *Mass Persuasion: The Social Psychology of a War Bond Drive* (New York: Harper, 1946).

92. "Keep War Drives Burning, Council Urges Advertisers," *Advertising Age*, August 21, 1944, 1.

93. "The War Isn't Over Yet," *Advertising Age*, April 3, 1944, 12; "Advertising's Continuing Job," *Advertising and Selling*, November 1944, 44.

94. "Full Steam Ahead," *Advertising and Selling*, January 1944, 34. *Advertising Age* expressed similar concerns; see "We Still Have a Job to Do," *Advertising Age*, November 13, 1944, 12.

95. Letter to Sherman K. Ellis, May 10, 1944, TDBP, Box 7, Folder 11; Don Wharton, "The Story Back of the War Ads," *Readers' Digest*, July 1944, 103–5.

96. Memorandum to "Board of Directors" from T. S. Repplier, October 20, 1944, ACA, RG 13/2/201, Box 1, Folder: War Advertising Council Board of Directors Minutes, September–October 1944, 3.

97. War Advertising Council, "Stirring Call to Action Issued by War Advertising Council" (news release), January 15, 1945, ACA, RG 13/2/305, Box 6, Folder: War Advertising Council News Releases 1945, 1.

98. War Advertising Council, *Are We Getting a Little Tired of the War?* (New York: War Advertising Council, 1945); "Council Seeking Wider Advertising Support to Combat Possible War-Weariness," *Printers' Ink*, January 12, 1945, 19; "Advertising News and Notes," *New York Times*, January 15, 1945, 25; "Council Booklet Calls for Support of War Theme Ads," *Advertising Age*, January 22, 1945, 55.

99. "Minutes of Meeting—Board of Directors and Sponsor Members—War Advertising Council, Inc., December 8, 1944 and February 2, 1945," ACA, RG 13/2/201, Box 1, Folder: War Advertising Council—Board of Directors and Sponsor Members—Minutes, November–December 1944.

100. "Indoctrination Meeting," January 12, 1945, ACA, RG 13/2/305, Box 4, Folder: Indoctrination 1944, 1945, 9.

101. War Advertising Council, "The Council Looks Ahead," ACA, RG 13/2/300: War Advertising Council File, 1941–45, Box 1, Folder: War Advertising Council Publications, 1945–46, n.p.

102. Irwin Robinson to T. S. Repplier, February 7, 1944, ACA, RG 13/2/305, Box 1, Folder: ANPA File, 1944.

103. "Reconverting Advertising," *Advertising Age*, February 7, 1944, 12.

104. "War Ad Council Urges Postwar Aid-U.S. Drives," *Advertising Age*, November 20, 1944, 38.

105. "Minutes of Meeting—Board of Directors and Sponsor Members—War Advertising Council, Inc., December 1, 1944," ACA, RG 13/2/201, Box 1, Folder: War Advertising Council—Board of Directors and Sponsor Members, Minutes, November–December 1944.

106. "War Ad Donations Put at $352,650,000," *New York Times*, March 23, 1944, 25; "Minutes of Meeting—Board of Directors and Sponsor Members—War Advertising Council, Inc., July 27, 1944," ACA, RG 13/2/201, Box 1, Folder: War Advertising Council—Board of Directors and Sponsor Members—Minutes, July–August 1944; "War Ad Council Urges Drives."

107. "War Ad Council Urges Drives."

108. Franklin D. Roosevelt to Harold B. Thomas, December 7, 1944, ACA, RG 13/2/305, Box 5, Folder: The President's Letter.

109. "Words That Work." For a list and brief description of the WAC's 1944 campaigns, see "Words That Work," 10–16.

110. "Words That Work," 18.

111. Memo to Thomas from Winger, August 17, 1944, 1.

Chapter 7. Peace and the Reconversion of the Advertising Council

1. "Minutes of Meeting Board of Directors and Sponsor Members War Advertising Council, Inc., August 24, 1944," and "Minutes of Meeting Board of Directors and Sponsor Members War Advertising Council, Inc., August 10, 1944," both ACA, RG 13/2/201: Meeting Minutes, 1942–98, Box 1, Folder: War Advertising Council—Board of Directors and Sponsor Members—Minutes, July–August 1944. See also "We Still Have a Job to Do," *Advertising Age*, November 13, 1944, 12.

2. War Advertising Council, "The Council Looks Ahead," ACA, RG 13/2/300: War Advertising Council File, 1941–45, Box 1, Folder: War Advertising Council Publications, 1945–46, n.p.

3. "Social Responsibilities," reprinted from *Tide* magazine, March 15, 1945, James Lawrence Fly Papers, Rare Books and Manuscripts Room, Butler Library, Columbia University, New York, Box 49 (hereafter JLFP), Folder: *Tide* Magazine, 3.

4. "What Are the Social Responsibilities of Advertising?" (transcript of a guided discussion directed by Leo Nejelski and sponsored by *Tide* magazine), February 9, 1945, JLFP, Folder: *Tide* Magazine, 19. For Lasswell's pioneering work on propaganda, see Harold D. Lasswell, *Propaganda Technique in the World War* (New York: Alfred A. Knopf, 1927).

5. War Advertising Council, "Confidential Memorandum," n.d., ACA, RG 13/2/305, Box 5, Folder: Post War Planning, 2–3. Similar concerns were expressed by the editors of Time-Life-Fortune. See "Meeting of Post War Planning Committee with Editors of Time-Life-Fortune," ACA, RG 13/2/305, Box 3, Folder: Council Future Plans, 1945 (2), 2.

6. Franklin D. Roosevelt to Harold Thomas, December 7, 1944, ACA, RG 13/2/305: Washington Office Subject File, 1942–81, Box 5, Folder: The President's Letter, 1944. See also "Roosevelt Lauds Ad Group's Work," *New York Times*, December 19, 1944, 28. The president's letter was prompted by a request from Thomas. See Harold Thomas to Franklin D. Roosevelt, November 29, 1944, FDR PPF, Box 9003, Folder: War Advertising Council. For a copy of the president's letter, see TDBP, Box 7, Folder 11.

7. "Ad Council Sheds War Mantle to Embark upon Peace Program," *New York Times*, November 1, 1945, 38. Several government officials, including President Truman, expressed great appreciation for the council's war work and welcomed its decision to continue into the postwar era. See H. B. Lewis to T. S. Repplier, November 13, 1945, ACA, RG 13/2/305, Box 3, Folder: Council—Future Plans, 1945. For a comment from Secretary of the Treasury Fred M. Vinson, see "Minutes of Meeting Board of Directors and Sponsor Members War Advertising Council, September 7, 1945," ACA, RG 13/2/201, Box 2, Folder: War Advertising Council Minutes, September–October

1945; "Truman Critical of, but Believer in War Advertising," *Advertising Age*, April 16, 1945, 1; Harry Truman to James Webb Young, October 15, 1945, ACA, RG 13/2/305, Box 4, Folder: Government Information Set-Up, 1945. See also *Tide* newsletter, October 19, 1945, ACA, RG 13/2/305, Box 6, Folder: War Advertising Council—Publicity, 1; "Truman Approves WAC Continuation," *Broadcasting*, October 22, 1945, 85; "President Backs Plan for Business Public Service" (news release), October 18, 1945, ACA, RG 13/2/305, Box 6, Folder: WAC News Releases, 1945.

8. "Minutes of Meeting Board of Directors and Sponsor Members, The Advertising Council, Inc., November 30, 1945," ACA, RG 13/2/201, Box 2, Folder: Advertising Council, November–December 1945, 2; War Advertising Council, "From War to Peace," ACA, RG 13/2/300, Box 1, Folder: War Advertising Council Publications, 1945–46. In addition to Clark, the Public Advisory Committee consisted of Olive Clapper, the wife of famous Washington reporter Raymond Clapper and a publicist; Kermit Eby, research director at the Congress of Industrial Organizations; Chester Davis, president of the Federal Reserve Bank of St. Louis and chairman of the Famine Emergency Committee; Clarence Francis, chairman of the General Foods Corporation; Dr. George Gallup, director of the American Institute of Public Opinion; Dr. Alan Gregg, director of medical science at the Rockefeller Foundation; Helen Hall, director of the Henry Street Settlement; Paul Hoffman, president of the Studebaker Corporation; A. E. Lyon, executive secretary of the Railroad Executives Association; Eugene Meyer, publisher of the *Washington Post*; Dr. Reinhold Niebuhr, professor of applied Christianity at the Union Theological Seminary; Boris Shishkin, an economist for the American Federation of Labor; and Dr. George N. Shuster, the president of Hunter College. "Public Advisory Group Will Aid Ad Council," *Advertising Age*, May 6, 1946, 73. See also Evans Clark, "What Leaders in All Fields Say of the Campaign," Association of National Advertisers, *New Dimensions for Advertising*, the 39th Annual Meeting of the Association of National Advertisers, October 27, 1948, ACA, Box 496, 6–7; For a list of members of the Industrial Advisory Committee, see ibid., 36.

9. "Minutes of Meeting Board of Directors and Sponsor Members War Advertising Council, Inc., October 6, 1944," ACA, Box 1, Folder: War Advertising Council Board of Directors Minutes, September–October 1944; War Advertising Council, "From War to Peace," n.p.; "War Ad Council Launches Peacetime Service Plan," *Advertising Age*, September 17, 1954, 1–2.

10. "Minutes of Meeting Board of Directors and Sponsor Members War Advertising Council, Inc., May 4, 1945," ACA, RG 13/2/201, Box 1, Folder: War Advertising Council Board of Directors and Sponsor Members, Minutes, May–June 1945.

11. "Memorandum to the Planning Committee," n.d. (probably from May or June 1945), TDBP, Box 5, Folder 1, 2–4.

12. "Minutes of Meeting Board of Directors and Sponsor Members War Advertising Council, Inc., June 1, 1945," ACA, RG 13/2/201, Box 1, Folder: War Advertising Council Board of Directors and Sponsor Members, Minutes, May–June 1945, 4; War Advertising Council, "Confidential Memorandum," 5.

13. "A Post-War Plan for the War Advertising Council," June 27, 1945, TDBP, Box 5, Folder 1, 1.

14. "Minutes of Meeting Board of Directors and Sponsor Members, War Advertising Council, Inc., September 28, 1945," ACA, RG 13/2/201, Box 2, Folder: War Advertising Council Minutes, September–October 1945, 3.

15. "Business Men Urged to Weigh Social Responsibilities," Advertising Council Press Release, November 20, 1945, ACA, RG 13/2/305, Box 6, Folder WACouncil, News Releases 1945, 3, emphasis in the original.

16. "Where Does Advertising Go from Here?," *Advertising and Selling*, September 1945, ACA, RG 13/2/305, Box 5, Folder: Postwar Planning, 1945, 34; "Minutes of Meeting Board of Directors and Sponsor Members War Advertising Council, Inc., May 11, 1945," ACA, RG 13/2/201, Box 1, Folder: War Advertising Council Board of Directors and Sponsor Members, Minutes, May–June 1945, 3. For the proposal to continue the WAC into the postwar period, see War Advertising Council, "Confidential Memorandum," n.d., ACA, RG 13/2/305, Box 5, Folder: Post War Planning. Others also advised postwar advertising to stay clear of "politics and pressure groups" but warned that this could be rather difficult. See, for example, "Advertising as a Social Force," *Advertising Age*, November 27, 1944, 12.

17. "In the Public Service," *Advertising Age*, April 30, 1945, 12. See also "A Better Advertising Climate," *Advertising Age*, June 25, 1945, 12; "Let's Start by Saving Lives," *Advertising Age*, September 24, 1945, 12. The proposal to continue the WAC into the postwar period received twenty-two affirmative votes and one negative vote. Three board members cast "unknown" votes. "Minutes of Meeting Board of Directors and Sponsor Members War Advertising Council, Inc., July 27, 1945," ACA, Box 2, Folder: War Advertising Council Minutes, July–August 1945.

18. "A Plan to Sell the Post-War Council," August 9, 1945, ACA, RG 13/2/201, Box 2, Folder: War Advertising Council Minutes, July–August 1945.

19. "War Ad Council Launches Peacetime Service Plan"; "Advertising News and Notes," *New York Times*, September 17, 1945, 24; "Ad Council Maps $30,000,000 Public Service Program," *Printers' Ink*, September 21, 1945, 55; "Minutes of Meeting Board of Directors and Sponsor Members War Advertising Council, Inc., November 30, 1945," ACA, RG 13/2/201, Folder: War Advertising Council Minutes, September–October 1945, 2; "Minutes of Meeting Board of Directors and Sponsor Members, Advertising Council, Inc., October 26, 1945," ibid., Folder: Advertising Council Minutes, November–December 1945; "Minutes of Meeting Board of Directors and Sponsor Members, Advertising Council, Inc., December 28, 1945," ibid. One trade journal guessed that the annual amount would be "at least" $40 million. See "Ad Plan Lives On," *Business Week*, September 22, 1945, 95–96. Confidentially, the WAC estimated these contributions to be between $30 million and $75 million a year; see "Post-War Plan," 5.

20. "Ad Council Maps $30,000,000," 70, 74.

21. The seven paying sponsors included the AAAA, the ANPA (and its Bureau of Advertising), the ANA, the National Association of Broadcasters, the National

Publishers Association, the Outdoor Advertising Association of America, and the Point of Purchase Advertising Institute. Twenty-seven organizations in the printing, engraving, publishing, and advertising fields were affiliated with the council as well. "Ad Council Maps $30,000,000"; "Advertising News and Notes," *New York Times*, October 4, 1945, 28; "Progress Report to the Chairman," October 23, 1945, ACA, RG 13/2/305, Box 3, Folder: Council—Future Plans (1), 1945, 4.

22. By 1948, the council had rented the entire floor of the central building located at 25th West Forty-Fifth Street in New York City. See "Advertising Council Gets Floor," *New York Times*, December 14, 1948, 53.

23. "Snyder Agrees to Talk 'Clearance' Plan with Council," *Advertising Age*, September 24, 1945, 65.

24. "Truman Acts to Aid Task of Ad Council," *New York Times*, October 18, 1945, 27; "Dudley Back Again as 'Advertising Manager of U.S.,'" *Advertising Age*, October 29, 1954, 7. After one year on the job, Dudley left his position to assist Eugene Meyer, the president of the International Bank for Development and Reconstruction. See "Dudley Takes Bank Post; Ad Council Hunts New Liaison," *Advertising Age*, November 4, 1946, 2.

25. "Council Assumes OWI Radio Allocation Plans," *Advertising Age*, September 17, 1945, 76; "Executive Office of the President—Office of Government Reports," Files of Charles W. Jackson, Harry S. Truman Papers, Harry S. Truman Library, Independence, Mo. (hereafter CWJ), Box 1, Folder: Advertising Council's 5th Anniversary. See also Gerd Horten, *Radio Goes to War: The Cultural Politics of Propaganda during World War II* (Berkeley: University of California Press, 2002).

26. Anthony Hyde to Mr. Steelman, November 15, 1946, NA2, RG 250, Office of War Mobilization and Reconversion, Entry 16, Subject Numeric File II General Classified File, May 1945–December 1945, Box 176-D, "Public Relations—4, Information Program."

27. "Business Steps Up Its Candle Power," vol. 5, *Year of the Advertising Council*, ACA, RG 13/2/202: Annual Reports, 1943–, Box 1, Folder: Ad Council Annual Reports, 1946–47, 8; Hyde to Steelman, November 15, 1946; "Executive Office of the President—Office of Government Reports"; "Truman Acts to Aid Ad Council"; Theodore S. Repplier, "Advertising Dons Long Pants," *Public Opinion Quarterly* 9, no. 3 (Fall 1945): 269–78.

28. See, for example, "Conference—The White House, September 17–18, 1946," John W. Gibson Papers, Harry S. Truman Library, Independence, Mo. (hereafter JWGP), Box 3, Folder: White House Conference, September 1946.

29. Advertising Council, "Report on Major National Problems," n.d., NA2, RG 250, Office of War Mobilization and Reconversion, Entry 20, Box 186, Folder: Advertising Council Meetings, 1.

30. Ibid. See also John Steelman to "Jack," September 23, 1946, NA2, RG 250, Office of War Mobilization and Reconversion, Entry 5, Central Files, General Classified Files, Box 47, Folder: Meetings—Advertising Council; J. D. Small to "John," Sep-

tember 4, 1946, ibid. See, for example, "Conference—The White House, September 17–18, 1946."

31. Edgar Kobak to John Steelman, February 14, 1949, Harry S. Truman Papers, Harry S. Truman Library, Independence, Mo. (hereafter HSTP), Official File, Box 1706/2597 Feb '49, Folder #2.

32. Office of War Mobilization and Reconversion, September 17, 1946, HSTP, Official File, Box 684, Folder: OF 196, 1.

33. Theodore S. Repplier, "Now the American Enterprise System Is Being Re-sold to the American People" (speech before the Association of National Advertisers Convention, Atlantic City, October 1, 1946), Files of Dallas C. Halverstadt, HSTP, Box 1, Folder: The Advertising Council misc.; Robert Jackall and Janice M. Hirota, *Image Makers: Advertising, Public Relations, and the Ethos of Advocacy* (Chicago: University of Chicago Press, 2000), chap. 2.

34. Kim McQuaid, *Uneasy Partners: Big Business in American Politics, 1945–1990* (Baltimore: Johns Hopkins University Press, 1994), 18. See also Elizabeth Fones-Wolf, *Selling Free Enterprise: The Business Assault on Labor and Liberalism, 1945–60* (Urbana: University of Illinois Press, 1994).

35. C. Hartley Grattan, "What British Socialism Is Up Against," *Harper's Magazine* 193 (July 1946): 38–48.

36. McQuaid, *Uneasy Partners*, 18. See also Fones-Wolf, *Selling Free Enterprise*.

37. Patrick Renshaw, *American Labor and Consensus Capitalism, 1935–1990* (Jackson: University Press of Mississippi, 1991), 108.

38. Win Cline, "Sell Public the Idea *behind* All This Post-War Planning," *Printers' Ink*, November 19, 1943, 18, emphasis in the original. For information about these issues, see Robert H. Ziegler, *American Workers, American Unions, 1920–1985* (Baltimore: Johns Hopkins University Press, 1992), chap. 4; Renshaw, *American Labor*, chap. 4.

39. The CED was an independent business organization with no formal ties to the government. The BAC, on the other hand, was part of the government's Commerce Department. The BAC had been created by big business at the request of New Deal leaders to maintain mutual advisory contacts when the National (Industrial) Recovery Administration negotiated its economic reforms. See Robert M. Collins, "Positive Business Response to the New Deal: The Roots of the Committee for Economic Development, 1933–1942," *Business History Review* 52, no. 3 (Autumn 1978): 369–91; McQuaid, *Uneasy Partners*, 19. For a discussion of the CED in the postwar period, see Karl Schriftgiesser, *Business and Public Policy: The Role of the Committee for Economic Development, 1942–1967* (Englewood Cliffs, N.J.: Prentice-Hall, 1967). For a treatment of labor issues in the 1940s, see, for example, Ziegler, *American Workers*, chaps. 3–5; Nelson Lichtenstein, *Labor's War at Home: The CIO in World War II* (New York: Cambridge University Press, 1992); George Lipsitz, *Rainbow at Midnight: Labor and Culture in the 1940s* (Urbana: University of Illinois Press, 1994). Elizabeth A. Fones-Wolf maintains that the USCC had more liberal tendencies than

the NAM. This became apparent during World War II, when the USCC's organizational setup and leaders reflected a more conciliatory attitude toward labor and liberal ideas. Fones-Wolf, *Selling Free Enterprise*, chap. 1; Daniel L. Lykins, *From Total War to Total Diplomacy: The Advertising Council and the Construction of Cold War Consensus* (Westport, Conn.: Praeger, 2003), chap. 3.

40. The term *nonpolitical* most likely meant *nonpartisan*.

41. Lykins, *From Total War*, 40.

42. McQuaid, *Uneasy Partners*, 18–20; Fones-Wolf, *Selling Free Enterprise*, 23–24. See also Roger William Riis, "Industry's Plan for Prosperity," *Advertising and Selling*, March 1943, 15–16.

43. Lykins, *From Total War*, 40.

44. Riis, "Industry's Plan for Prosperity," 16, emphasis in the original; Jackall and Hirota, *Image Makers*, 46–47.

45. "Stuart Chase Book Points Way to Postwar Goals," *Advertising Age*, November 23, 1942, 40. This survey was quoted in a book that Stuart Chase, the leader of Consumers' Research in the 1920s and 1930s, was commissioned to write for the Twentieth Century Fund.

46. "What's Free Enterprise," *Advertising Age*, November 15, 1943, 12. Confusion over the exact meaning of *free enterprise* was not limited to the general public; business interests were uncertain as well. Attempting to clarify the matter, *Printers' Ink* asked industry representatives to submit definitions of the term. The trade journal appointed a jury to select the best three proposals and asked the business community to use these definitions whenever it referred to *free enterprise*. See "Here, Mr. Dreyfuss, Are Some Definitions of 'Free Enterprise,'" *Printers' Ink*, April 7, 1944, 21. Whereas only 30 percent of adult Americans knew the meaning of *free enterprise* in 1943, a majority expressed a "somewhat informed" opinion a year later. See Frank LaClave, "How Sales and Advertising Executives Can Use Public Relations," *Printers' Ink*, October 20, 1944, 93–94.

47. "What the Public Thinks about You," ACA, RG 13/2/305, Box 3, Folder: Future Plans 1945 (2), 16–17. In spite of opposition from radical groups such as the People's Lobby, Inc., an organization closely affiliated with Consumers Union, business emerged as the clear winner in the postwar fight over control of federal production plants and equipment. Most were sold to a small group of large manufacturers at minimal prices, often pennies on the dollar. Kim McQuaid declares big business a clear winner in what he terms "a program of state-sponsored oligopoly"; *Uneasy Partners*, 24. See also The People's Lobby, Inc., "Which Way Will America Choose," ACA, RG 13/2/305, Box 3, Folder: Council Future Plans, 1945 (2); "Reconversion the Hard Way," *Advertising Age*, February 28, 1944, 12.

48. Richard S. Tedlow, *Keeping the Corporate Image: Public Relations and Business, 1900–1950* (Greenwich, Conn.: JAI Press, 1979), 121–22.

49. William L. Bird Jr., *Better Living: Advertising, Media, and the New Vocabulary of Business Leadership, 1935–1955* (Evanston, Ill.: Northwestern University Press, 1999), 160; "Minutes of Meeting of the Board of Directors of the War Advertising Council,

Inc., February 4, 1944," ACA, RG 13/2/201, Box 1, Folder: War Advertising Council Board of Directors Minutes, January–February 1944, 1; "Minutes of Meeting Board of Directors and Sponsor Members War Advertising Council, Inc.," February 9, 1945, 1, and January 19, 1945, 2–3, ACA, RG 13/2/201, Box 1, Folder: War Advertising Council Board of Directors and Sponsor Members Minutes, January–February 1945; "Minutes of Meeting Board of Directors War Advertising Council, Inc., December 10, 1943," ACA, RG 13/2/201, Box 1, Folder: War Advertising Council—Council and Board of Directors Minutes, November–December 1943. For a discussion of the advertising community's (favorable) view of the CED and advertising's role in promoting the commission's goals, see, for example, "Advertising in Post-War Era Must Combat State Socialism," *Commercial and Financial Chronicle*, July 8, 1943, 114; "Advertising's Responsibility in the Postwar Economy," *Advertising and Selling*, December 1944, 74. See also "The C.E.D.'s Tax Plan," *Advertising and Selling*, October 1944, 40; "Preconditioning Postwar Markets," *Advertising Age*, September 20, 1943, 12; "Production Comes First," *Advertising Age*, May 31, 1943, 12. Elizabeth A. Fones-Wolf discusses the many postwar organizations that were established to defend free enterprise. The (War) Advertising Council, with its recognition of labor's right to free collective bargaining, found a home among the more liberal segment of this group. Fones-Wolf, *Selling Free Enterprise*, 38–39.

50. "Asks Ad Council Aid to Win the Peace," *New York Times*, November 18, 1944, 21.

51. War Advertising Council, "The Council Looks Ahead." The WAC's vice-chairman warned advertisers that peace would not automatically solve all of its problems. The situation called for a well-planned strategy. "Minutes of Meeting Board of Directors and Sponsor Members War Advertising Council, Inc., May 18, 1945," ACA, RG 13/2/201, Box 1, Folder: War Advertising Council Board of Directors and Sponsor Members Minutes, May–June 1945.

52. "Help of Business in Cold War Cited," *New York Times*, August 25, 1949, 1; The Advertising Council, "Progress Report—November, 1949," CWJF, Box 19, Folder: Advertising Council Monthly Summaries (3 of 3), 1.

53. Jackall and Hirota, *Image Makers*, 46.

54. Ibid.; Lykins, *From Total War*, 34–35.

55. Fones-Wolf, *Selling Free Enterprise*, 199.

56. Robert Griffith, "The Selling of America: The Advertising Council and American Politics, 1942–1960," *Business History Review* 57, no. 1 (Autumn 1983), 395.

57. Ibid., 396; Fones-Wolf, *Selling Free Enterprise*, 199.

58. Griffith, "Selling of America," 398.

59. Lykins, *From Total War*, 75; "Clark Explains Funds for 'Freedom Train,'" *New York Times*, June 19, 1947, 44. See also John Vianney McGinnis, "The Advertising Council and the Cold War" (Ph.D. diss., Syracuse University, 1991), chap. 5.

60. Griffith, "Selling of America," 399. A "listener impression" refers to one individual listening to one particular message. If one person listened to two hundred "Freedom Train" announcements, he or she would generate two hundred impressions. Thus, the number of impressions was larger than the number of people reached.

61. "For Radio, September 16, P.M.," n.d., Papers of Tom C. Clark, Harry Truman Papers (hereafter TCC), Box 38, Folder: Freedom Train (2).

62. Stuart J. Little, "The Freedom Train: Citizenship and Postwar Political Culture, 1946–1949," *American Studies* 34, no. 1 (1993): 37–38.

63. Lykins, *From Total War*, 69.

64. Little, "Freedom Train," 55.

65. Paul Robeson, "Plain Talk" (newspaper clipping from unidentified source), TCC, Box 38, Folder: Freedom Train (2).

66. "For Radio."

67. Little, "Freedom Train." 56–60.

68. Ibid., 59.

69. Griffith, "Selling of America," 399.

70. Patricia Cayo Sexton, *The War on Labor and the Left: Understanding America's Unique Conservatism* (Boulder, Colo.: Westview Press, 1991), 141–42. See also Richard M. Fried, *Nightmare in Red* (New York: Oxford University Press, 1990). For a discussion of communist accusations against the 1930s consumer movement, see Stole, *Advertising on Trial*, chap. 7.

71. Fones-Wolf, *Selling Free Enterprise*, 6.

72. "Ad Drive Set to Aid Free Enterprise," *New York Times*, April 18, 1947, 1.

73. Ibid.; T. J. Repplier to John R. Steelman, August 5, 1947, HSTP, Box 685, Folder OF 196 (1947), 1, 2.

74. "Ad Drive Set to Aid Free Enterprise," *New York Times*, April 18, 1947, 31.

75. "Advertising Council Backs ANA–4-A Drive to Improve Understanding of U.S. System," *Printers' Ink*, April 25, 1947, 109.

76. "Ad Drive 'to Sell' U.S. System Ready," *New York Times*, April 24, 1947, 37.

77. "Advertising Council Backs ANA–4-A Drive."

78. "'Free Enterprise' Theme Sought," *New York Times*, October 25, 1947, 41; "'Enterprise' Ads Meet Resistance," *New York Times*, January 25, 1948, 1.

79. "'Free Enterprise' Snag Denied," *New York Times*, November 11, 1947, 42:3.

80. "Radio Advertising Declared Lacking," *New York Times*, May 29, 1947, 30.

81. By the fall of 1948, nearly fifty different firms were reported to have adapted the basic plan; Brendan M. Jones, "Nation-Wide Advertising Campaign Aimed at Combating Communism," *New York Times*, October 17, 1948, sec. 3, 1.

82. "'Enterprise' Ads Meet Resistance"; "'Free Enterprise' Theme Sought"; Brendan M. Jones, "Nation-Wide Advertising Campaign."

83. Brendan M. Jones, "Nation-Wide Advertising Campaign."

84. The Advertising Council, "Progress Report, November, 1949," CWJ, Box 19, Folder: Advertising Council Monthly Summaries (3 of 3), 1.

85. The Advertising Council, "Monthly Progress Report—March, 1950," CWJ, Box 19, Folder: Advertising Council Monthly Summaries (3 of 3), 1; The Advertising Council, "Progress Report—January 1950," ibid., 1–2.

86. The Advertising Council, "Progress Report—February, 1950," CWJ, Box 19, Folder: Advertising Council Monthly Summaries (3 of 3), 1.

87. "Canadian Groups Examine Proposal for Ad Council," *Advertising Age*, October 6, 1947, 20; "World Advertising Action Now," *Advertising Agency and Advertising and Selling*, April 1952, 82–83.

88. "Ad Drive Is Aimed at Communism," *New York Times*, November 11, 1948, 43.

89. Summary of the Advertising Council's Activities for November, 1948, CWJ, Box 19, Folder: Advertising Council Monthly Summaries (1 of 3), 6–7.

90. "Talks in the Treaty Room: A Catch-as-Catch-Can (but Confidential) Report on a Two-Day Session in Washington, February 15 and 16, 1950," February 21, 1950, CWJ, Box 21, Folder: Advertising Council—White House Meeting, Feb '50 (2 of 2), 5.

91. "Ad Men Urged to Back U.S. Total Diplomacy," *Advertising Age*, April 3, 1950, 32.

92. "Help of Business in Cold War Cited"; Brendan M. Jones, "'Education' Urged on World Affairs," *New York Times*, March 12, 1950, sec. 3, 1.

93. John Stuart, "Freedom Crusade Is 'Rolling In High,'" *New York Times*, September 9, 1951, sec. 3, 8.

94. "Advertising and Marketing News," *New York Times*, September 9, 1952, 41.

95. Advertising Council, "Give us this day . . . Our daily *truth*," ad prepared by the Advertising Council for the Crusade for Freedom campaign ca. 1952. ACA, Historical File, 1941- (RS 13/2/207), Folder 556, Crusade for Freedom/Radio Free Europe.

96. LB (Leo Burnett) to T. S. Repplier, January 15, 1951, CWJ, Box 21, Folder: Advertising Council—White House Meeting, Feb '50 (1 of 2). For a copy of the report, see "Briefing on America," January 1951, ibid.; "Round Table Discussion on the Basic Elements of a Free, Dynamic, Society, Sponsored by the Advertising Council Ink," April 1951, Files of Spencer R. Quick, HSTP, Box 1, Advertising Council Misc. Corr. 1951; The American Round Table, Digest Report of the Second Session, "Our Concept of Political and Civil Liberties," May 26, 1952, Sponsored by the Advertising Council Ink, April 1951, ibid.; The American Round Table, Digest Report of the First Session, "The Moral and Religious Basis of the American Society," Sponsored by the Advertising Council Ink, April 1951, ibid.

97. "General Eisenhower's Comments at the A.N.A. Meeting, Association of National Advertisers," *New Dimensions for Advertising*, the 39th Annual Meeting of the Association of National Advertisers, October 27, 1948, Box 496, 12–13.

98. Griffith, "Selling of America," 404–10; Robert H. Ziegler, "The Paradox of Plenty: The Advertising Council and the Post-Sputnik Crisis," *Advertising and Society Review* 4, no. 1 (2003), http://muse.jhu.edu/journals/advertising_and_society _review/summary/v004/4.1zieger.html (accessed September 27, 2011).

99. This observation was made in late October 1941 at a convention for the Pacific Council, American Association of Advertising Agencies, "Sees End to Government Advertising Opposition," *Editor and Publisher*, November 1, 1941, 6.

100. Cohen, *Consumers' Republic*.

Epilogue

1. See, for example, McGovern, *Sold American*; Stole, *Advertising on Trial*; Cohen, *Consumers' Republic*; Glickman, *Buying Power*; Fox, *Madison Avenue Goes to War*.

2. Advertising Council, Inc., "In the Wake of War," Files of Dallas C. Halverstadt, Harry S. Truman Library, Independence, Mo., Box 1, Folder: The Advertising Council, Inc., 5–7; Repplier, "Advertising Dons Long Pants," 271–75; "1307 Days" (press release issued by James W. Young, chairman, War Advertising Council), September 4, 1945, ACA, RG 13/2/305: Washington Office Subject File, 1942–81, Box 6, Folder: War Advertising Council News Releases 1945; "Advertisers' Work for Victory Cited in Young Report," *Advertising Age*, September 3, 1945, 8; "How the War Affected Marketing," *Printers' Ink*, September 21, 147–48; "Business Supported over 100 Council Drives; Contributed $1,000,000,000," *Printers' Ink*, September 7, 1945, 45. For an industry account of advertising's war contributions, see Raymond Rubicam, "Advertising," in *While You Were Gone: A Report on Wartime Life in the United States*, ed. John Goodman (New York: Simon and Schuster, 1946), 421–46.

3. John W. Jeffries, *Wartime America: The World War II Home Front* (Chicago: Ivan R. Dee, 1996), 183.

4. The term *People's Capitalism* had been coined by the president of the United States Chamber of Commerce, Eric Johnston, in the 1940s and was the title of a mid-1950s council campaign. See Johnston, *America Unlimited* (Garden City, N.Y.: Doubleday, Doran, 1944), chap. 8; Robert H. Ziegler, "The Paradox of Plenty: The Advertising Council and the Post-Sputnik Crisis," *Advertising and Society Review* 4, no. 1 (2003), http://muse.jhu.edu/journals/advertising_and_society_review/summary/v004/4.1zieger.html (accessed September 27, 2011); Lykins, *From Total War*, 112.

5. Mills, *Power Elite*, chap. 12.

6. Griffith, "Selling of America," 388.

7. McGovern, *Sold American*, 352.

8. John Fisher, "Truman and Co., Ltd.," *Advertising Age*, July 11, 1949, 14, 15.

9. "20th Century Find Monopoly Study Is Critical of Role of Advertising," *Advertising Age*, January 26, 1951, 59.

10. "Plan to Tax Advertising Is Proposed, Then Pooh-Poohed by Congress Committee," *Tide*, April 13, 1951, 15–16.

11. Griffith, "Selling of America," 412.

12. "A Report to Management from the Wage Earner Forum, Sponsored by MacFadden Publications Inc., Directed by Everett R. Smith," vol. 8, no. 4 (May 9, 1951), HSTP, Official File, Box 685, Box: OF 196 (1951–53), 7.

13. Ibid., 6.

14. Susan M. Hartman, *The Homefront and Beyond: American Women in the 1940s* (Boston: Twayne, 1982), 8.

15. Cohen, *Consumers' Republic*, 123; James L. Baughman, *The Republic of Mass Culture: Journalism, Filmmaking, and Broadcasting in America since 1941* (Baltimore: Johns Hopkins University Press, 1992), chap. 3.

16. "Wartime Advertising," *Bread and Butter*, April 1, 1944, 1; Daniel Pope, *The Making of Modern Advertising* (New York: Basic Books, 1983), 29.

17. Dannagal Goldthwaite Young, "Sacrifice, Consumption, and the American Way of Life: Advertising and Domestic Propaganda during World War II," *Communication Review* 8, no. 45 (2005): 27–52.

18. Henthorn, *From Submarines to Suburbs*, 200.

19. In spite of polls showing a high degree of public support for the Office of Price Administration and Civilian Supply's extension, the NAM allied with the National Retail Dry Goods Association, and congressmen representing agricultural and industrial interests launched an intensive public relations program to end the OPA's reign. The compromise was, for consumers, a very weak bill, passed in December 1946, two days before the existing price control bill was to expire. "The result was a 14 percent increase in food prices with meat doubling and overall living expenses increasing 6 percent." Cohen, *Consumers' Republic*, 103.

20. Colston Warne to Elizabeth Rohr, October 29, 1945, CEWP, Box 112, Folder 1.

21. "Legislative-Research Program of CU," CEWP, Box 82, Folder 2 (Board of Directors General 1946–52).

22. Colston E. Warne to Harold Aaron, May 12, 1949, CEWP, Box 83, Folder 2: "Board of Directors General, 1946–52."

23. Stole, *Advertising on Trial*, chap. 7.

24. "Threat to Business," CEWP, Box 62, Folder 1.

25. Leland J. Gordon to Colston (Warne), February 7, 1942, CEWP, Box 5, Folder 3; "Un-American Activities in California" (Report of the Joint Fact-Finding Committee to the Fifty-Fifth California Legislature, Sacramento, 1943, Jack B. Tenney), CEWP, Box 98, Folder 3.

26. "Un-American Activities in California." For the classics mentioned in the text see Arthur Kallet and F. J. Schlink, *100,000,000 Guinea Pigs: Dangers in Everyday Foods, Drugs, and Cosmetics* (New York : Grosset and Dunlap, 1935); M. C. Phillips, *Skin Deep: The Truth about Beauty Aids—Safe and Harmful* (New York: Vanguard Press, 1934); Arthur Kallet, *Counterfeit—Not Your Money but What It Buys* (New York: Vanguard Press , 1935); F. J. Schlink, *Eat, Drink and Be Wary* (New York : Arno Press, 1935; reprint, New York: Covici, Friede, 1976); J. B. Matthews, *Guinea Pigs No More* (New York: Covici, Friede, 1936).

27. For a collection of letters accusing CU of communist behavior and CU's response, see CEWP, Box 98, Folder 3.

28. Claude V. Courter to Colston Warne, July 5, 1951, CEWP, Box 98, Folder 3 (3rd package of 3 in folder).

29. Special Committee to Arthur Dondineau, July 26, 1951, CEWP, Box 99, Folder 3.

30. "NBBB letter sent on 1/17/52," CEWP, Box 98, Folder 4; Colston E. Warne to Thomas D'A. Brophy, January 31, 1952, CEWP, Box 98, Folder 3.

31. Courter to Warne, July 5, 1951.

32. "Where Does CU Stand? A Statement by the Consumers Union Board of Direc-

tors," reprinted from *Consumer Reports*, April 1953, CEWP, Box 99, Folder 4; "E. F. Tomkins Reveals: Half Million in U.S. Duped into Aiding Attack by Reds," *Freeman*, editorial page, pt. 1—Monday, July 28, 1952, CEWP, Box 99; Jean L. Whitehill to Mr. L. F. Gray, July 27, 1953, CEWP, Box 98, Folder 4; "The Following Statement Was Unanimously Approved by the Members of the Consumers Union Board of Directors on December 4, 1952," CEWP, Box 98, Folder 4.

33. Affidavit of Arthur Kallet, June 8, 1953, CEWP, Box 99, Folder 4, 26.

34. Ibid., 17.

35. Norman D. Katz, "Consumers Union: The Movement and the Magazine" (Ph.D. diss., Rutgers University, 1977), 239–64; Norman Isaac Silber, *Test and Protest: The Influence of Consumers Union* (New York: Holmes and Meier, 1983), 30–31. For a chart of *Consumer Reports*' growth between 1936 and 1961, see Richard L. D. Morse, *The Consumer Movement: Lectures by Colston E. Warne* (Manhattan, Kans.: Family Economics Trust, 1993), 150; Glickman, *Buying Power*, 268–70.

36. Colston Warne, "A Consumer Looks at Advertising" (talk given at First District AFA Advertising Conference, Poland Springs, Maine), July 1, 1949, CEWP, Box 117, Folder 6, 9; Colston E. Warne to Mr. Rascoe A. Day, May 6, 1953, CEWP, Box 98, Folder 4; Colston E. Warne to Boris (Shiskin), May 3, 1952, CEWP, Folder 3.

37. Daniel M. Potter, *People of Plenty: Economic Abundance and the American Character* (1954; reprint, Chicago: University of Chicago Press, 1962); David Riesman, *The Lonely Crowd: A Study of the Changing American Character* (New Haven, Conn.: Yale University Press, 1953); Vance Packard, *The Hidden Persuaders* (New York: David McKay, 1958); John Kenneth Galbraith, *The Affluent Society* (Boston: Houghton Mifflin, 1958).

38. Victor Pickard, "The Revolt against Radio: Postwar Media Criticism and the Struggle for Broadcast Reform," in *A War on Many Fronts: Advertising, Its Critics and the Government during World War II*, ed. Janice Peck and Inger L. Stole (Milwaukee: Marquette University Press, 2011), 35–56.

39. Griffith, "Selling of America," 412. See also T. J. Jackson Lears, "A Matter of Taste: Corporate Cultural Hegemony in Mass-Consumption Society," in *Recasting America*, ed. Larry May (Chicago: University of Chicago Press, 1989), 38–57; Warren Susman with the assistance of Edwin Griffin, "Did Success Spoil the United States? Dual Representation in Postwar America," in May, *Recasting America*, 19–37; and Stephanie Koontz, *The Way We Never Were: American Families and the Nostalgia Trap* (New York: Basic Books, 1992).

40. *Valentine v. Chrestensen*, 316 U.S. 52 (1942); *Virginia State Pharmacy Board v. Virginia Citizens Consumer Council*, 425 U.S. 748 (1976).

41. *Citizens United v. Federal Election Commission*, 558 U.S. 08-205 (2010).

Index

INGER L. STOLE is an associate professor of communications at the University of Illinois at Urbana-Champaign and the author of *Advertising on Trial: Consumer Activism and Corporate Public Relations in the 1930s.*

THE HISTORY OF COMMUNICATION

The University of Illinois Press
is a founding member of the
Association of American University Presses.

Composed in 10.5/13 Minion Pro Regular
with Meta display
by Celia Shapland
at the University of Illinois Press
Manufactured by Thomson-Shore, Inc.

University of Illinois Press
1325 South Oak Street
Champaign, IL 61820-6903
www.press.uillinois.edu